Contents

KU-540-694

4 Creating Teams 59

5 Channels and Tabs 83

6 Text Chatting 99

902857593 6

Ni

Microsoft Teams

In easy steps is an imprint of In Easy Steps Limited
16 Hamilton Terrace · Holly Walk · Leamington Spa
Warwickshire · United Kingdom · CV32 4LY
www.ineasysteps.com

Copyright © 2021 by In Easy Steps Limited. All rights reserved. No part of this book may be reproduced or transmitted in any form or by any means, electronic or mechanical, including photocopying, recording, or by any information storage or retrieval system, without prior written permission from the publisher.

Notice of Liability
Every effort has been made to ensure that this book contains accurate and current information. However, In Easy Steps Limited and the author shall not be liable for any loss or damage suffered by readers as a result of any information contained herein.

Trademarks
Microsoft® is a registered trademark of Microsoft Corporation. All other trademarks are acknowledged as belonging to their respective companies.

In Easy Steps Limited supports The Forest Stewardship Council (FSC), the leading international forest certification organization. All our titles that are printed on Greenpeace approved FSC certified paper carry the FSC logo.

MIX
Paper from
responsible sources
FSC® C020837

Printed and bound in the United Kingdom

ISBN 978-1-84078-931-7

1 The Workplace Revolution

Millions of people spend their working lives in offices, and this chapter shows how this has evolved.

The Changing Face of the Workplace

The concept of an office workplace, where a group of people are located together to perform a range of productivity tasks, can be traced back to the Romans, who had government establishments in their towns to manage and run the towns' affairs. These were known by the name "officium", from where the modern word used today comes.

Office work – and its environment – has evolved significantly over the centuries, largely as a result of political, social, and technological changes and advances. Three of the main areas that have driven these changes are communication, productivity and collaboration, and each of them can be linked to technological developments that have changed the way in which office work is performed. All of these factors have also helped to shape the modern office workspace, which relies heavily on digital technology and, increasingly, tools such as Microsoft Teams.

New technology in the workplace is only as good as the people who use it, so it is important for organizations to invest in comprehensive training for employees whenever any new technology is introduced.

Communication

Communication is one of the most important aspects of office work, and the telephone was one of the most significant breakthroughs in this area. Being able to communicate with someone in another town, city, country or continent transformed the speed at which business could be done: one telephone call potentially replacing the need to send a letter to another part of the world. Once telephony communication was established, it made the concept of global business much more attainable.

Productivity

As with most workplaces, the office environment is largely concerned with producing output. One way in which this was increased considerably was with the invention of the humble typewriter. This led to documents being produced in a fraction of the time than previously, resulting in this skill becoming one of the main features of the office workplace.

Collaboration

Being able to quickly share documents electronically around different locations is another landmark in making the modern office more efficient and productive. One of the first ways of doing this was achieved by a device that is now frequently viewed with amusement and gentle ridicule: the fax machine. Despite its slightly archaic nature to workers brought up with the internet, email and social media, the fax machine was revolutionary in its time, with its ability to send copies of documents to locations around the world, using existing telephone infrastructure.

The modern office workplace

While the modern office workplace may seem a long way from the days of typewriters and fax machines (although they are still used in some instances) there has been a natural evolution in terms of communication, productivity and collaboration tools. Computing technology has been the main driving force behind this – in some cases, consolidating all of these functions into a single device.

The natural development of the modern workplace is now being seen in collaboration apps that combine all of the main functions in the workplace. Microsoft Teams (Teams) epitomizes this, with its ability to connect groups of office workers – or those in other environments such as education – so that they can communicate, share documents and even collaborate on creating new documents. The functions of Teams can be traced back through the history of the workplace, but it is definitely a very modern tool that can provide invaluable assistance to office workers.

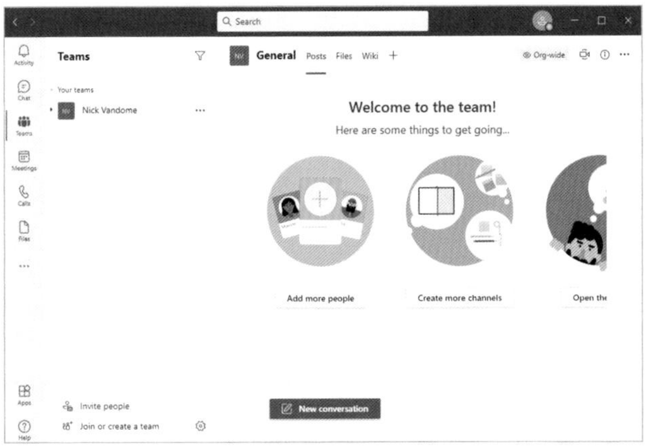

Teams is free to download and use, and there is also an upgraded version that can be purchased as part of the Microsoft 365 suite of apps or from within the free version of Teams. The upgraded version includes unlimited users (the free version allows up to 300), an increased amount of storage for documents (1TB per user for the paid-for version; 1GB per user for the free version). There are also additional administrative functions in the paid-for version.

Working From Home

In terms of working from home, the Covid-19 pandemic has accelerated a process that was already taking a firm hold in the digital workplace. For people who work primarily with computers, there are few arguments to prevent them working from home for at least part of their time at work.

As with any major shift in working practices, there are numerous areas to consider when working from home, for both the employer and the employee. If these issues are addressed constructively, practically and progressively, then working from home can bring enormous benefits for all concerned and transform the way in which we look at our working lives.

Hot tip

Just because employees have more free time as a result of working from home, this does not mean that they should feel they have to use it in an outwardly constructive way, such as starting a new hobby. The important thing is that the time available should be appreciated and it can be used in any way that people see fit, even if that is to do nothing in particular.

Benefits

Although there are some concerns that should be addressed when employees are working from home, there are many benefits:

- **Work/life balance**. The concept of striking the right balance between your working life and your home life is something that is widely talked about in modern society. With the traditional 9-5 model of office work, this can be hard to achieve effectively. However, working from home offers a genuine option for workers to adapt their time at work so that they can maximize the benefits of their free time.

- **Financial**. For workers who have to commute to work, the option of working from home can result in considerable financial savings. If people have to commute large distances then the savings can be dramatic, particularly when calculated over a year. Even if a daily commute is relatively short, savings can soon mount up over time. Added to this are savings that can accrue from miscellaneous expenditure during the working day, and it soon becomes clear that the financial benefits to the employee are one of the most attractive features of working from home.

Savings from working from home have to be offset against additional expenditure, such as increased utility bills.

- **Corporate savings**. Employers can also benefit from their employees working from home. Maintaining office space for workers is a considerable expense for businesses, and if they have hundreds – or thousands – of employees, this can quickly run into large sums. If some of the workforce can work from home, the subsequent savings from downsizing on office space is something that most organizations should consider.

...cont'd

Getting the right balance

While working from home offers the chance for employees to strike a better work/life balance, this does not mean that working from home constantly is always the best option. Some aspects of office life are important from both a corporate and social perspective and many organizations are now favoring a hybrid model, where employees spend some time in the office and some at home. The ideal situation for employees is if they can choose their own balance between working from home and going into the office.

If a hybrid model is used, incorporating working from home and also in the office, an effective hot-desking policy should be implemented to ensure that home workers can book desks in the office when required.

Managing people

One area that can cause issues in relation to working from home is the management of employees. Some managers like to physically see their staff, as they believe this ensures that they are working and being productive. However, this is not always the case, and a considerable amount of the working day in an office can be wasted by employees not doing much work. In reality, employees can be more productive when working from home and, in some cases, there needs to be a shift in the approach of managers, which can come about once they see that productivity can be improved by employees being located at home.

Home workspace

If employees are going to be working from home for an extended period, it is important that they have an adequate workspace in which to work. Not everyone will be able to have a dedicated office space, but organizations should ensure that their employees have proper space in which to work and the appropriate equipment for the job (see pages 12-15 for details).

Human contact

Human interaction is important in many aspects of our lives, and this is particularly true in a working environment. Attention should be given to ensure that people working from home still have sufficient contact with their colleagues so that they do not feel cut off or isolated. Activities such as virtual coffee breaks and social meetings should be encouraged for home workers, and they should also be given the opportunity to meet up with their friends and colleagues when they work in the office. Human Resources departments should have a working-from-home policy that includes details of maintaining social contact and interaction.

Getting Set Up

In an ideal world, home working should be backed up by a robust policy that includes the provision of appropriate office and IT equipment, and a health and safety inspection to assess the workspace being used. However, this is not always the case, particularly in instances where home working has to be accelerated due to unforeseen circumstances, such as the Covid-19 pandemic. Even in these circumstances though, there are some areas that should be looked at carefully in terms of working from home, such as workspace and equipment.

Don't forget

If you are in a household with other people, make sure that you have an open discussion with them about what is expected for when you are working from home. This is particularly important if there are children in the household.

Workspace

When people are working from home, their actual location will be largely dependent on their own circumstances and where they live. However, if this is going to be a long-term situation for you, then some care and attention should go into where you are going to work. Some areas to consider are:

- Try to ensure you have enough space. If you cannot use a work desk, try to use a flat surface and ensure that your workspace has enough room for your work equipment and also any documents, books or folders that you may have to access.
- Natural light is important. Try to work somewhere where there is enough natural light so that you do not feel like you are working in a cave. This does not have to be direct sunlight, but try to avoid working in any area where there are no windows or sources of natural light.
- Be prepared to clear away your equipment at the end of the working day or working week, if necessary. If you use a space that is regularly in use by other members of a household, you may have to make the space available when you have finished working. If you have to do this, make sure that your equipment is kept somewhere safe and secure. This is just one of the many trade-offs that working from home can entail.
- Ensure that your workspace is somewhere where you can conduct audio and video conversations. If there are other people in the household, particularly children, then it may be necessary to schedule these types of calls at times when you are least likely to be disturbed.

If you are working near a window in your home, there may be occasions where the glare from sunlight can make it hard to view your computer screen. If this happens, make sure you are somewhere where you can draw curtains or a blind and, in some cases, use a glare guard over your screen.

If possible, it is best to use a work desk when you are working from home. This will not only help you organize your equipment, but will also create a more professional workspace.

Try to keep your desk as free from clutter as possible. This will create a more efficient workspace and help maintain a more focused mindset for work.

A workspace using a large table, near a window, is a good option if you cannot have a dedicated desk in your home.

A reliable and fast broadband connection is usually required when working from home. In some instances this may be provided by the organization, but frequently it will be up to individuals to provide their own broadband.

...cont'd

Equipment

In terms of equipment for working from home, your organization should provide a minimum of any IT equipment that you need, such as a desktop computer, monitor, keyboard, mouse, laptop and printer. There is also a range of other equipment that could be provided, to help with your workplace setup. This includes:

- **Foot rests**. These can be used below a table or desk so that the user can have their legs raised slightly, which can help with circulation and make sitting more comfortable.
- **Back rests**. These can be attached to a chair to give back support. They are usually adjustable so that you can position them where they can give you the most support and comfort.
- **Wrist rests**. These can be used with a keyboard or a mouse, to give your wrist support when you are typing or maneuvering your mouse. Wrist rests are frequently filled with a firm gel, to increase support and flexibility.

- **Computer stands**. These can be used to position a computer or a laptop at the correct height on a table or a desk. Ideally, your eyeline should be in line with the top of the monitor.
- **Headsets for audio or video calls**. These can be used to make hands-free calls so that the user can simultaneously perform another task, such as typing a text message, as required.

If you change your work pattern so that some – or all – of your time is spent working from home, you may be able to claim tax deductions for certain items, such as utility bills. Check with an accountant or financial advisor for the tax rules for your particular working situation.

Headsets are more effective for audio and video calls than the speakers and microphone on a computer because they enable the two elements to be isolated and used separately, unlike the ones on a computer, where only one element can be used at a time.

The most important item of equipment for working from home is undoubtedly your chair, since you will probably be spending many hours a day in it. Ideally, a dedicated office chair should be used: if your organization does not provide one then it is worth getting your own one, rather than sitting on a kitchen chair that may become uncomfortable. A fully adjustable office chair is probably one of the best investments you will make when working from home (and it may be tax-deductible; see first Hot tip on the previous page).

Back problems are common among people who work regularly with computers, and one option that can provide relief from this is to use a standing desk. This is a type of desk where the user stands at a workstation rather than sitting on a chair, thereby helping their posture and, hopefully, putting less strain on their back. This is not a solution for everyone, but it has the added advantage of being more mobile around the home.

Some standing desks are foldable, to make them easier to store away in the home.

Teams Comes of Age

One of the areas of digital communication that have flourished due to the increase in the number of people working from home is that of collaboration tools, and Microsoft Teams (Teams) is very much at the forefront of this revolution.

It is easy to think of Teams as a video communication tool, along the likes of Zoom or Skype, but in reality it offers an impressive range of features that can link people throughout an organization so that they can communicate and collaborate in a range of ways.

For many organizations, Teams has become the default option for collaboration through teams, video calls, text chat and file sharing.

Teams at work or in education

Teams is very much a tool for a professional environment, and it can be equally effective in the business world or in all levels of formal education. During the Covid-19 pandemic, large numbers of schools and universities have embraced Teams to ensure that their students can continue their studies, wherever they are located.

The power of Teams

Some options that Teams offers are:

- **Creating teams of people with common work interests or duties**. The team can then communicate and collaborate with each other, in an environment that is limited to the people in the team. These are the teams that give the app its name.
- **Enabling audio or video meetings**. Meetings can be held with members of a team or can be started (or scheduled) with a member of the organization, presuming they have permissions for this. It is a quick and efficient way to conduct online meetings with colleagues or students.
- **Providing a text chat facility**. Teams also contains a powerful text function, which can be used to send text messages around the organization, and even to post text comments during an audio or video meeting.
- **Sharing files with people within the Teams environment**. This is an excellent feature for sharing work presentations or a range of coursework in an educational environment. Documents can be shared by displaying items on your own screen during a video meeting, or files can be uploaded to their own dedicated area within Teams, where other members of the organization can access them to view them, and also edit them as required.

Versions of Teams

Teams is a cross-platform app that can be used on devices with a range of operating systems. It can be used on desktop computers and laptops using Windows, or macOS on Apple devices. There are also mobile versions of Teams that can be used on iPhones using iOS; iPads using iPadOS; and Android smartphones and tablets. This gives users the ultimate flexibility in terms of how and where they use Teams.

For more details about using Microsoft 365 apps within Teams, see pages 170-173.

Integration with Microsoft products

As Teams is a Microsoft product, it is only natural that it is closely aligned with other Microsoft productivity apps. Teams can be downloaded, for free, as a stand-alone app and it is also included in the Microsoft 365 suite of apps. This is a subscription service that can be used on a monthly or an annual basis. A lot of organizations will already be using Microsoft 365, and so its apps will be available within Teams. If not, it can be subscribed to from the Microsoft website. Microsoft 365 apps can be accessed from within Teams, in which case they appear within the Teams interface. The components of Microsoft 365 include:

- **Word**. This is the widely used word processing app that helped revolutionize the way that documents are produced in the workplace.

- **Excel**. This is an app for creating spreadsheets so that data can be viewed and managed using complex mathematical formulae, if required.

- **PowerPoint**. This can be used to create presentations for the business environment, although it should not be over-used.

- **OneNote**. This is a powerful note-taking app that can be used to create lists and reminders and also display a range of different content.

- **Outlook**. This is a powerful email client that links up with the other Microsoft 365 apps.

- **OneDrive**. This is Microsoft's online storage facility and it can be used within Teams so that content can be accessed wherever users are located, either in an office or on the move.

When using Teams, documents can be stored on your own computer or in OneDrive. Documents stored in OneDrive will be available to you from any of your devices on which you are using Teams. Teams will also enable the OneDrive documents to be available to others Teams members.

Security Issues

Cyber security is a vital issue when working in any computing environment, particularly one in which people will be collaborating and sharing information. This applies to Teams just as much as using other apps or any online activity. While the technical side of cyber security should be taken care of by your organization's IT department or supplier, there are also certain steps that individuals can take to ensure their interactions on Teams are as secure as possible:

- **Reading your organization's policy regarding the use of Teams**. This should lay out what you can, and cannot, do with Teams. Some of the areas that may be covered include creating and editing teams and channels, sharing documents, and communicating with people outside your organization. If your organization does not have a specific policy for Teams, a general IT policy may cover the pertinent points.
- **Being aware when discussing sensitive information**. When communicating with a collaboration app such as Teams there is always a chance of a conversation being recorded, either by the app or by someone using a smartphone. Because of this, it is essential that only appropriate information is discussed in an audio or a video call. Never say anything that you would not want to appear somewhere else at a later date.
- **Being careful when sharing documents with people outside your organization**. Teams has a facility for including external users, but you should consult your organization's appropriate policy to see what is allowed in terms of sharing documents or information in this way. If in doubt, don't do it.
- **Referring unsolicited requests for information**. If you are contacted by someone outside your organization with a request for documents or information, contact your IT security officer if there are any aspects about the request with which you feel uncomfortable. It is always best to check first and keep a record of the request and your referral.
- **Removing sensitive background items during video calls**. When conducting video calls, make sure that there is nothing offensive in the background of your video feed and there are no sensitive financial items in view, such as bank statements or credit cards.

Beware

If your organization's Teams policy states that something is not allowed, then this function should be disabled for use. However, even if you can use it, resist the temptation to do so if you know that it is referred to in the policy.

2 Setting Up Teams

This chapter details how to obtain and get started with Microsoft Teams.

What is Microsoft Teams?

Apps for enabling communication, collaboration and managing meetings are becoming increasingly important for the modern workplace, particularly when employees are located in different locations, either in offices or working from home. Microsoft Teams (Teams) is one such app and it is quickly becoming established as one of the most popular workplace collaboration tools. While there are other apps that provide similar functionality, Teams has the advantage of being developed specifically for the workplace and other areas of professional collaboration.

Teams can link all of the employees in an organization and enable them to do the following:

- Create teams so that people with a shared subject or interest can interact with other like-minded individuals.

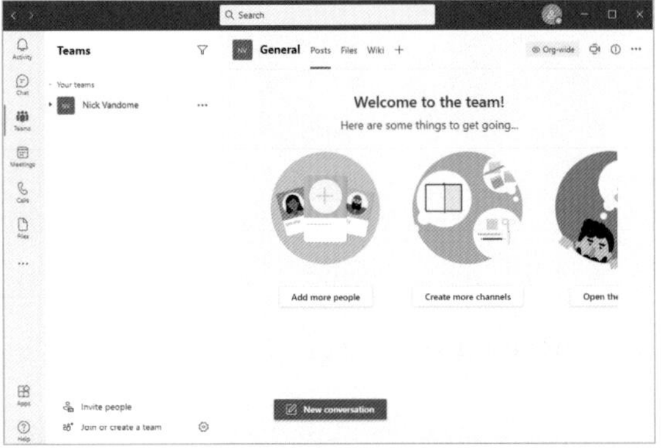

- Conduct text chats, either with people within a specific team or with anyone else in the organization, with the Teams app.

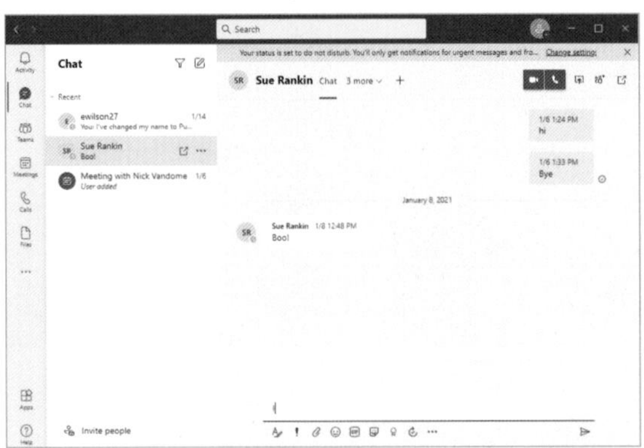

Don't forget

There is a free version of Teams that is very powerful and effective. However, for increased functionality, there is a paid-for upgrade that has added features, such as increased online storage and more powerful administration tools and functions.

Each team that is created covers a specific subject, category or group of people. Numerous teams can be created for each user of the app. Sub-categories can also be created within a team and these are known as channels – see pages 84-93 for more details.

- Perform video calls, either with individuals or a group of people in your own organization, or externally.
- Perform voice calls, in the same way as making a video call, just without the camera.
- Organize and manage meetings, which can then be conducted within the Teams environment.

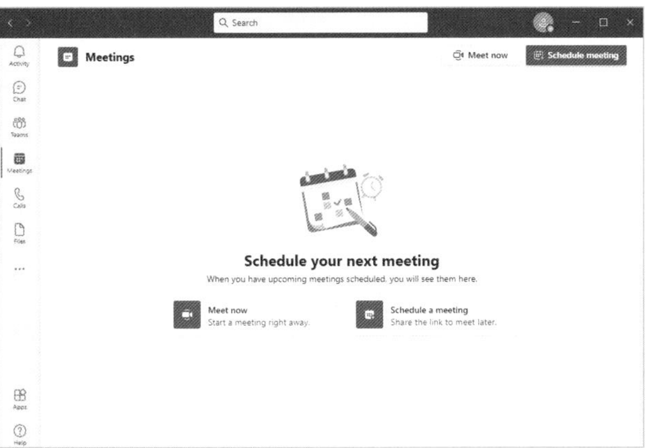

- Share files with colleagues and allow them to edit them.
- Share the screen on your computer with other people on an audio or a video call. It is also possible to change what is on the screen, just as if someone were looking at your computer.

Any screen that you have open on your computer can be shared with other Teams members on an audio or a video call.

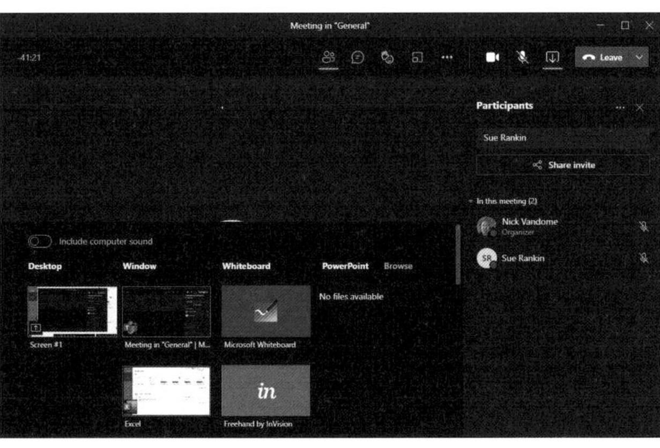

- Add apps to Teams, to enable even more options.

Obtaining Teams

If you are using Teams within an organization, it may be pre-installed and ready for you to use. However, it can also be downloaded by organizations where it is not pre-installed, and also by individuals who want to use it for group communication. Teams can be downloaded to a variety of platforms and devices (Windows, Mac, Android, iOS and iPadOS), which can all be linked together with the same Teams app. This is the process for downloading Teams onto a Windows desktop computer or laptop:

The download page will usually identify your location and ask if you would like to be redirected to a download page for that location. For instance, the download page for the UK is www.microsoft.com/en-gb/microsoft-teams/download-app

1. Go to the website **www.microsoft.com/en-us/microsoft-teams/download-app**, for the US

2. Click on the **Download for desktop** button

3. Click on the **Download Teams** button

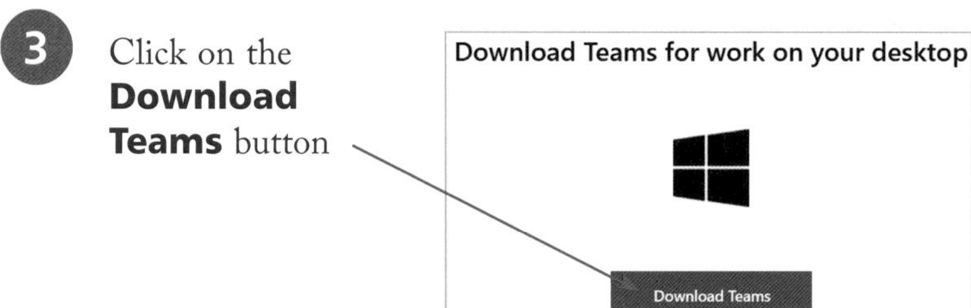

4. Double-click on the Teams file in the web browser's Downloads section

5. Click on the **Save File** button to install the Teams app

6 Click on the **Teams** app to perform the registration process and link the app to a Microsoft Account

7 Click on the **Sign in** button to sign in to Teams with an existing Microsoft Account

8 Click on the **Send code** button to send a code to your Microsoft Account email, to confirm your identity for signing in to Teams

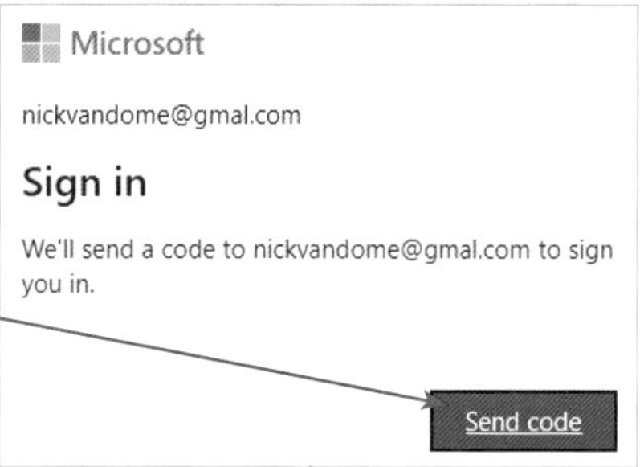

9 Enter the code and click on the **Sign in** button

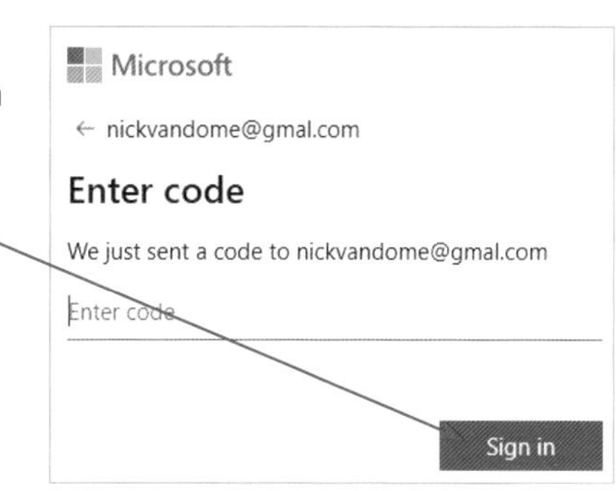

On a Windows desktop or laptop, the Teams app will be located in the Start menu.

If you do not have a Microsoft Account, there will be an option to create one in Step 7.

The process for setting up Teams is a fairly lengthy one, but once it has been done you can use Teams at any time by clicking on the **Teams** icon.

...cont'd

10 Click on the **Sign up for Teams** button to register with the Teams app and start creating a Teams environment

If you are already using Teams on another device, you can sign in using the **Already using Teams? Sign in now** link in Step 11.

11 Click on the **Sign up for free** button to start the sign-in process for Teams

12 Enter an email address and click on the **Next** button. (You do not have to use your Microsoft Account email at this point, but it is recommended)

13 Select an option for how you would like to use Teams (school, family, or work) and click on the **Next** button

14 Enter the password for the email used to register for Teams (ideally your Microsoft Account password) and click on the **Sign in** button

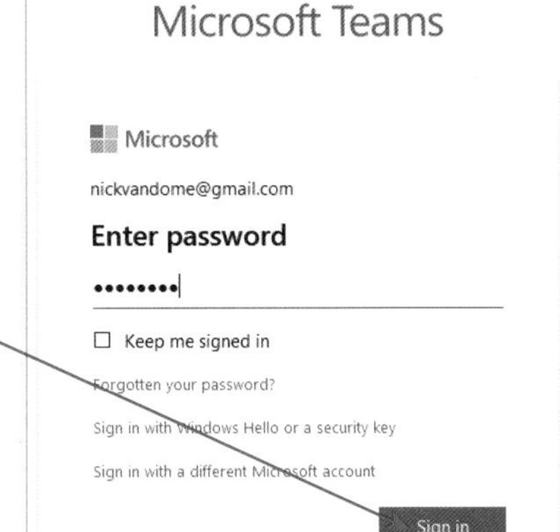

15 Review your security information for the selected account and click on the **Looks good!** button, or the **Update now** button if you have changed any of the details

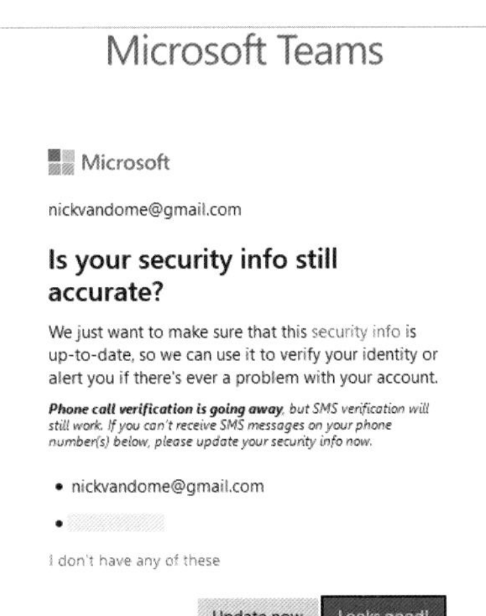

Security details can include your email address and a cell/mobile phone number. These are used if verification is required for any security aspect relating to Teams, or your Microsoft Account. Click on the **I don't have any of these** link in Step 15 to add the required security details.

...cont'd

16 Microsoft offers an option for downloading an app to your smartphone so that you can sign in to your Microsoft Account without the need to enter a password. Click on the **Get it now** button to download the app to your smartphone

The name used in Step 17 will be the one displayed in Teams – e.g. if you send a text message or organize a meeting. However, this can be changed by editing your profile – see pages 38-39 for details.

17 Enter your name, company name (if applicable) and location, and click on the **Set up Teams** button

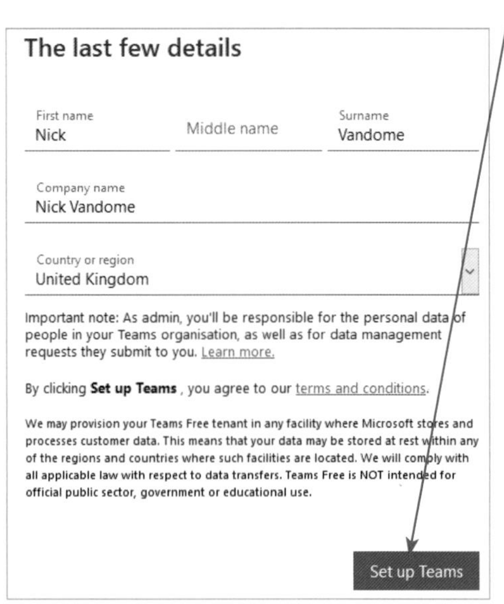

18 Click on the **Microsoft Teams** option to enable Teams to use a link to open the app, and click on the **Open link** button

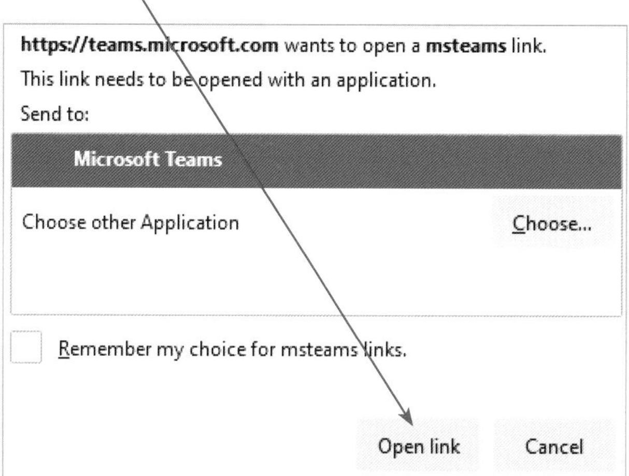

19 Once the registration process has been completed a Welcome window will be displayed. Click on the **Continue** button to start using Teams

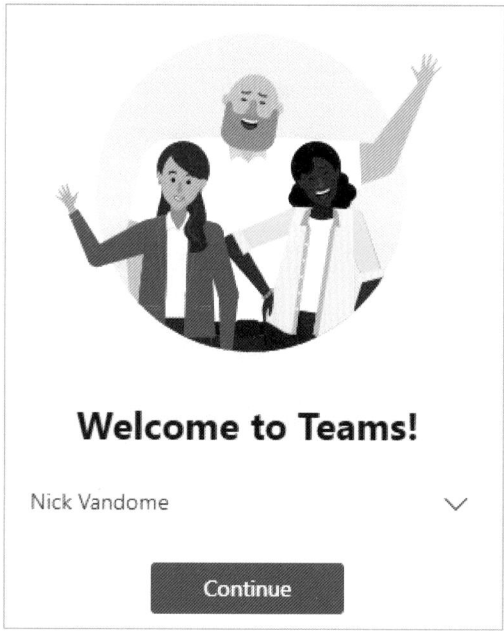

If you set up the Teams app you will be the administrator of the Teams environment. This means that, by default, you will have more control over the operation of Teams than other members who are added to Teams.

Teams for Mac

Teams is a multi-platform app, which means that it can be used on a range of different devices and with different operating systems. For Mac users (Mac Pro, iMac, Mac mini and MacBook), the version of Teams can be downloaded and used in an almost identical way to the Windows version. To do this:

1. Go to the website **www.microsoft.com/en-us/microsoft-teams/download-app**, for the US (or **www.microsoft.com/en-gb/microsoft-teams/download-app**, for the UK)

2. Click on the **Download for desktop** button

3. Click on the **Download Teams** button

4. Click here at the top of the Safari browser, to access the installation file for Teams. Double-click on the installation file and follow the same registration process as for the Windows version of Teams on pages 22-27

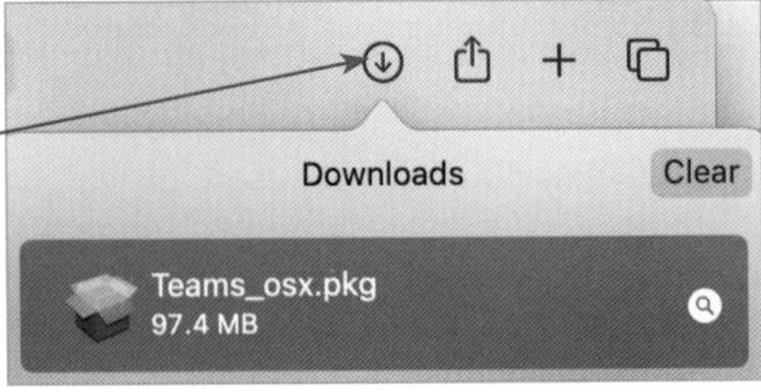

The Apple symbol in Step 3 is an indication that you are downloading the Mac version of Teams.

5. Open the Launcher on your Mac and click on the **Microsoft Teams** icon to open the app

6. Select your own account name for using Teams, and click on the **Continue** button. (In some cases further verification may be required, by having a code sent to your cell/mobile phone)

7. The interface for the Mac version of Teams is almost identical to the Windows one, with the left-hand sidebar for navigation; the left-hand panel for the headings of items selected in the sidebar; and the main window for content relating to the selection in the left-hand panel

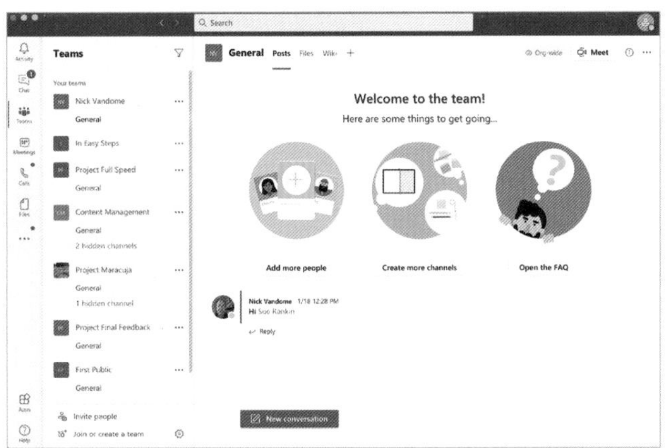

To open the Launcher, which displays all of the available apps on your Mac, click on this button on the Dock, situated along the bottom of the screen:

When you first open Teams on your Mac, you will require your Microsoft Account email address and password in order to log in.

Mobile Versions of Teams

Teams is primarily designed to be used on a desktop computer or laptop, in an office or educational environment, or for someone working or studying from home. However, the significance of being mobile is also recognized, with versions of the app for smartphones and tablets. These can be used on Android and Apple devices, and downloaded from a browser or from the device's relevant app store.

Downloading from a browser

To download a mobile version of Teams to a smartphone or a tablet from a web browser:

The mobile version of Teams does not have the same range of functionality as the desktop or laptop versions, but it is an excellent option for keeping in touch with people and up-to-date with what is happening, when you are away from your home or work desk.

1. Go to the website **www.microsoft.com/en-us/microsoft-365/microsoft-teams/download-app**, for the US (or **www.microsoft.com/en-gb/microsoft-teams/download-app**, for the UK)

2. Click on the **Download for mobile** button

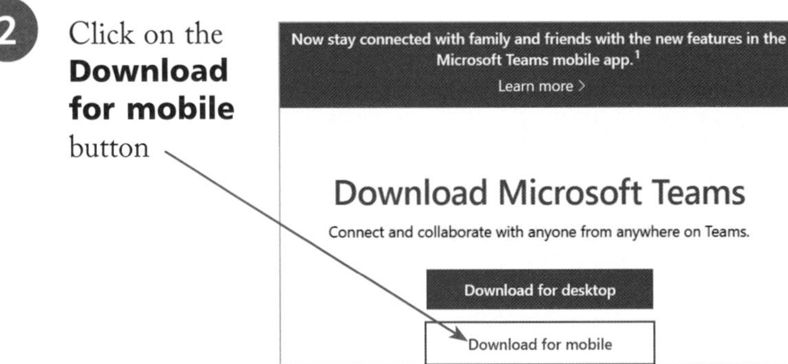

3. Enter your email address and click on the **Send now** button. A link for downloading Teams will be sent to your email address. Open this on the mobile device on which you want to use Teams and follow the instructions via the link in the email

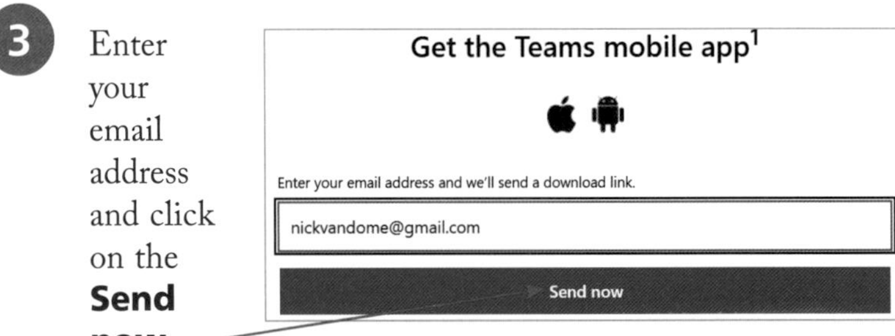

Teams for Android

To download the mobile version of Teams to an Android device, from the Google Play Store:

1. Access the Google Play Store and navigate to the Microsoft Teams app. Click on the **Install** button

2. The Teams app is downloaded to the Home screen of your Android smartphone or tablet. Tap on it to open Teams

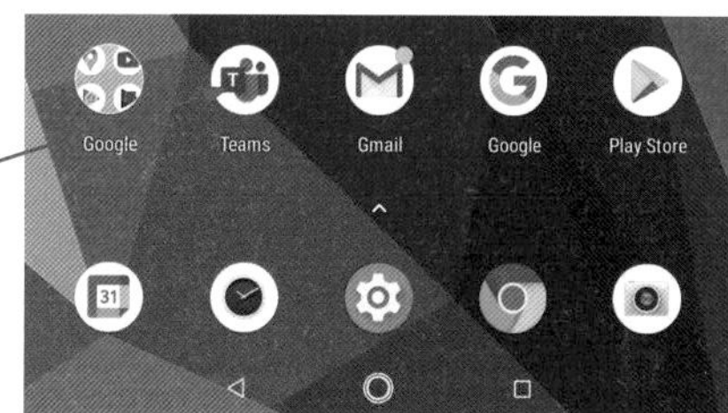

3. The mobile Teams interface for Android contains the main navigation buttons at the bottom of the window. These mirror most of the ones used on the desktop/laptop version of Teams – e.g. **Activity**, **Chat**, **Teams**, **Meetings** and **Calls**. Click on the **More** button to access additional options, including accessing and uploading files

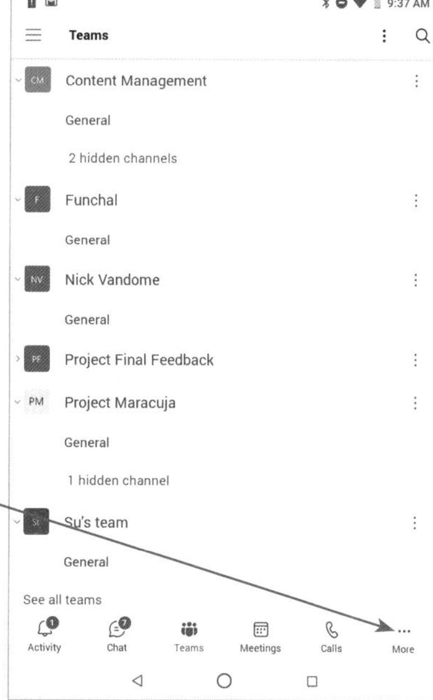

The option for creating a **Wiki** (see Chapter 11) on an Android mobile device is accessed from the **More** button.

...cont'd

Teams for Apple (iOS and iPadOS)

To download the mobile version of Teams to an iPhone (using iOS) or an iPad (using iPadOS) from the Apple App Store:

1. Access the App Store and navigate to the Microsoft Teams app. Click on the **GET** button

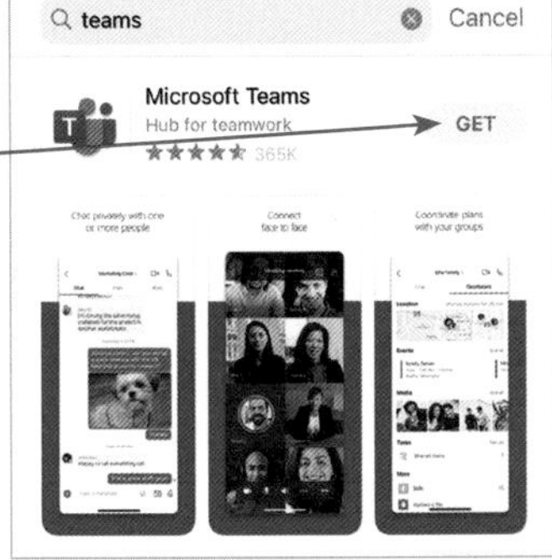

With Teams on an iPhone, the **Calls** option is accessed from the **More** button.

2. The Teams app is downloaded to the Home screen of your iPhone or iPad. Tap on it to open Teams

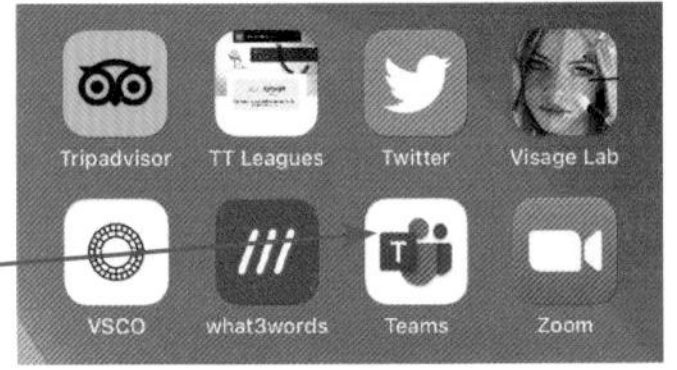

3. The mobile Teams interface contains the main navigation buttons at the bottom of the window. These mirror most of the ones used on the desktop/laptop version of Teams – e.g. **Activity**, **Chat**, **Teams**, and **Meetings**. Click on the **More** button to access additional options, including accessing and uploading files

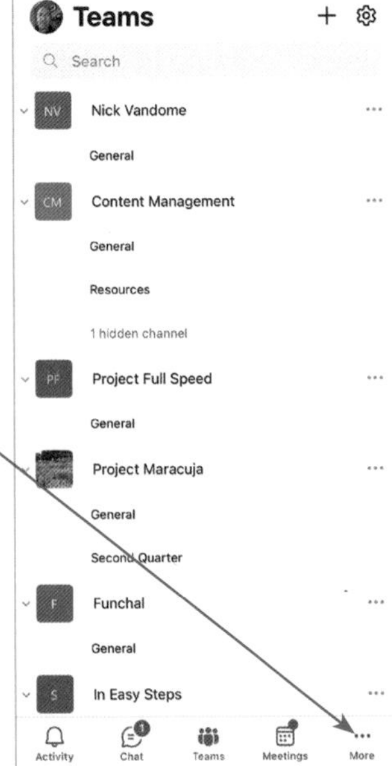

The option for creating a **Wiki** (see Chapter 11) on an Apple mobile device is accessed from the **More** button.

3 Getting Started with Teams

Teams is a powerful communication, collaboration and sharing tool that has great advantages for office workers. This chapter explains the Teams interface, with the different sections and features. It also shows how you can customize your own information that is displayed within Teams.

The Teams Interface

Once Teams has been downloaded and installed you can get started with communicating and collaborating with your colleagues. To get started with the Teams interface:

Your account icon can be used to access your own profile within Teams and edit it, if required. See pages 38-39 for details about editing your profile.

Not all sections have a left-hand panel, depending on their functionality.

1. Click on the **Teams** app 

2. The Teams interface is displayed:

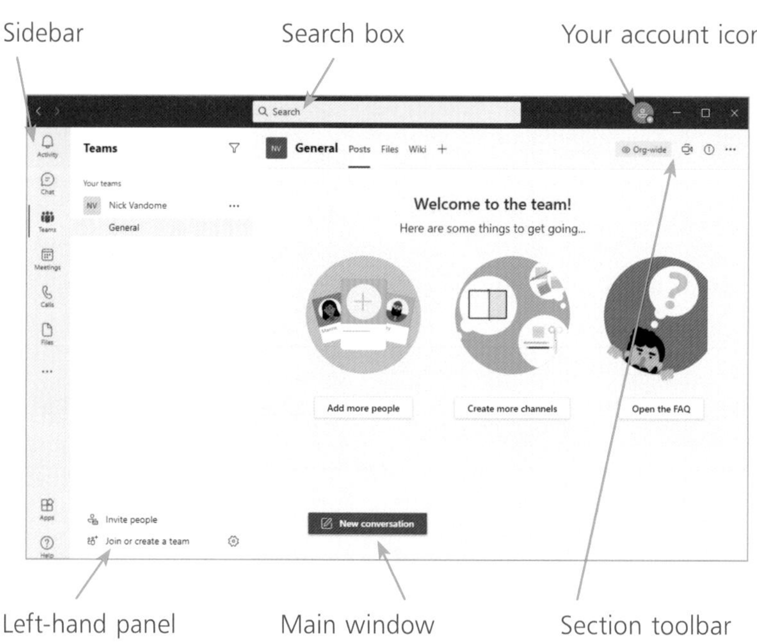

3. Click on the options in the sidebar to view, from top to bottom: **Activity**, which displays all of your latest actions in Teams; **Chat**, to start – or continue – a chat with an individual or group (this is separate from a chat within a specific team); **Teams**, which displays all of the teams of which you are a member and enables you to create new ones; **Meetings**, for scheduling and managing meetings; **Calls**, to make voice or video calls to individuals; **Files**, to upload and view shared files; **Apps**, to add more functionality within Teams; and **Help**, to access Help files

4. The **Teams** section has options to get started with creating teams and also a **Frequently Asked Questions** (**FAQs**) option with help features for the Teams app

5. Each section has its own interface, such as the **Meetings** section for scheduling and managing meetings

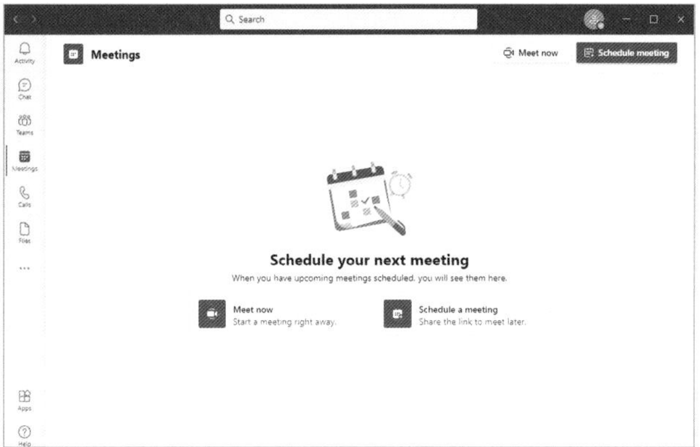

6. Some sections, such as the **Apps** option, contain items that can be selected to increase the functionality of the Teams app

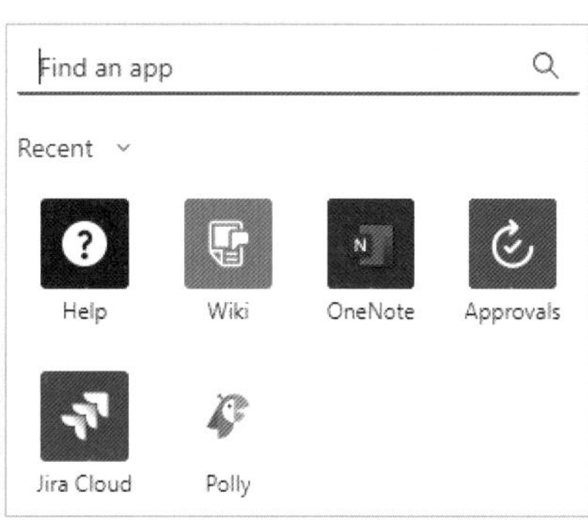

Menu buttons are used throughout the Teams app, to access additional options for certain items. Click on a menu button to view its options.

Setting Your Status

One of the first things to do when you start using Teams is to set your status. This provides other Teams members with information about your availability, or customized details that you have added. To set your status:

1. Click on your account icon in the top right-hand corner of the Teams app

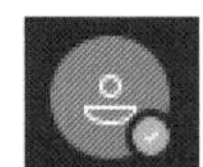

2. Click on current status; e.g. **Available**

Microsoft Teams free

NV Nick Vandome
Edit profile

Available

Set status message

3. Click on another option to display that as your current status; e.g. **Do not disturb**

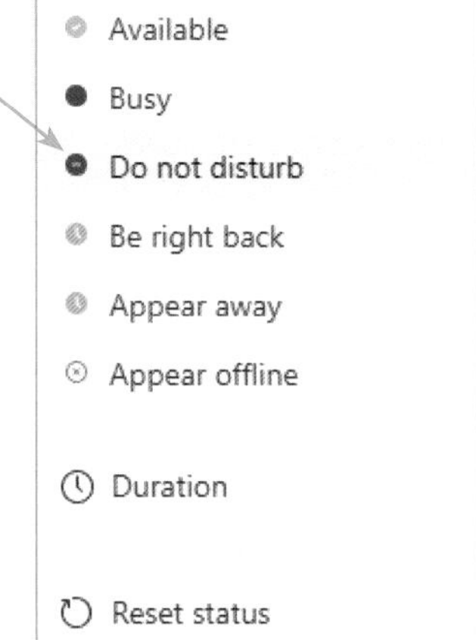

4. The badge on your account icon changes according to your status

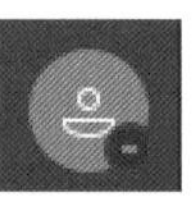

5. Move the cursor over the account icon to view your current status

Your current status is the one that other users will see when they view your details in their Teams app, which can be done by moving the cursor over the relevant icon.

Creating a customized message

To set a customized message, in addition to your status:

1. Click on the **Set status message** option

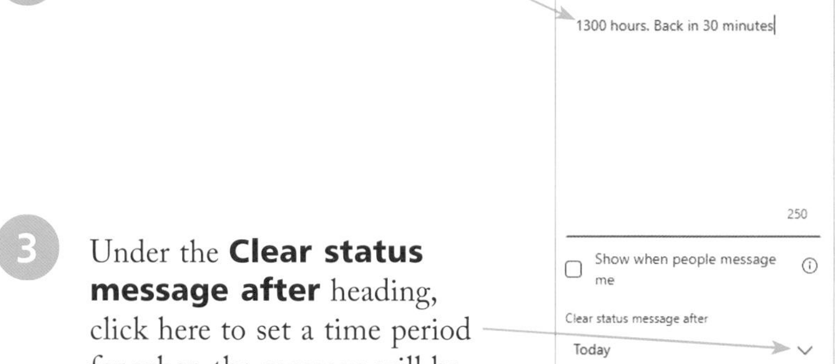

2. Enter the required message here

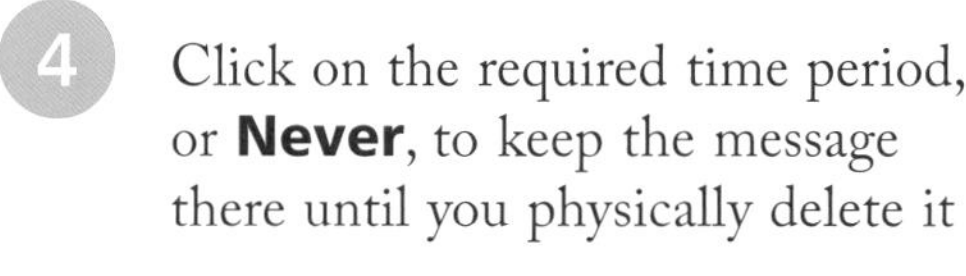

3. Under the **Clear status message after** heading, click here to set a time period for when the message will be removed

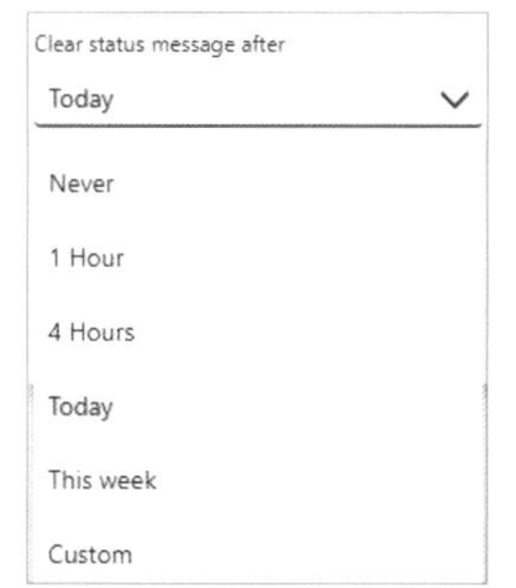

4. Click on the required time period, or **Never**, to keep the message there until you physically delete it

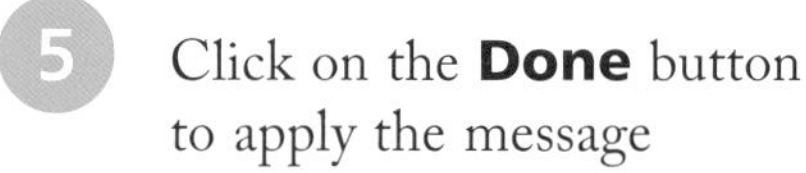

5. Click on the **Done** button to apply the message

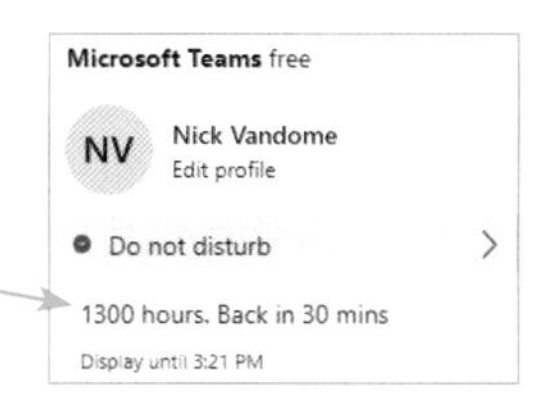

6. The message will appear on your Teams profile and this will be seen by other users

If you set your status to say that you will be back after a certain period of time, put the time the message was created so that your colleagues have a reference for how long you will be away. See Step 2 for an example of this.

Editing Your Profile

In addition to setting your status there is a range of options for editing your profile within Teams, to determine various elements that other people can see. This includes the name that other Teams users see and your profile picture.

Changing your profile name

To change the name that your colleagues see:

1. Click on your account icon in the top right-hand corner of the Teams app

2. Click on the **Edit profile** button

Microsoft Teams free
NV
Nick Vandome
Edit profile

3. Your current profile name is displayed here

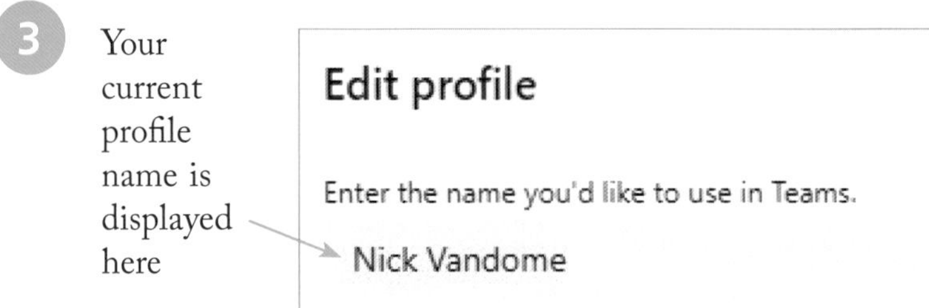

4. Double-click on the name and overtype with a new name, as required

Edit profile
Enter the name you'd like to use in Teams.
Nicholas Vandome

5. Click on the **Save** button to apply the new profile name

Save

Some organizations do not allow users to change their own profile names, as they are set centrally to ensure consistency throughout the organization.

Use your own real name for your Teams profile, rather than a nickname or a humorous name.

Adding a profile picture

To add, or change, your profile picture:

1. Access the profile window as shown on the previous page

2. Click on the **Upload picture** button

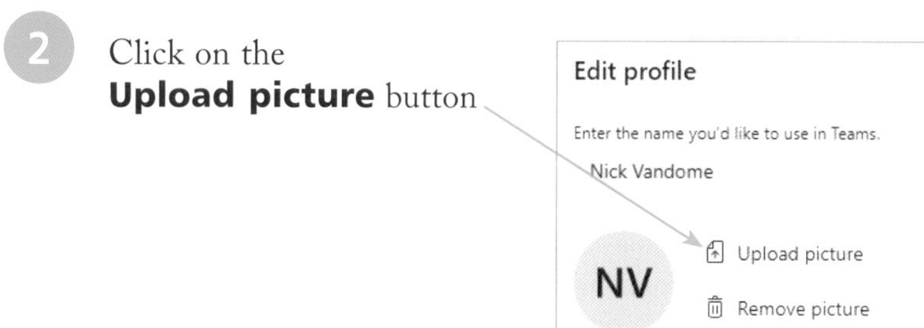

As with profile names, some organizations will apply profile pictures centrally. This will frequently be the photo that is used for your official work pass – again, to ensure consistency.

3. Navigate on your computer to the photo that you want to use, click on it to select it, and click on the **Open** button

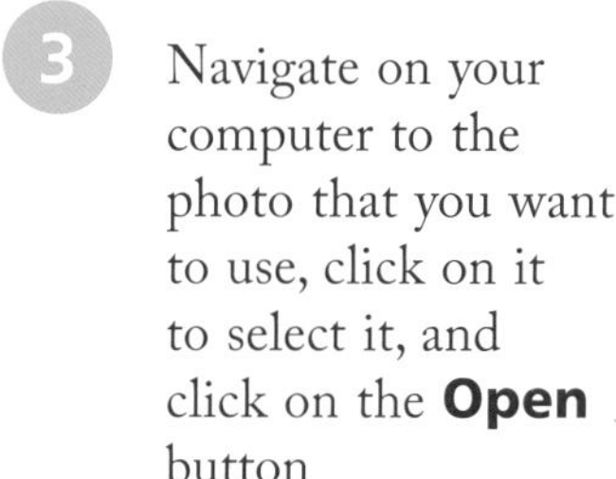

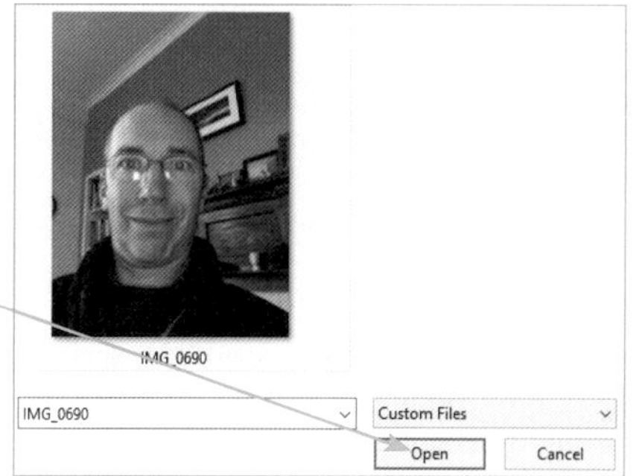

4. The photo is displayed in the **Edit profile** window. Click on the **Save** button if this is the photo you want to use

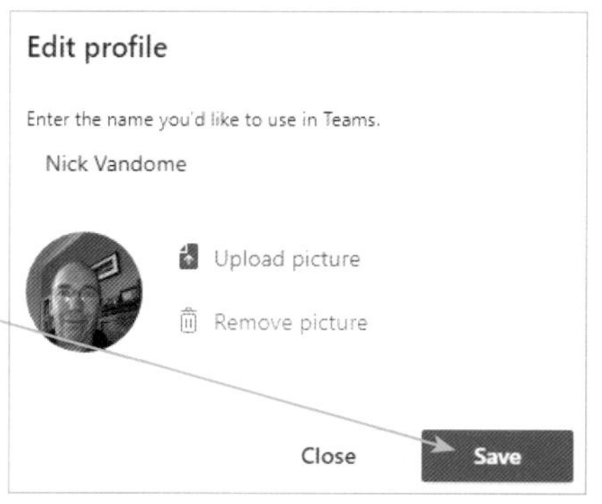

Use a photo in which your face can be seen clearly, since it will appear quite small on the account icon.

5. The photo is displayed as your account icon and this is what other Teams users will see when you add content in the Teams environment

Settings

The appearance and operation of Teams can be customized, to a certain extent, through the use of Settings. To do this:

1. Click on your account icon in the top right-hand corner of the Teams window 

2. Click on the **Settings** option 

3. Click on the **General** tab in the left-hand sidebar, for options for the appearance of Teams and how the app opens, and the language used by it

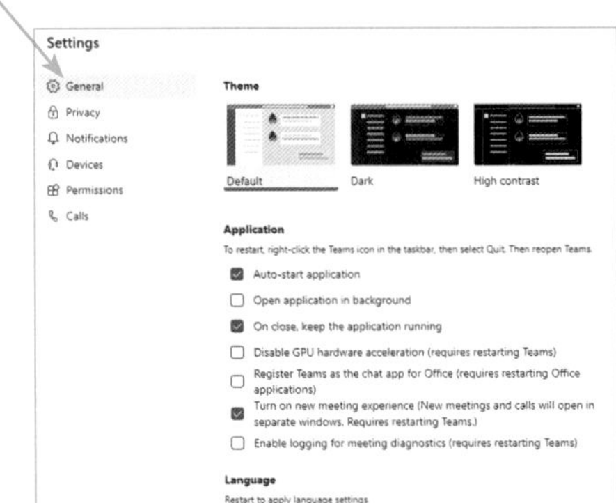

4. Click on the **Privacy** tab in the left-hand sidebar, for options for configuring Do not disturb settings, blocking contacts, applying read receipts for messages, as well as an option for participating in Teams surveys

As with some other aspects of Teams, certain settings may be applied centrally by an organization and not be able to be changed by individual users.

5 Click on the **Devices** tab in the left-hand sidebar, for options for the speakers and microphone that are used with Teams for voice and video calls

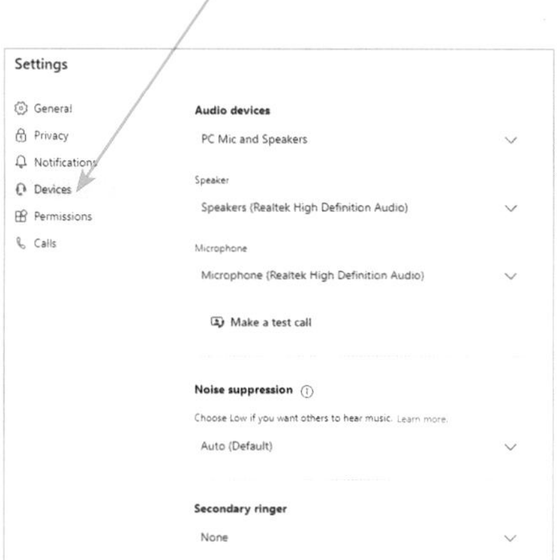

6 Click on the **Permissions** tab in the left-hand sidebar, to specify which items can access your computer

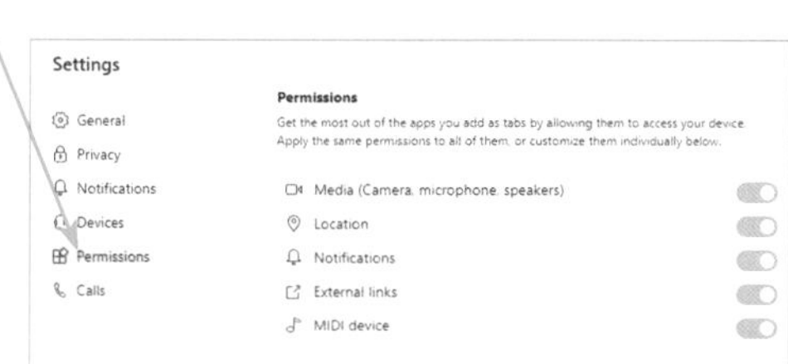

7 Click on the **Calls** tab in the left-hand sidebar, for options for when you make and receive calls

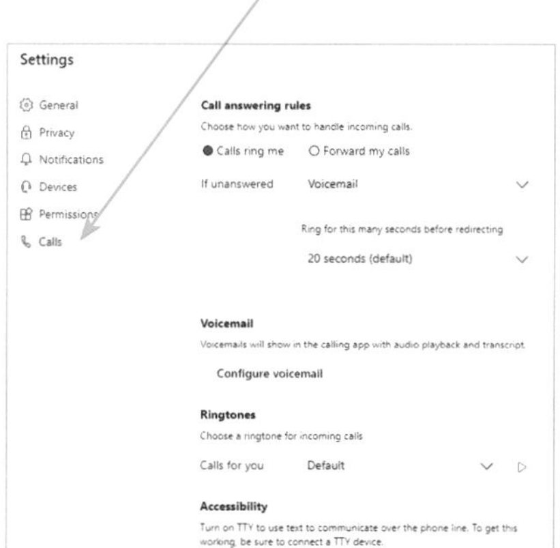

The **Notifications** settings are specific to the Activity feed section and this is looked at on pages 42-43.

Activity Feed Section

The Activity feed is a panel that shows messages you have sent or received, and items from other people where you have been mentioned in a conversation using the @ symbol. Notifications also appear in the Activity feed. To use it:

If you click on a new item in the left-hand sidebar when you are in the Activity feed, this will be replaced by the new selection. However, if you click on the **Activity** button again, it will become available.

1. Click on the **Activity** button in the left-hand sidebar

2. The Activity feed panel appears to the right of the left-hand sidebar. Whichever window you were previously viewing is still available in the right-hand panel

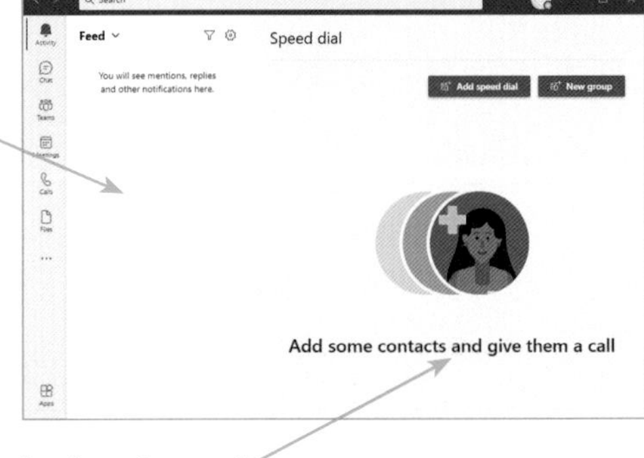

3. Click here at the top of the Activity feed panel to select either the **Feed** or **My Activity** option

4. The **Feed** section displays items that have been posted by other users, either to you or mentioning you

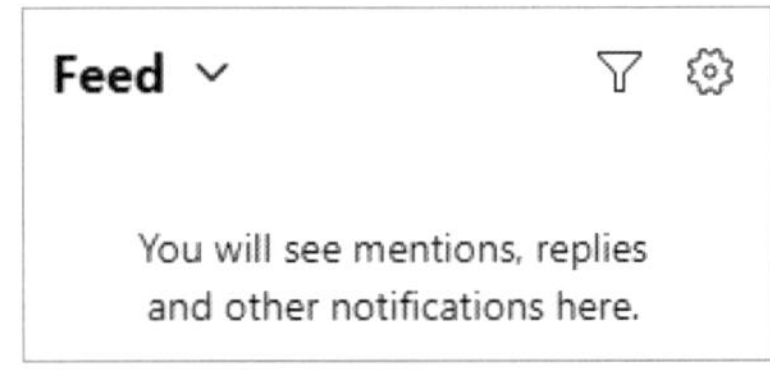

5. The **My Activity** section displays messages that you have sent to other people

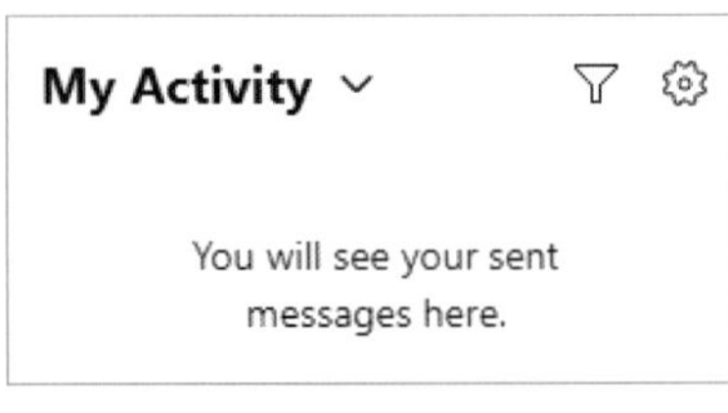

The **Feed** section can contain a variety of information, including text messages you have received; mentions of your name in a message; meeting requests; and teams to which you have been added.

Activity feed settings

Within the Activity feed, there are settings that can be applied for how a range of notifications are displayed. To do this:

1. Click on this button in the top right-hand corner of the Activity feed panel

2. Click on the **Notifications** tab in the left-hand sidebar

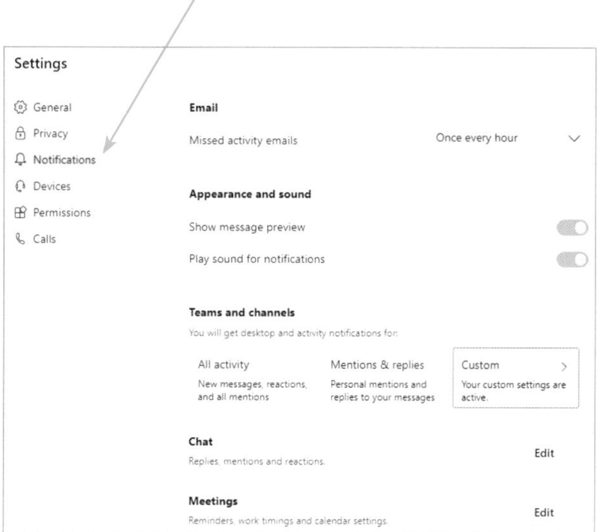

3. The Notifications settings include options for being notified about when email arrives; the appearance and sound for notifications; notifications for activity within Teams and channels; and notifications for text messages and meeting reminders

4. Click on the **Edit** button next to an item (e.g. for Chat) to access more options

Edit

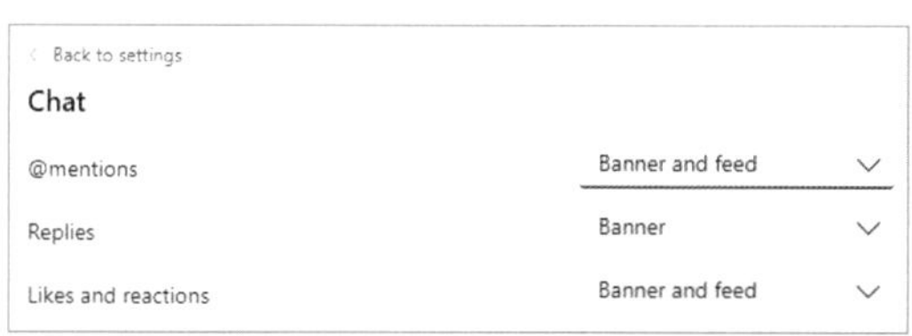

The **Notifications** settings can also be accessed from the account icon, as shown on page 39.

Chat Section

The second button on the sidebar is the Chat option. This can be used to conduct text and video chats with people throughout your organization. To use the Chat interface:

1. Click on the **Chat** button in the left-hand sidebar

2. The Chat window is accessed to the right of the sidebar. The left-hand panel contains details of conversations in which you are participating

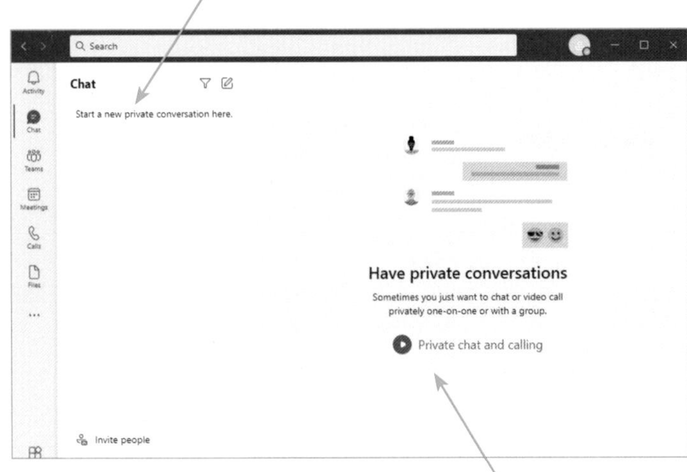

3. The main panel is where details of a selected conversation are displayed – e.g. it displays the individual messages from each member of a conversation

4. Click here to start a new conversation

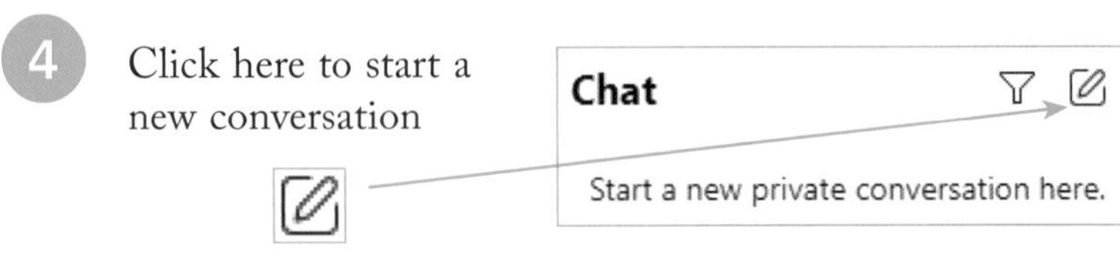

5. Enter details of the person or group with which you would like to have a conversation

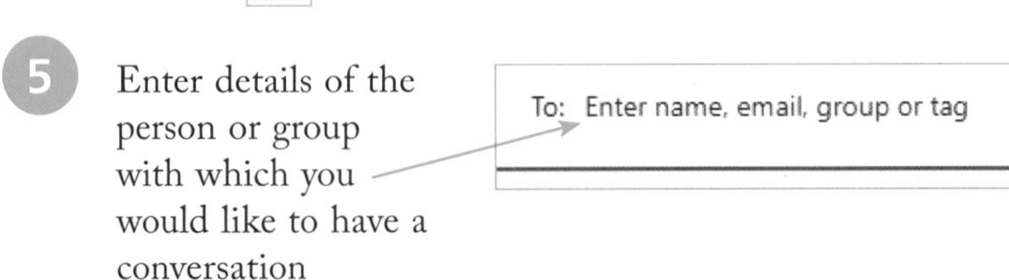

The **Chat** section can be used to have private chats with individuals or groups within Teams. Text chats can also be instigated from the **Teams** section, but these will be visible to everyone in the team.

6 Enter details of the message here

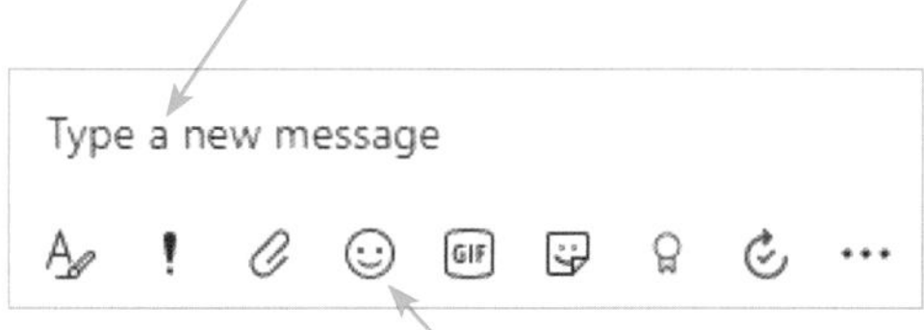

7 Use these icons to format the text in the message, and add content such as photos and emojis

8 Click on this button to send the message

9 Click on a conversation in the left-hand panel

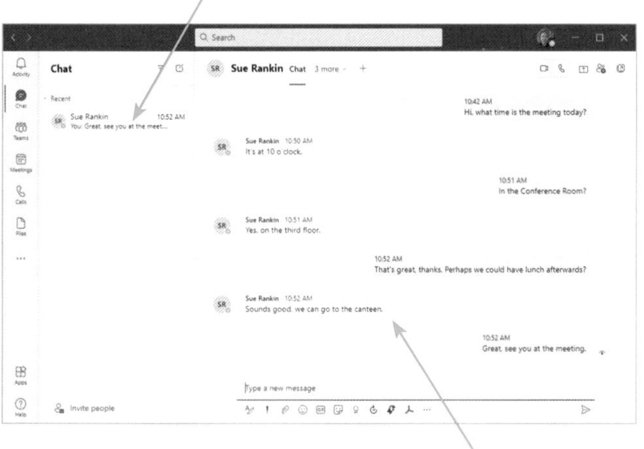

10 The conversation details are displayed in the main panel

11 The current conversation is also displayed at the top of the window. Click here to view other text conversations you are having

12 Click on these buttons on the top toolbar to have a video call with the person in the text chats, or have an audio call

Use these buttons (to the right of the buttons in Step 12) to, from left to right: share your screen with the person or people in a chat; add people to the chat; and pop out the chat, into its own window:

Teams Section

The Teams section is one of the most important in the Teams app, as this is where you will be able to create, manage and join teams so that you can link up with colleagues and perform a variety of tasks, from having a group video chat to sharing and editing documents. To use the Teams interface:

1. Click on the **Teams** button in the left-hand sidebar

2. The left-hand panel displays details of teams that have been created, and the channels within those teams

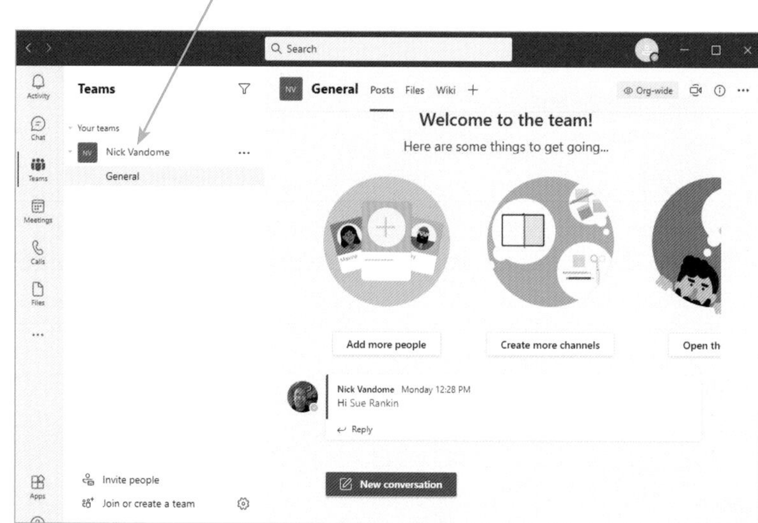

3. Click on a team name to view the channels within it

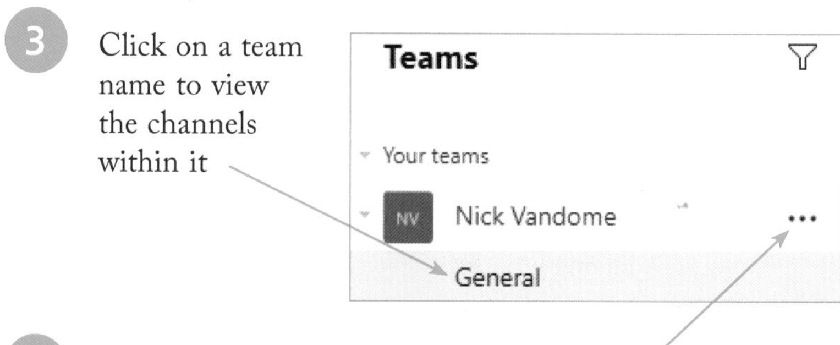

4. Click on this button to access the menu for managing the Teams panel

Think carefully before creating more teams, and channels within Teams. The more that there are, the harder it is to keep track of them all, for both you and the members of the teams.

For more details about viewing and adding channels within a team, see pages 84-93.

5 The Teams menu provides options for managing the Teams section, including adding channels to a team, adding team members, leaving a team, editing a team and deleting a team

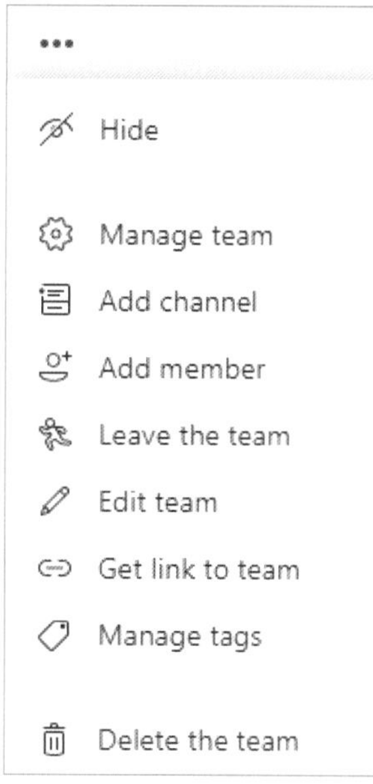

If you are not a Teams administrator, all of the options in Step 5 may not be available; i.e. you may not be able to delete the current team.

6 The top of the Teams section contains details of the current team and channel being viewed, and also tabs relating to elements of the team – e.g. posts, files and knowledge Wikis. Click on the **+** symbol to add tabs

Click on the different tabs in Step 6 to view their contents and add items, as required.

7 Use these buttons at the bottom of the left-hand panel to invite people to a team, join another team, or create a new team, which will appear as the next one on the Teams list

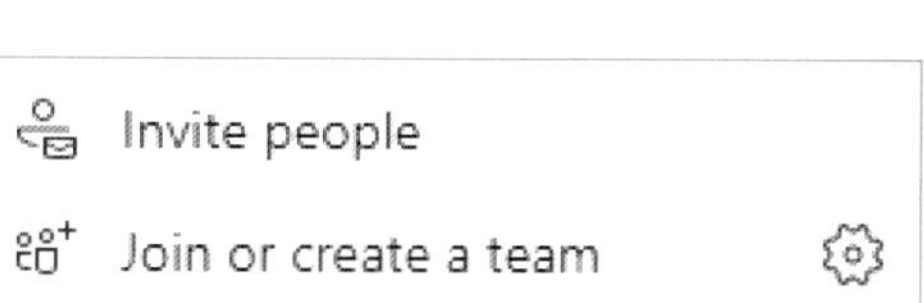

8 Click on these buttons on the top toolbar to, from left to right: start a video call or meeting; view information about the channel currently being viewed; and access additional options

Meetings Section

The Meetings section is where you can organize and manage meetings with colleagues throughout the organization. To use the Meetings interface:

1. Click on the **Meetings** button in the left-hand sidebar

2. The Meetings window does not have a left-hand panel, just one main window

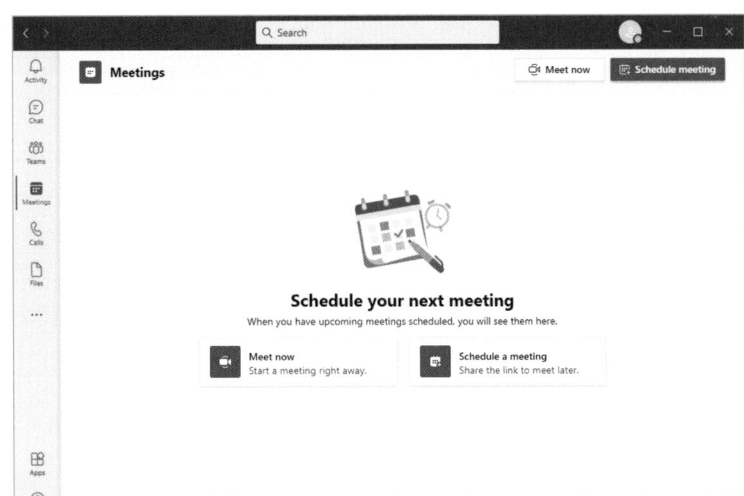

3. Click on the **Meet now** button to start a video meeting with selected people. The meeting starts as soon as you have invited people, and they accept

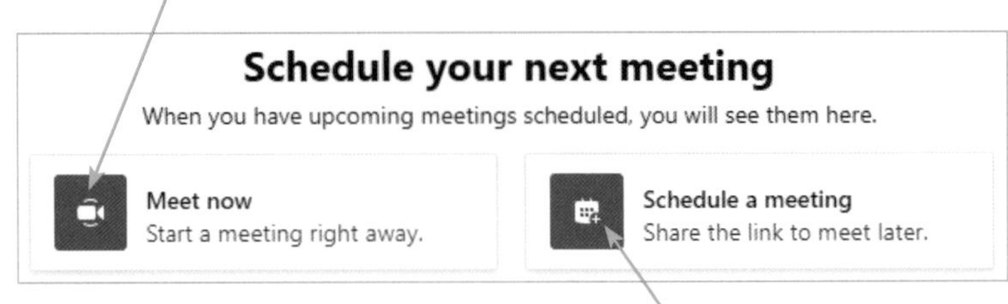

4. Click on the **Schedule a meeting** button to organize a meeting at a specific time

Meetings can also be conducted with audio only, with no video.

Meet now and **Schedule meeting** options are also available on the top toolbar of the **Meetings** section.

5 Click on the **Meet now** button to start a meeting, and make the relevant selections in the Meeting window, for audio and video

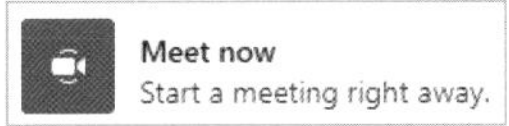

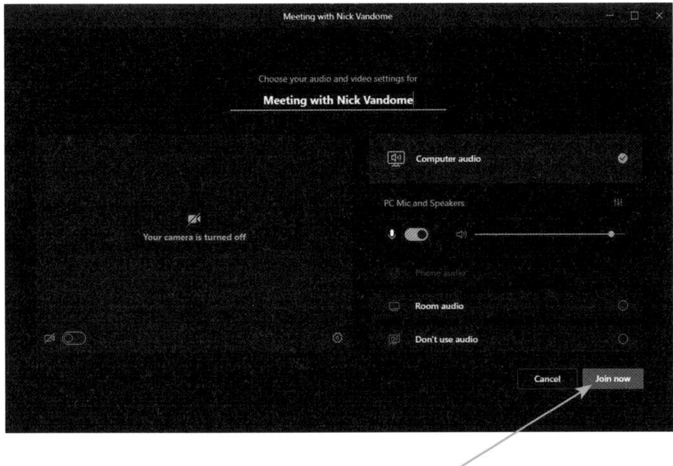

6 Click on the **Join now** button to start the meeting

7 Click on the **Schedule a meeting** button to set a date for a meeting in the future

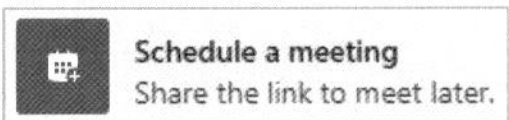

8 Select a date and time for the meeting and click on the **Schedule** button

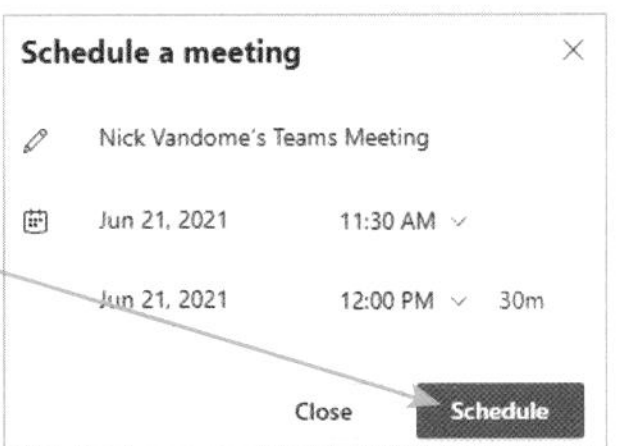

9 Use either the **Copy meeting invitation** or **Share via Google Calendar** button to invite people to the meeting

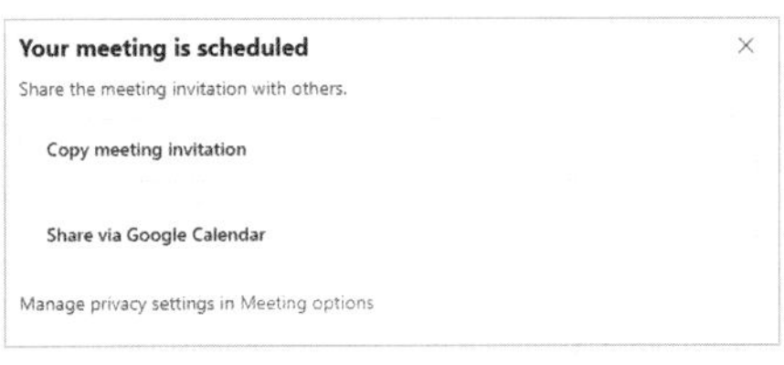

Meetings can be conducted with video and audio, or just audio. To do this, ensure that the camera button is turned **Off**. Drag it to the right to turn the camera **On**.

Once you have joined a meeting, you can invite other people.

Once you have scheduled a meeting, it will appear in the main **Meetings** window.

Calls Section

The Calls section is where you make calls via Teams, to either individuals or groups. To use the Calls interface:

1. Click on the **Calls** button in the left-hand sidebar

2. The left-hand panel displays options for making and managing calls, and the main window is where contacts and groups can be created

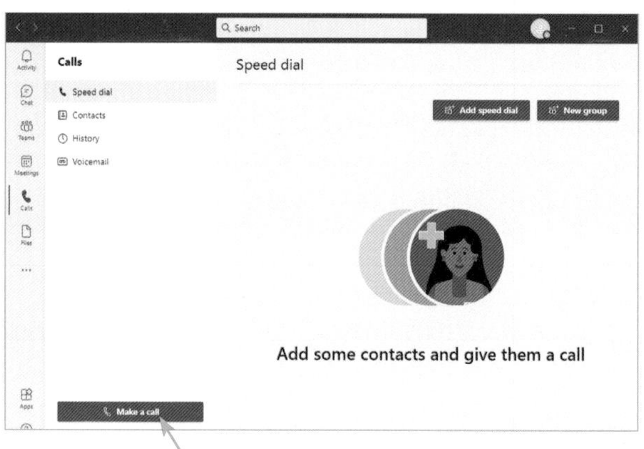

3. Click on the **Make a call** button

4. Click in the **Type a name** text box to enter the name of the person you want to call

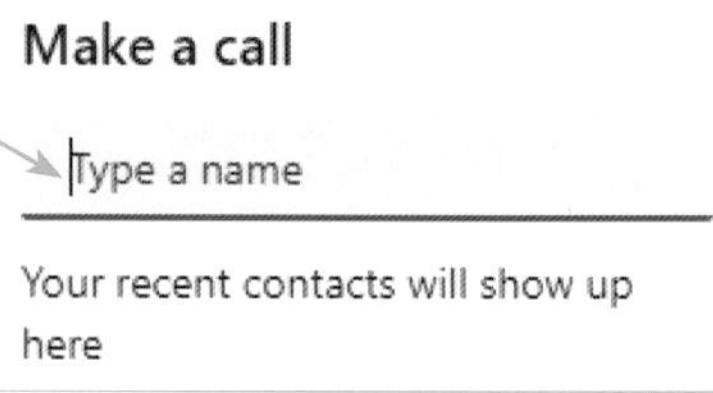

5. If a person is already in your contacts, their name will appear as you start to type it. Click on a person's name to start a call with them

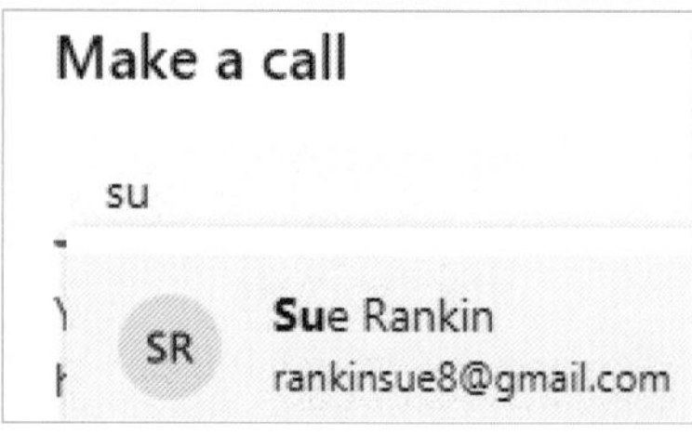

Use a headset with a good-quality microphone to make audio calls, and also video ones, as this will make the process much more enjoyable for everyone involved. Some organizations will provide headsets but, if not, it is worth investing in a good-quality one.

The more details that are entered in Step 5, the more refined the results will be. For instance, the letter "S" may result in multiple options, but if you enter "Steve", this will narrow it down considerably.

6. Click on the **New group** button in the main window

7. Enter a name for the group and click on the **Create** button. Follow the process to add people to the group

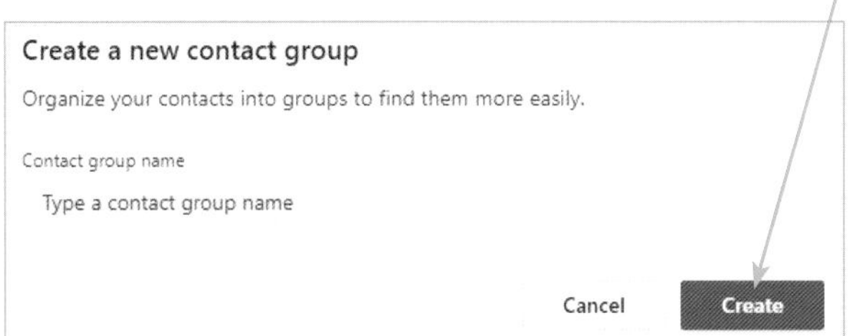

If a group is created, everyone in the group can be contacted with a single call.

8. Click on the **Add speed dial** button to a particular number to add it to your speed dial list

9. Enter the required number and click on the **Add** button

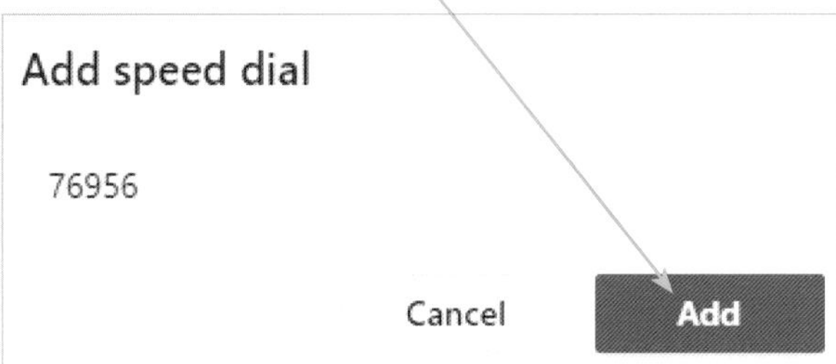

The numbers for speed dialing will frequently be internal ones that are used within an organization. However, it is also possible to enter external numbers, either mobile ones or landline numbers.

10. Click on these buttons in the left-hand panel to, from top to bottom: view speed dial numbers that have been added; view contacts that are available; view your call history; and listen to any voicemail messages. Details about each selected item are displayed in the main window

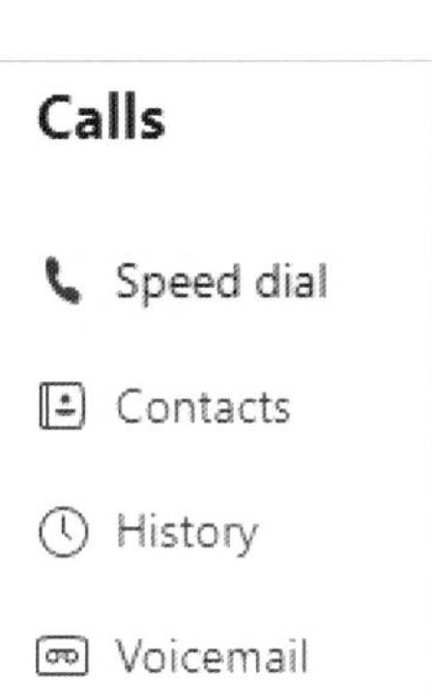

Files Section

The Files section is where you can share files with other people throughout your organization. Files can be uploaded and downloaded from here, and they can also be edited in this environment. To use the Files interface:

Files can also be shared and edited from within the **Files** tab of the **Teams** section.

1. Click on the **Files** button in the left-hand sidebar

2. The left-hand panel displays options for areas where files are shared, and the main window displays the files that have been shared, by you and other people

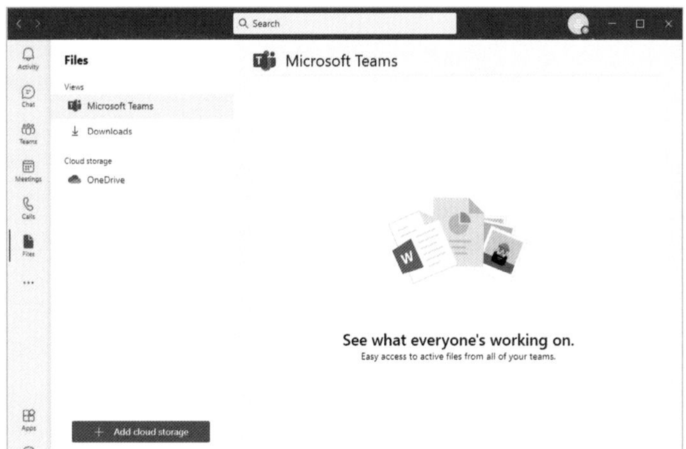

Click on the **Downloads** button in Step 3 to view items that have been downloaded into Teams, and also to access the Downloads folder on your computer.

3. The options in the left-hand panel contain locations from which you can view and add files to Teams

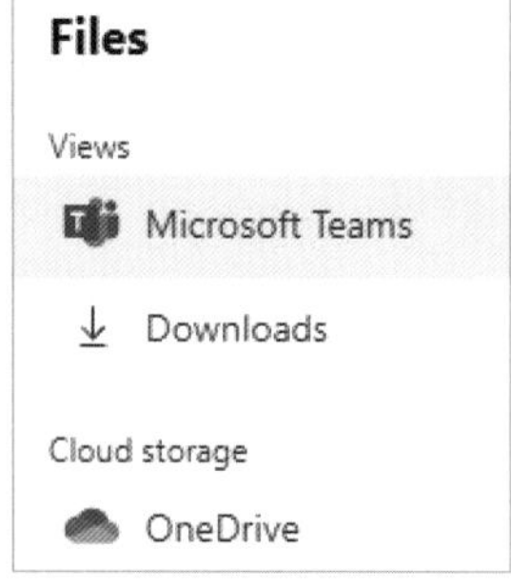

4. Click on the **Add cloud storage** button to add more online storage options; e.g. Dropbox

5 Click the online storage app that you want to use

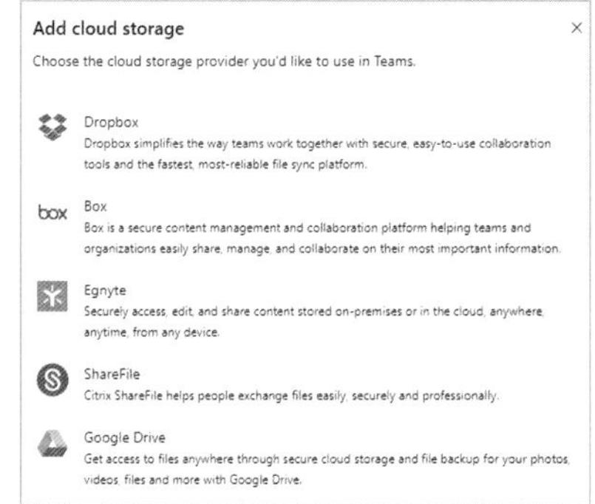

6 Enter the login details for the online storage app and click on the **Sign in** button. The storage app will then become available in Teams and the content in the app can be used within Teams

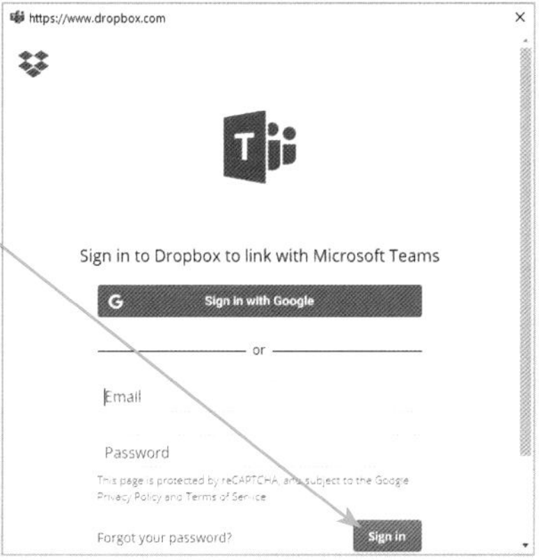

7 Click on an item in the left-hand panel to view its content in the main window

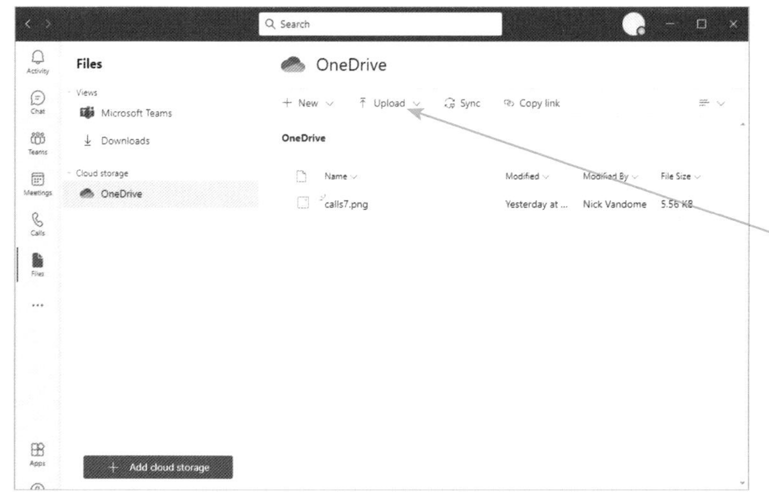

Files can be added to the online storage services, from within the Teams environment. Click on the **Upload** button on the top toolbar to add more files. These will then be available to other users who also have access to the same online storage.

Apps Section

The Apps section can be used to add more functionality to the Teams app, by adding more apps that can be used for a variety of different productivity tasks. To use the Apps interface:

1. Click on the **Apps** button in the left-hand sidebar

2. The left-hand panel displays options for searching for apps, including a Search box and a category list. The main window contains details of available apps

If you are using a specific app within Teams, other users will need to have added it too, for you to use the app to its full potential.

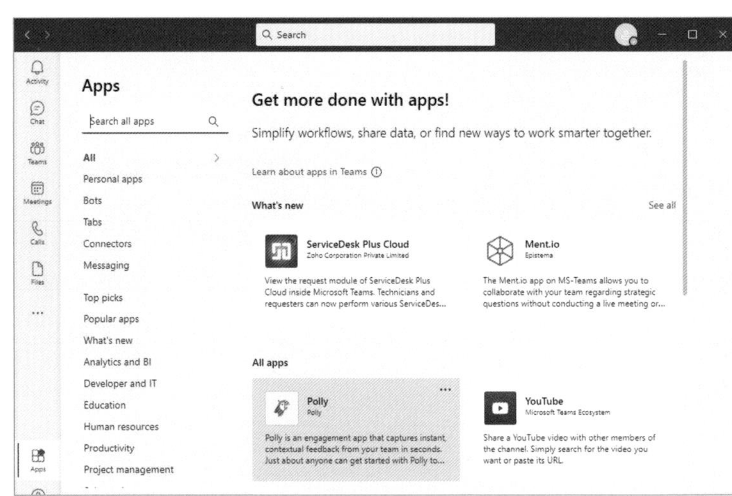

3. Use the left-hand panel to search for a specific app, in the Search box, or click on a category heading to view the available apps in that category

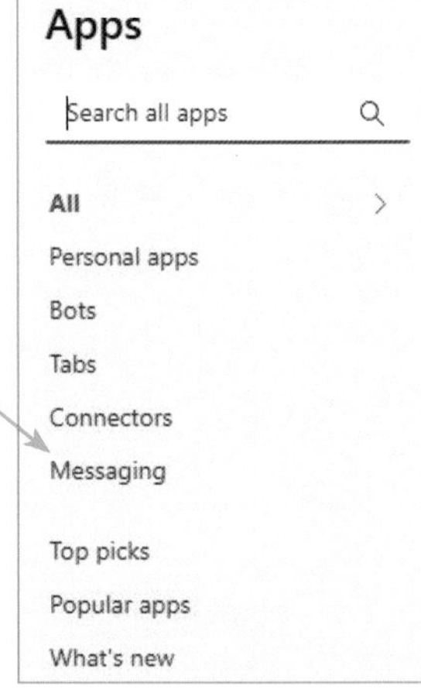

4 Click on an app to view its details

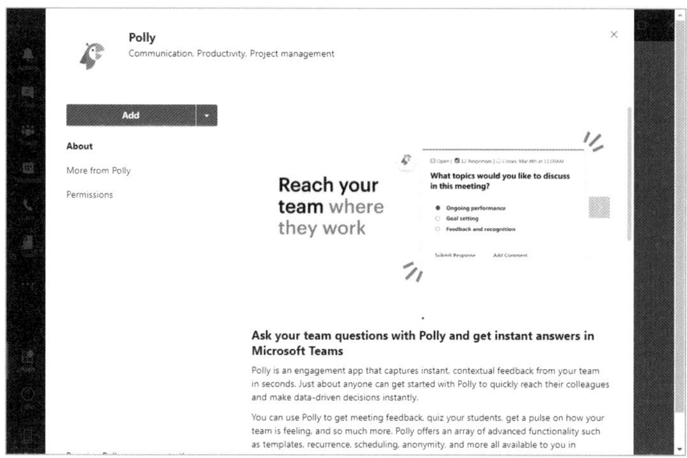

It is worth taking some time to read the descriptions of the apps available within Teams. This is because a lot of them will have functionality that is specific to being used within the Teams environment.

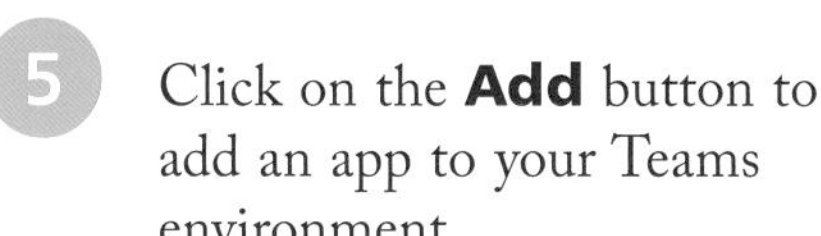

5 Click on the **Add** button to add an app to your Teams environment

6 Click on this button in the sidebar to view the apps that you have downloaded to Teams

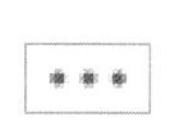

7 Click on an app to open it, or use the **Find an app** Search box to locate a specific app within your Teams environment

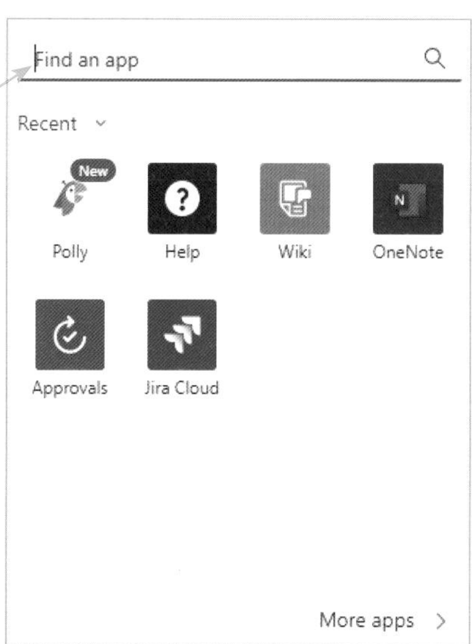

Click on the down-pointing arrow next to the **Add** button in Step 5 to access options for adding the app to a team or a chat, rather than just your own Teams environment.

Knowledge Wikis

Sharing knowledge and information is a vital way for organizations to develop and thrive. Within Teams there is an option for creating knowledge Wikis: shared information about a specific topic, which multiple people can add to and edit. To create and view a knowledge Wiki:

It is a good idea to have an organizational policy for creating Wikis within teams, to clearly define what is – and isn't – allowed in terms of content and subjects.

1. From within a team, or a channel, click on the **Wiki** tab on the top toolbar

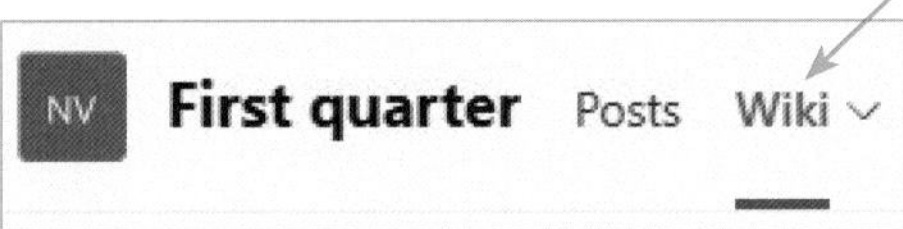

2. If a Wiki has already been created for a topic within the team or channel, it will be shown here. If a Wiki has not already been created, the page will have **Untitled** headings

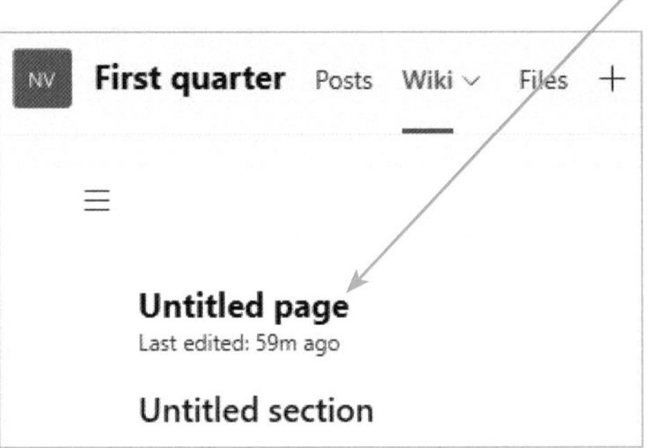

3. Double-click on the **Untitled page** heading and overtype it to give the Wiki a name. Double-click on the **Untitled section** heading and overtype it to give each section a name. Click here to add the Wiki's content

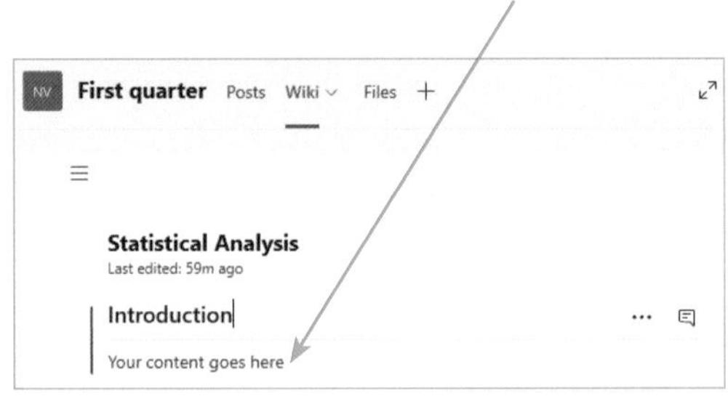

4. Move the cursor below the current content and click on the **Add a new section here** option, to add another heading

5. Move the cursor over a heading and click on the menu button next to a heading. Click on the options, as required, to manage items within the Wiki

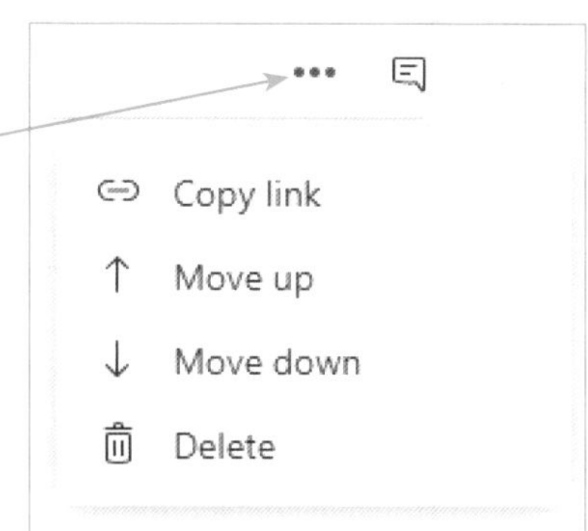

Be careful not to leave derogatory comments about a post within a knowledge Wiki. This type of comment can easily lead to conversations getting out of hand. If you have an issue with something that has been posted, it is usually better to discuss it with the person face to face.

6. Click on this button, to the right of the menu button in Step 5, to add comments about the Wiki. Enter a comment here and click on the **Send** button

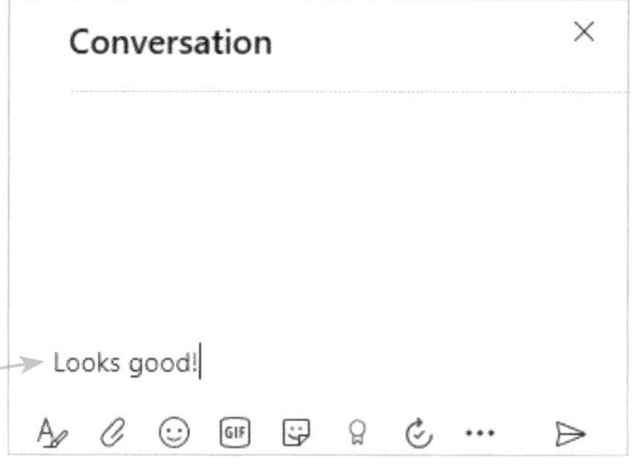

7. A conversation is created. This relates to the Wiki and can be added to by all of the team members

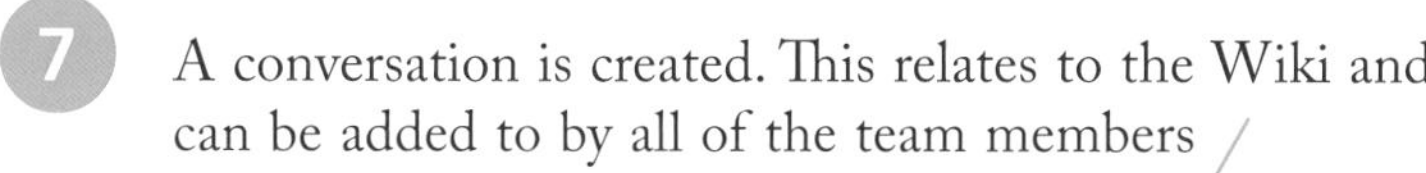

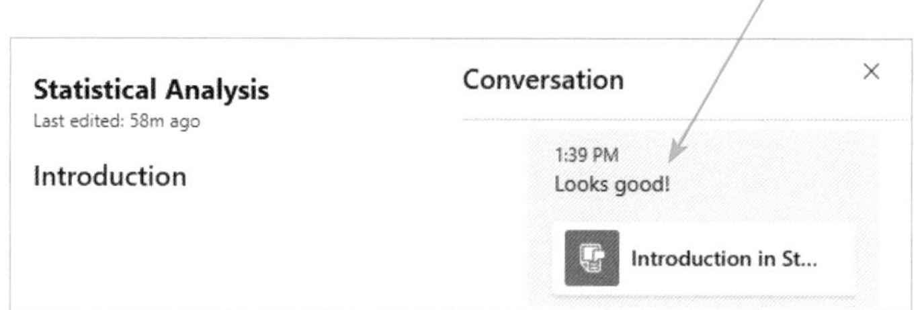

For more details about adding and formatting Wikis, see pages 180-186.

Help Section

The Help section provides a range of information and tips about using Teams. To use the Help interface:

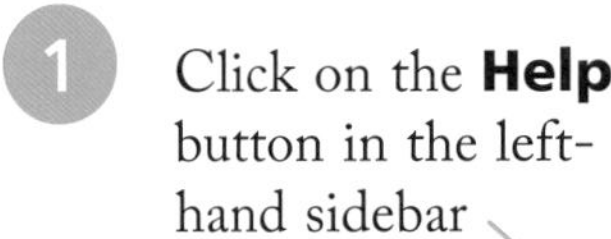

1. Click on the **Help** button in the left-hand sidebar

2. The various Help options are displayed. Click on one of these to view its details

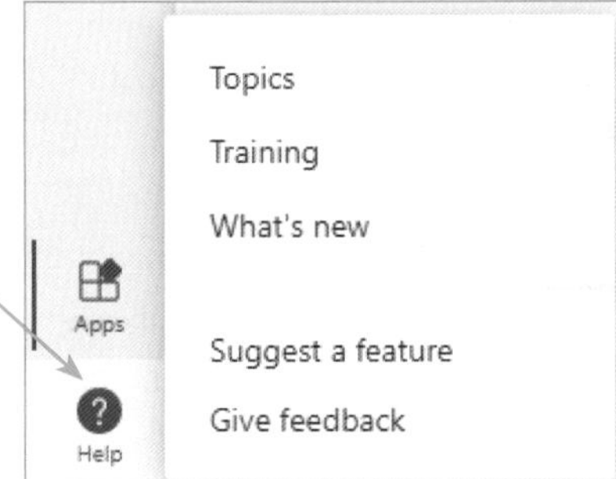

3. The Help topics are displayed within the Teams interface. Use the buttons on the top toolbar to find Help categories for **Topics**, **Training**, **What's new** and **About**

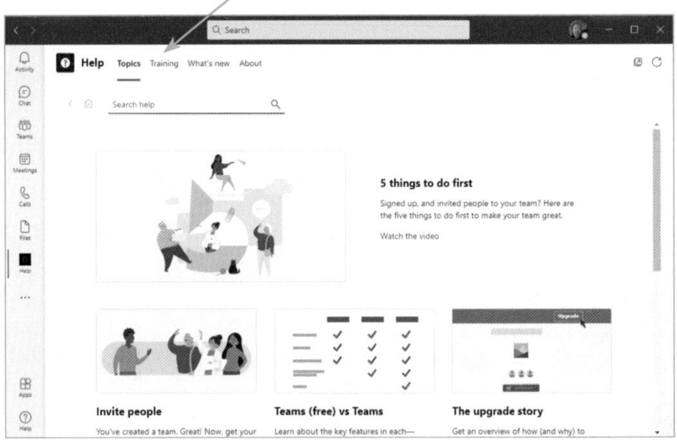

4. Each category has its own range of topics and headings

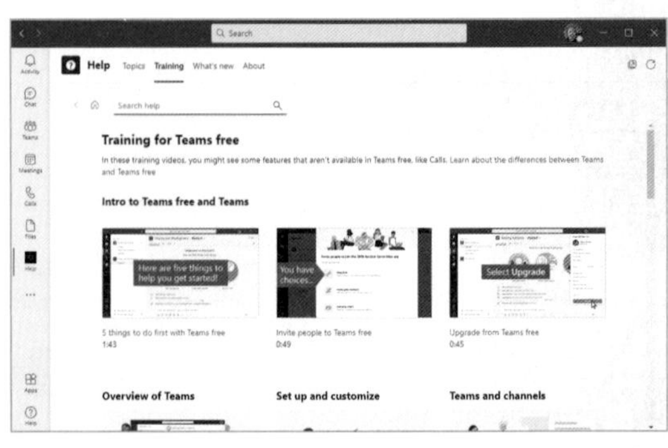

Each Help category contains animated videos for guiding users through specific tasks.

4 Creating Teams

Creating groups of people (teams) that can communicate and collaborate together is at the heart of the Teams app. This chapter shows how to get the most out of this in terms of creating different types of teams and managing them.

Creating a Private Team

The Teams app has considerable power and functionality in terms of the range of tasks that it can facilitate in the workplace. However, its central function is to allow teams of people to communicate and share information. This can be done on an organization-wide basis or through teams of specific individuals, and different teams can be set up accordingly. To get started with creating a new, Private, team:

Don't forget

New members have to be invited to a Private team by the organizer; they cannot join it themselves.

1. Click on the **Teams** button in the left-hand sidebar

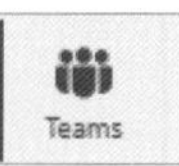

2. Click on the **Join or create a team** button at the bottom of the left-hand panel

3. Click on the **Create team** button

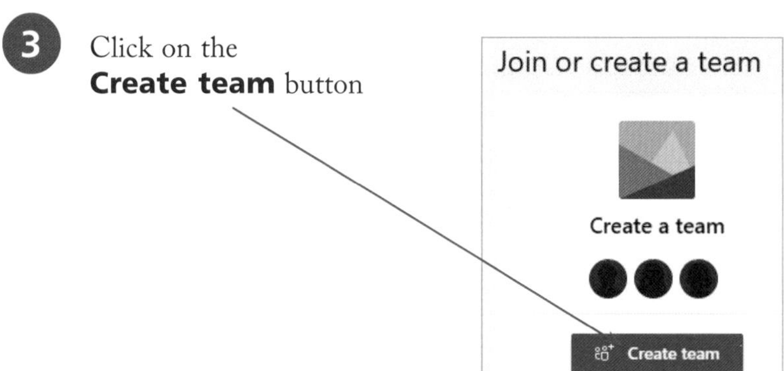

For details about creating a team using an existing group or team, see pages 67-69. For details about creating a team using a template, see pages 70-71.

4. There are several options for creating a new team. To create a basic team, click on the **From scratch** button

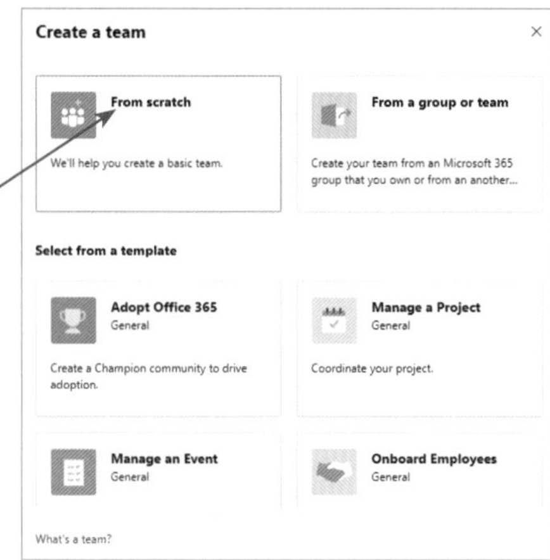

5 There are three options for creating a new team: **Private**, where you have to invite people to join the team, or they ask to; **Public**, where anyone in the organization can join the team; and **Org-wide**, where everyone in the organization is automatically part of the team. Click on the **Private** option to create your first team

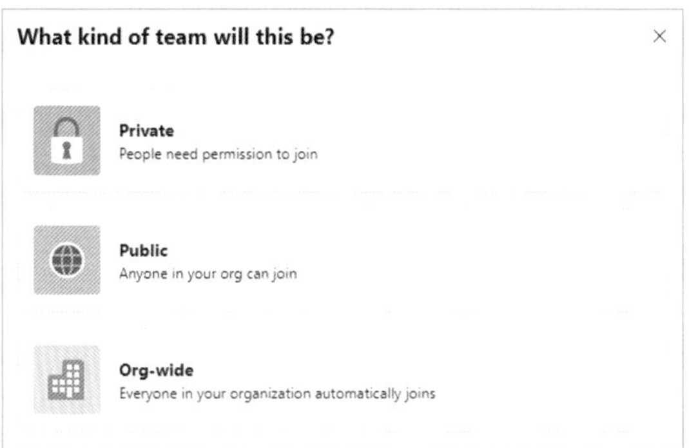

For details about creating a Public team, see pages 64-65. For details about creating an Org-wide team, see page 66.

6 Enter a name for the team, with a description of it in the text box below the team name

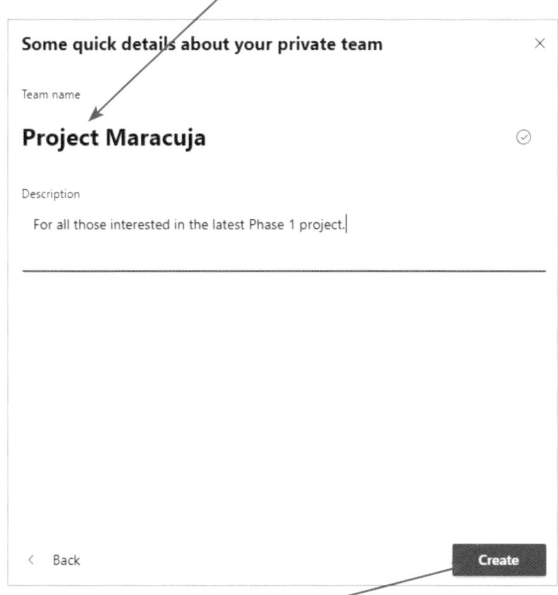

A description for the team does not have to be added but if one is used, make it as relevant to the subject matter of the team as possible.

7 Click on the **Create** button to create the team

...cont'd

8. For a Private team, members have to be invited by the organizer of the team. Members can be invited during the setup stage, or at a later time. To add members during the setup process, enter a name here

Add members to Project Maracuja

Start typing a name, distribution list, or security group to add to your team. You can also add people outside your organization as guests by typing their email addresses.

Start typing a name or group | Add

If groups of users have been created, these can be entered in Step 8. This is a good way to add numerous users with a single word or phrase.

9. When you start entering a name, options will be displayed from your contacts, or from within your organization. Click on a name to select it

Once someone has been added to a Private team, they will receive an email to alert them to this. They will not have to do anything themselves to join the team.

10. Once all of the required members have been selected, click on the **Add** button

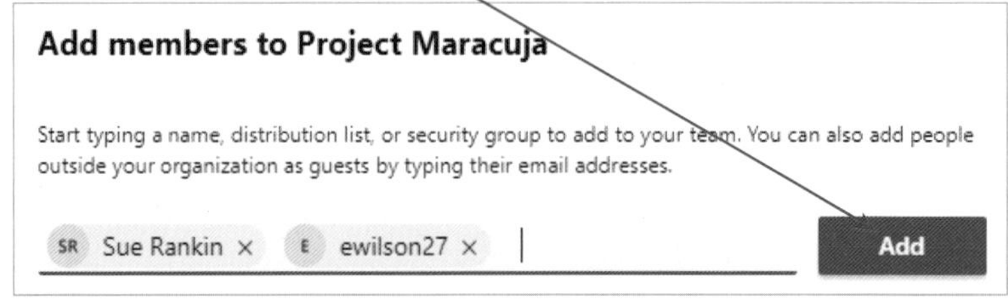

11 Once people have been added, they appear with **Member** next to their name

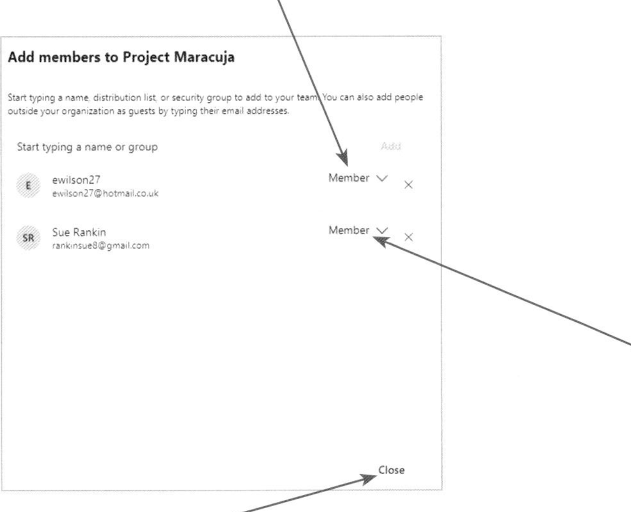

12 Click on the **Close** button once the required members have been added

13 The team name appears in the left-hand panel, below any existing teams, and with the **General** channel already available

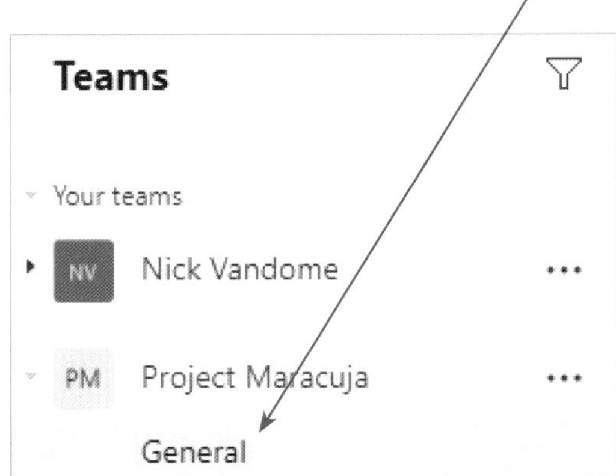

14 The type of team is displayed below your account icon. A Private team is displayed as **Team**

Hot tip

Click on the down-pointing arrow on the **Member** button to select an option for making the person an owner of the team. This will give them more options in terms of management of the team.

Hot tip

A Public team is displayed as **Org** below the account icon, and an organization-wide team is displayed as **Org-wide**.

Creating a Public Team

Public teams can be created within the Teams app, and anyone within an organization can join these types of teams. Individuals and groups can be invited when the team is created, or they can join the team themselves. To create a Public team:

A Public team displays the **Org** icon on the top toolbar.

1. Click on the **Create team** button, as shown on page 60

2. Click on the **From scratch** option

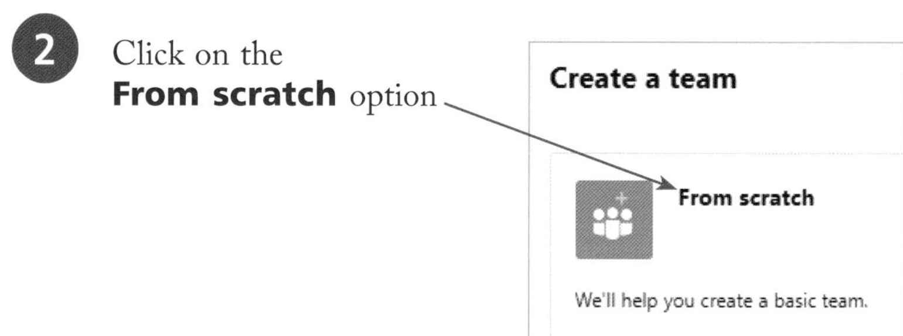

3. Click on the **Public** option

4. Enter a name for the Public team and a description of it, as required

5. Click on the **Create** button

If a team name is not entered in Step 4, you will not be able to create the team.

6. Click in the text box to add people to the team, in the same way as with a Private team. However, people do not have to be added at this point, as they can join a Public team themselves at a later time

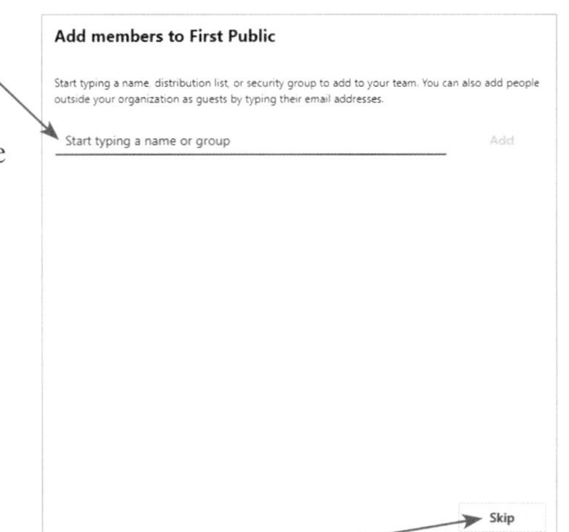

7. Click on the **Skip** button to create the team without adding any team members at this point

8. The team is added in the left-hand panel. Click on the menu button to access the menu

9. Click on the **Manage team** option to view details about the team

10. Details about the team are displayed, including the owner (who set up the team) and any members. If no-one was added in Step 6, there will be no members in the team at this point

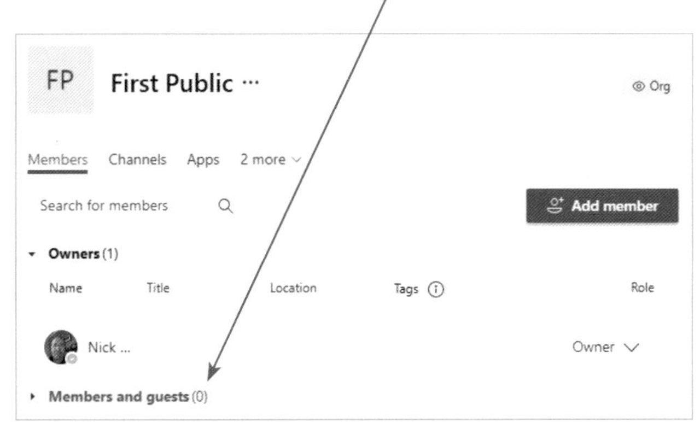

Anyone in the organization can join a Public team. To do this, access the **Join or create a team** window, as shown on page 60. Enter the name of the team in the **Search teams** box,

Search teams

move the cursor over the team, and click on the **Join team** button.

Click on the **Add member** button in Step 10 to add people to the team.

Creating an Org-wide Team

Organization-wide (Org-wide) teams are those that are automatically available to everyone within the organization, provided they are using Teams. To create an Org-wide team:

As soon as a new Org-wide team is created, it will automatically be available to everyone in the organization and will appear in the Teams section for all users.

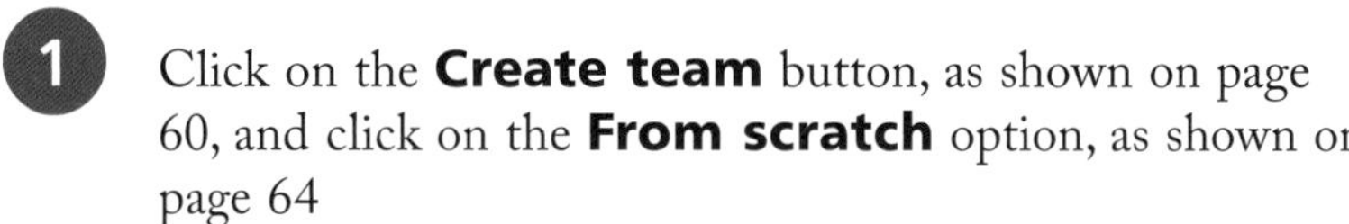

1. Click on the **Create team** button, as shown on page 60, and click on the **From scratch** option, as shown on page 64

2. Click on the **Org-wide** option

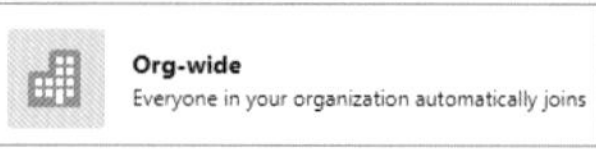

3. Enter a name and description for the team and click on the **Create** button

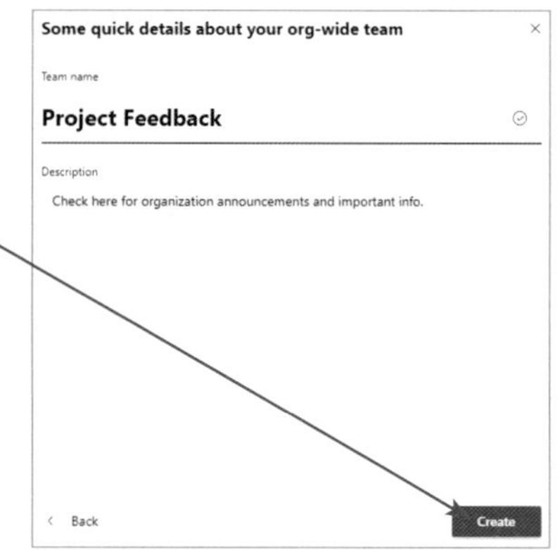

An Org-wide team displays the **Org-wide** icon on the top toolbar.

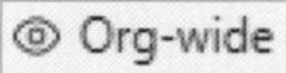

4. Access the **Manage team** option, as shown on page 65, to view the members in the team. This should be all of the people in the organization

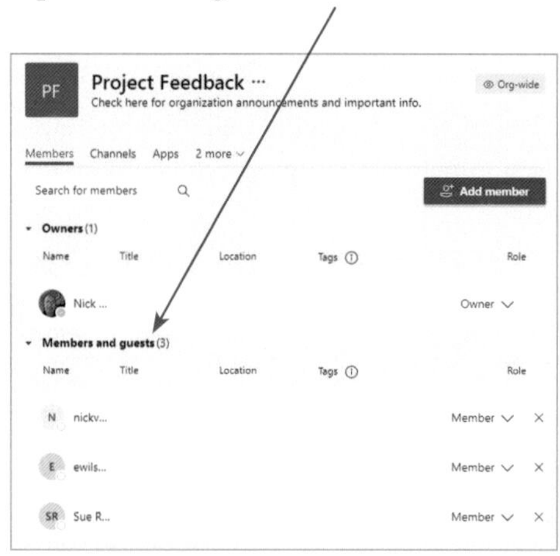

Creating From an Existing Team

Teams can become quite complex in terms of the channel structure and apps that are added to them. At times you may want to create a team with similar basic content, but on a new subject. This can be done by creating a new team from an existing one.

1. Click on the **Create team** button, as shown on page 60
2. Click on the **From a group or team** option

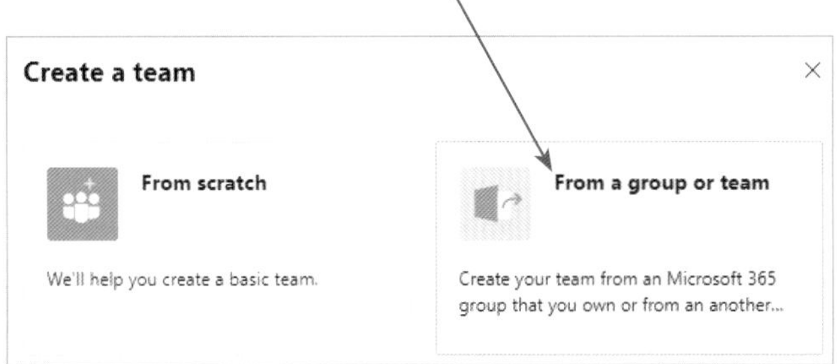

3. Click on the **Team** option

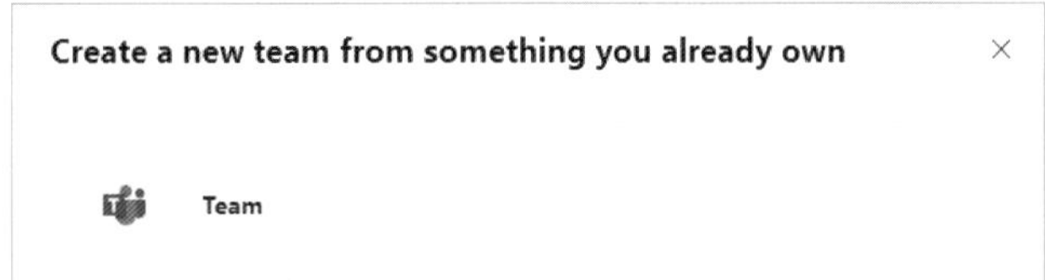

4. Click on one of your existing teams to use this as the basis for the new team

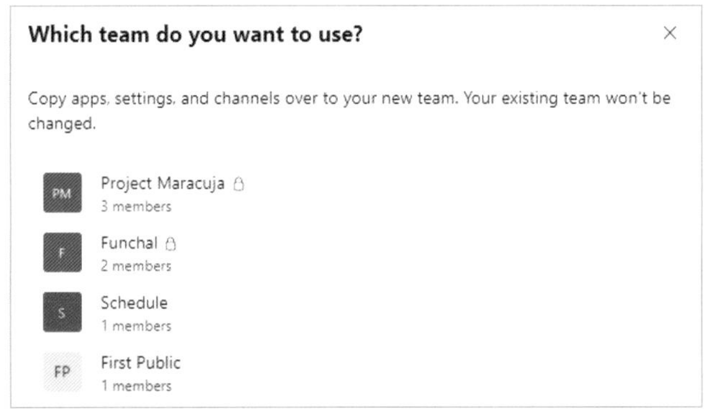

If you create a team from an existing team and then edit the new team, the original one will be untouched.

...cont'd

5. The new team window has various options to be applied to the team. The default name of the team is the one on which it is based, with the word **[copy]** after it

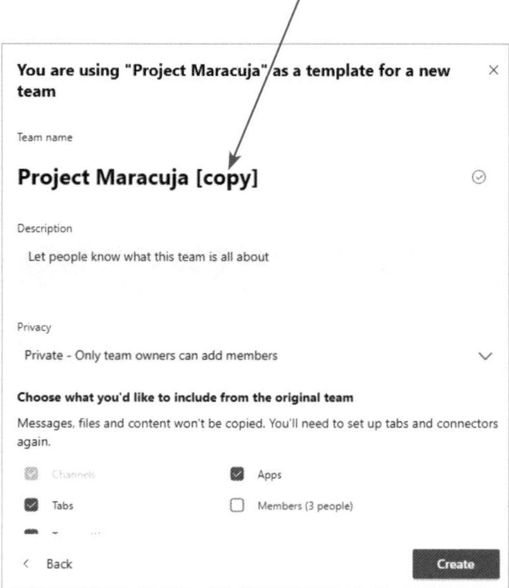
You are using "Project Maracuja" as a template for a new team

Team name

Project Maracuja [copy]

Description

Let people know what this team is all about

Privacy

Private - Only team owners can add members

Choose what you'd like to include from the original team

Messages, files and content won't be copied. You'll need to set up tabs and connectors again.

Channels
Apps
Tabs
Members (3 people)
Back
Create

Although the default name in Step 5 can be used for the team, it is recommended that a new one be used, to avoid any confusion.

6. Double-click on the name and overtype a new name

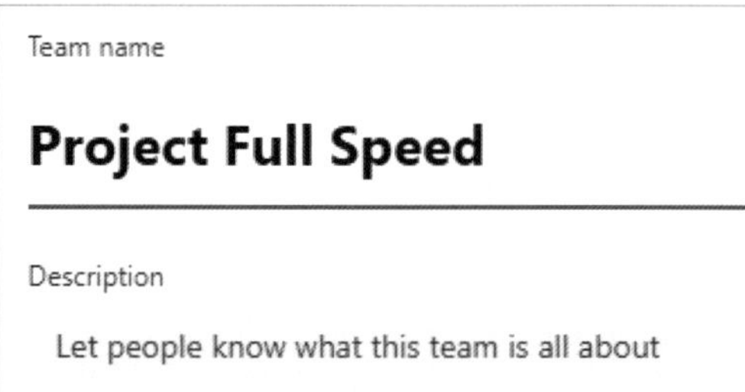

7. Below the **Privacy** heading, select whether you want the team to be a **Private** or a **Public** one

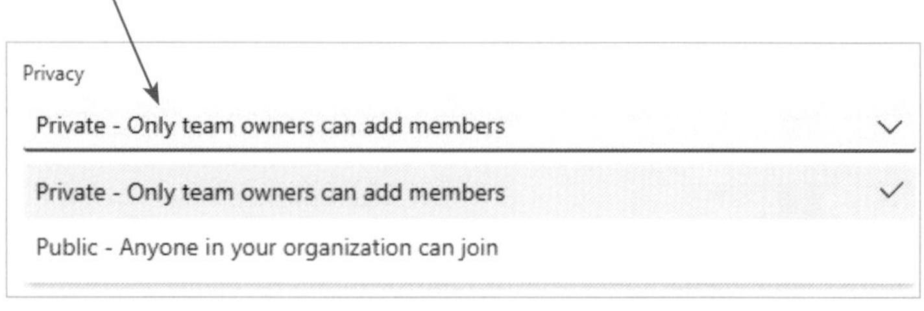

8 Check **On** the items from the original team that you want to include in the new one, including **Channels**, **Apps**, **Tabs** and team **Members**

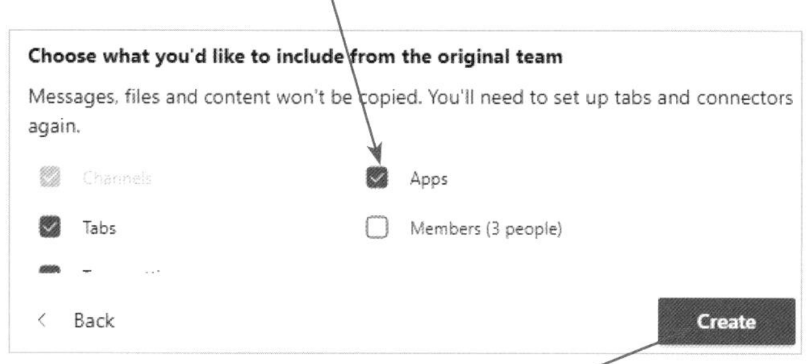

9 Click on the **Create** button

10 Add team members in the same way as for a standard team. Click on the **Add** button and then the **Close** button once all team members have been added

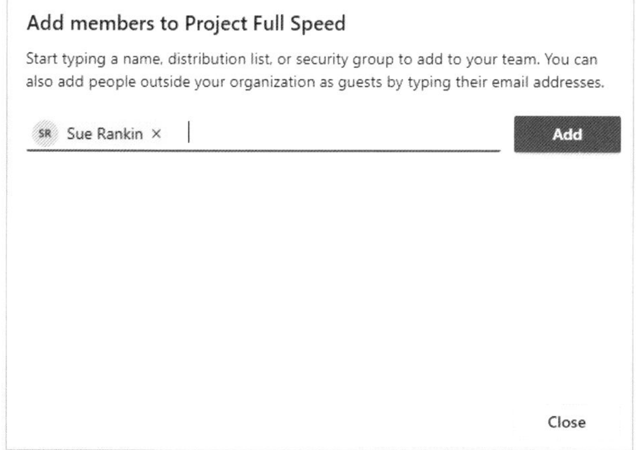

11 The new team is added to the Teams list in the left-hand panel

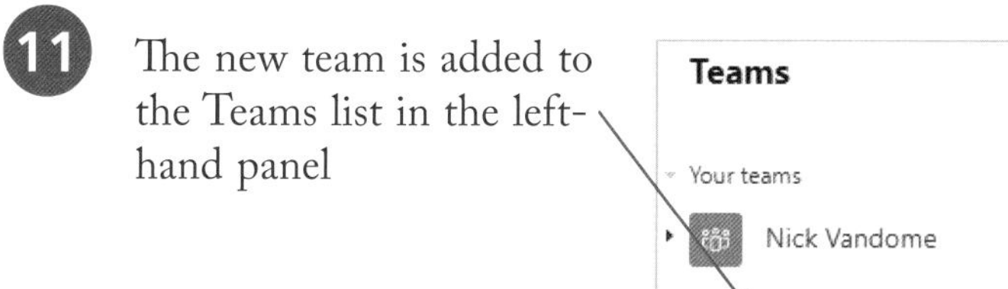

To join a team that someone else has created, click on the **Join or create a team** button in the left-hand panel and enter the team name in the **Search teams** box.

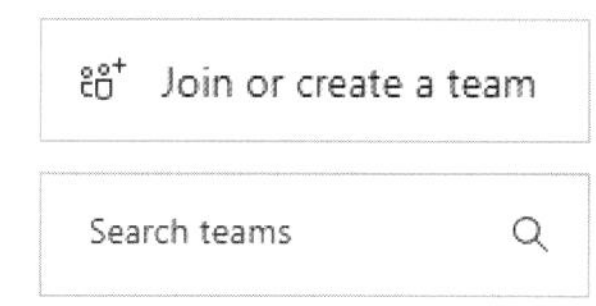

Creating Teams From Templates

A number of teams can cover the same type of subject matter; e.g. managing a project in an organization. Since the content of these types of teams is similar, a good option for creating a team is from a template that already contains the necessary items, in terms of channels and apps. To create a team from a template:

The Teams templates are created with items that are thought to be of most use in the workplace.

1. Click on the **Create team** button, as shown on page 60
2. Click on one of the options below the **Select from a template** heading

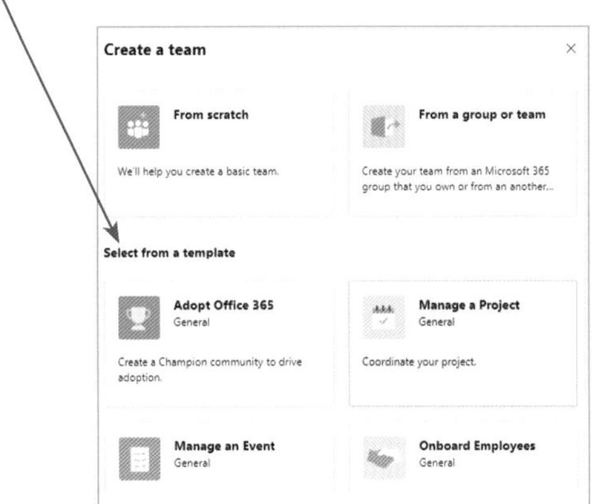

The items in a template, such as the channels and the apps, are a good way to find out about a recommended structure for a team in the workplace.

3. The items that will be included in the team are listed on the template page. Click on the **Start** button to begin creating the associated team

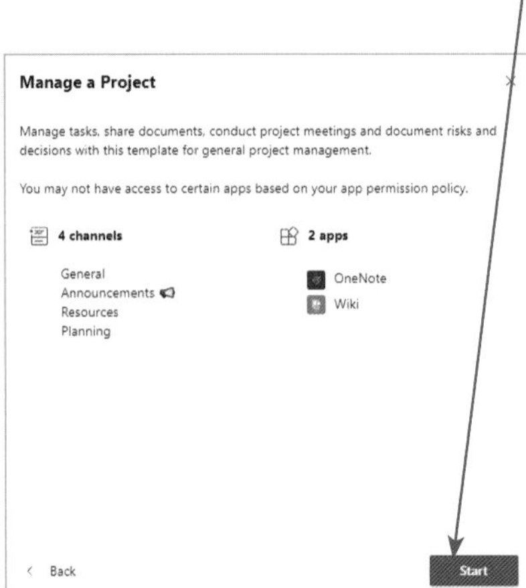

4. Select whether the team is to be **Private** or **Public**

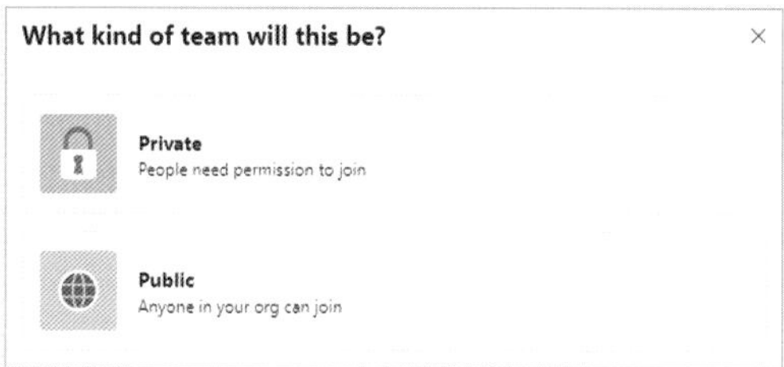

5. Enter a name for the team, and a description (if required) and click on the **Create** button

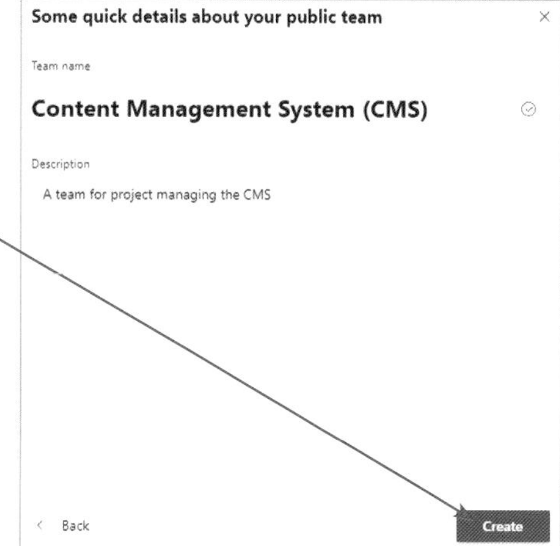

6. Select the team in the left-hand panel and access the **Manage team** option, as shown on page 65. Click on the **Apps** tab to view the apps that are included with the team, via the template from which it was created

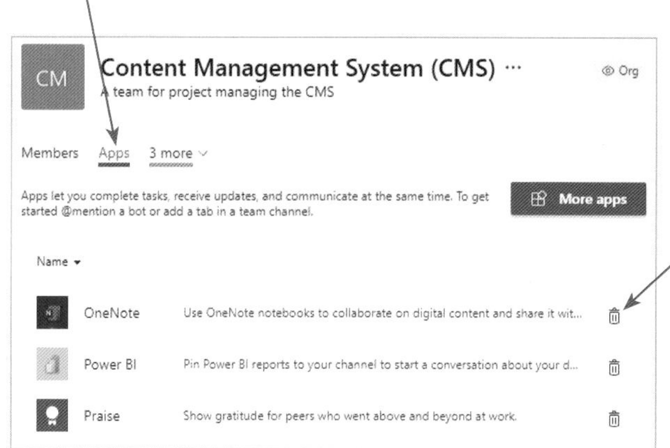

The default apps that are added to a team based on a template do not have to be kept. Click on the Trash icon in Step 6 to remove an app, if required.

Adding Team Members

People can be added to a team when it is first set up (unless it is Org-wide team, in which case everyone in the organization will automatically be added to it). It is also possible to add people to a team at any time. To do this:

1. Click on a team name in the left-hand panel
2. Click on the menu button next to the team
3. Click on the **Add member** button
4. Start entering the name of the person to add to the team and click on one of the results
5. Click on the **Add** button

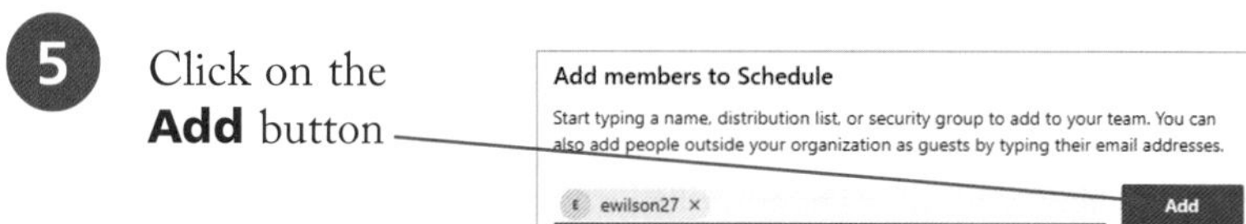

6. The new member is added here. Add more new members as required, and click on the **Close** button

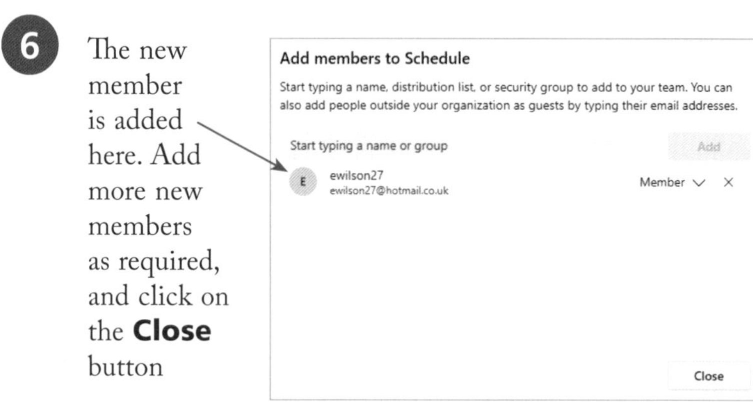

New team members can also be added from within the **Manage team** section. See pages 74-75 for details.

Editing a Team

Certain elements of a team can be changed using the Edit function. This is more limited in its options than the Manage team option; see pages 74-77 for details. To edit a team:

1. Click on a team name and click on the menu button, as shown on the previous page

2. Click on the **Edit team** button

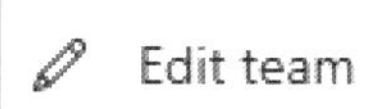

3. The general details of the team are displayed, including name, description and privacy settings

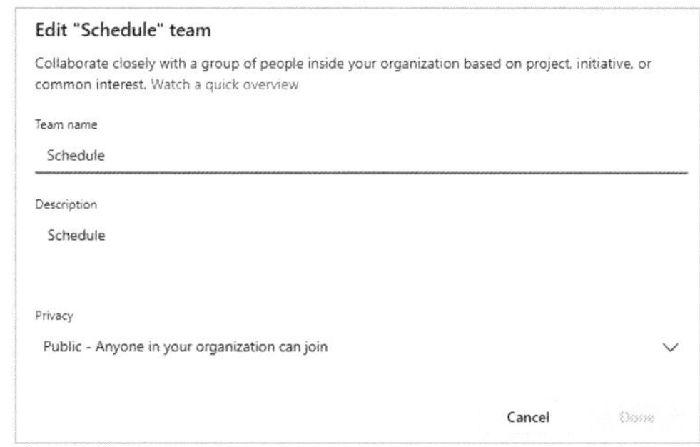

4. Double-click in the **Team name** and **Description** text boxes to change them as required

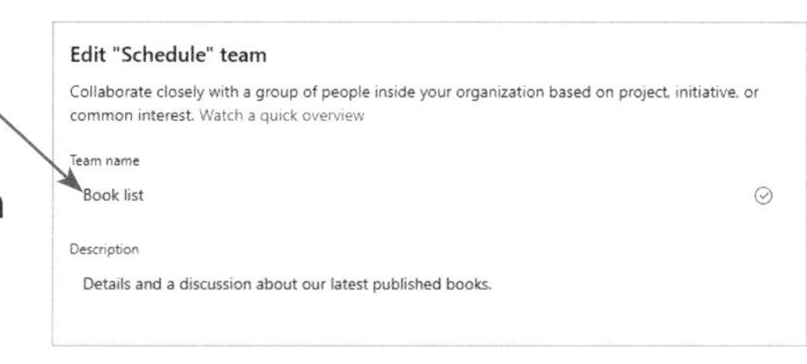

5. Click on the down-pointing arrow next to the privacy setting to select a new one

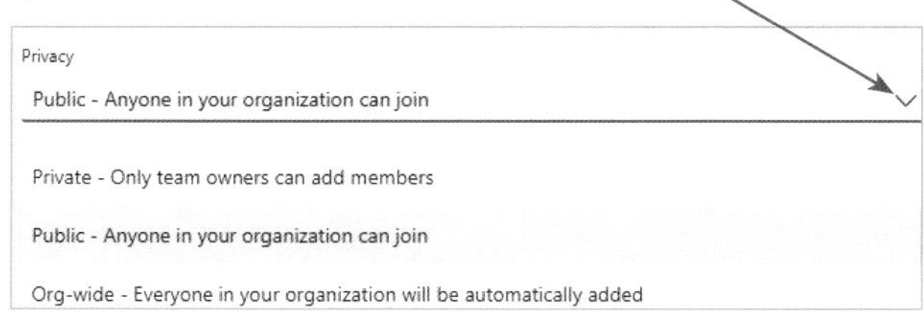

6. Click on the **Done** button to apply the editing changes

If you change the name or description of a team, this will be replicated in the team's list for all of the team members.

Managing a Team

For a more extensive range of options for editing numerous elements of a team (rather than just the name, description and privacy settings) the Manage team section is ideal for this:

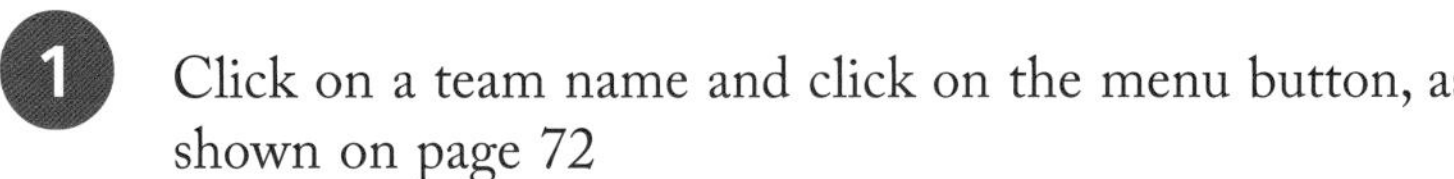

1. Click on a team name and click on the menu button, as shown on page 72

2. Click on the **Manage team** button

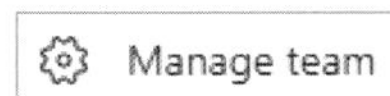

For Org-wide teams, all members of an organization are automatically included as members of these teams.

Viewing team members

To view everyone in the selected team:

1. Click on the **Members** tab

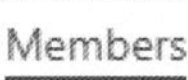

2. Details of the team owner(s) are displayed, and also a heading for team members and guests

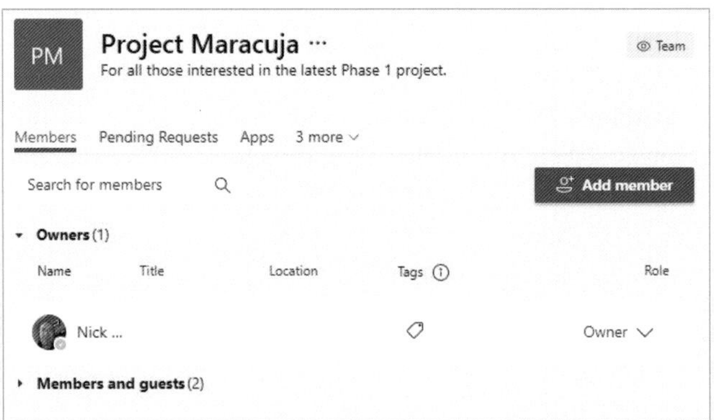

Guests are people outside the Teams app who have been invited to join a team or view information within the app. The invitation is usually sent by email.

3. Click here to view all of the team members and guests

Members and guests (2)
Name
Title
Location
Tags
Role
ewils...
Member
Sue R...
Member

4. Click on the **Member** button next to a team member's name and select whether to make them an owner or not

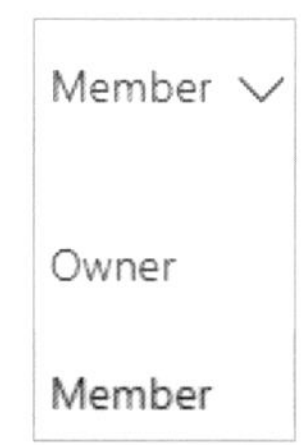

5. The status of each team member is shown here

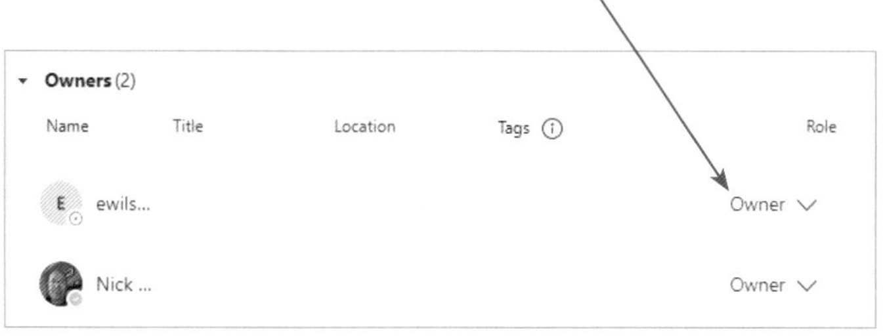

6. Click on the **Add member** button in the second Step 2 on the previous page to add more people to the team, as shown on page 72

Viewing pending requests

When people ask to join a team, their request has to be accepted. Before this is done, the request is pending. To view these pending requests:

1. Click on the **Pending Requests** tab

2. If there are any pending requests, they will be shown in this window

If someone has been made a team owner when the team was set up, or they were added to it, the word **Owner** will be displayed next to them in Step 4.

Team owners can make more changes to a team than team members.

...cont'd

Managing apps

Apps can be added to a team, to provide extra functionality. To do this:

1. Click on the **Apps** tab 

2. Details of the apps that are already available within the team are displayed. Click on the **More apps** button for more options

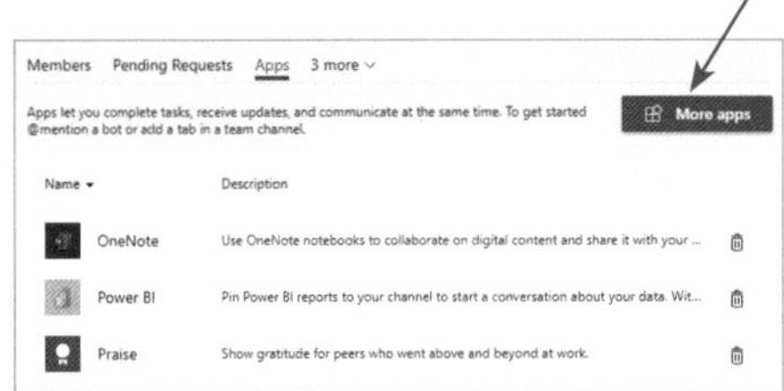

For more details about using apps within Teams, see pages 170-178.

3. The newest apps are displayed at the top of the window, with a full list below

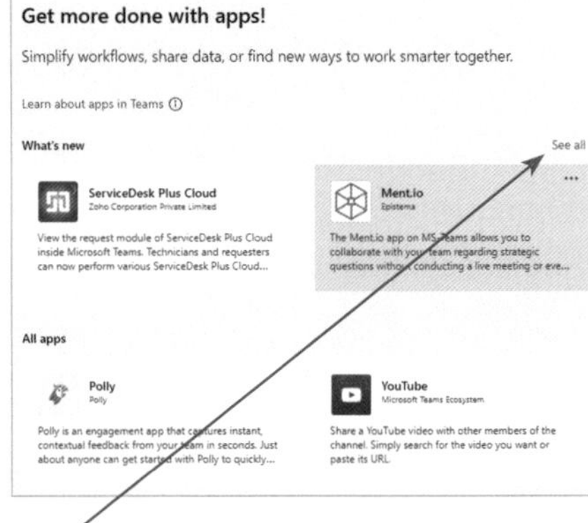

4. Click on the **See all** button for the **What's new** section, to view the latest apps 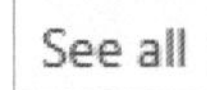

5. Click on an app to view its details, and click on the **Add** button to make it available within the team

Managing analytics

Analytical information can be displayed for an individual team from the Manage team section:

1. Click on the **Analytics** tab Analytics

2. Details about the team are displayed, including the number of users and apps; meetings that have taken place; and the number of posts, replies and mentions

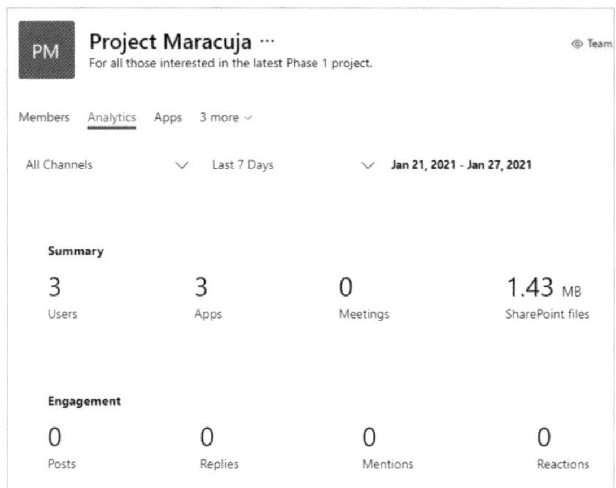

3. Click here to view options for viewing analytical information for specific channels

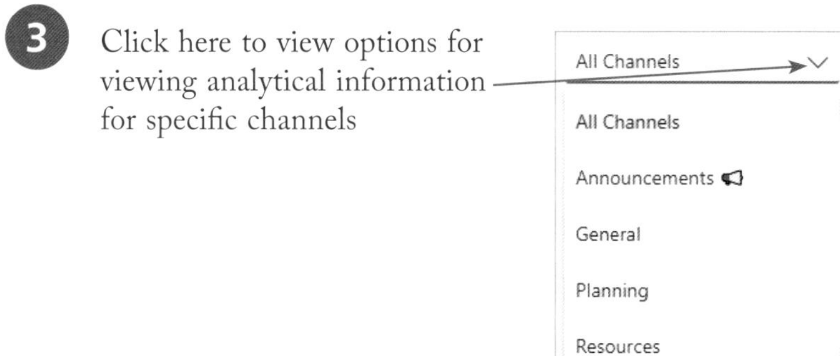

4. Click here to view analytical information over different timescales

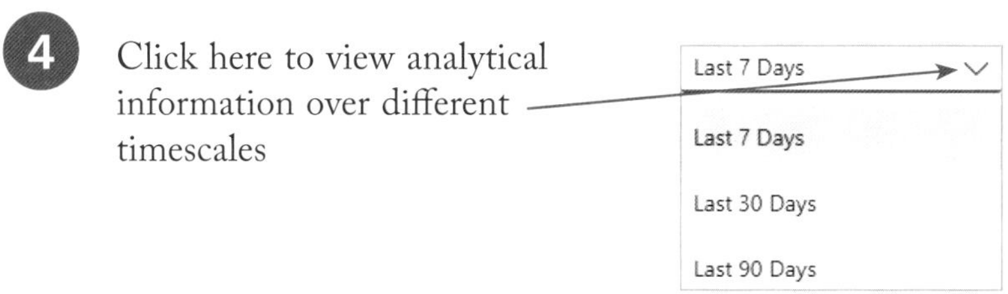

For details about viewing analytical information for all teams, see page 79.

More Team Management

In addition to the team management functions on pages 74-77, it is also possible to access some team management options from within the left-hand panel of the Teams interface. To do this:

1. Select a team and click on this button in the left-hand panel

2. Click on the **Teams** tab to view all of the currently available teams

3. Details of each team are displayed, including its name, description, number of members and type of team

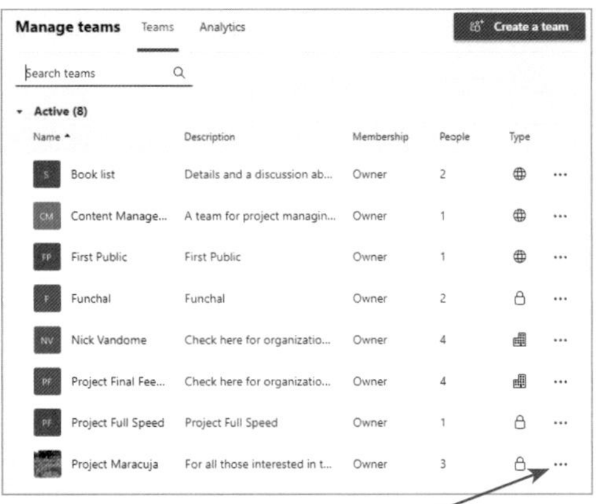

4. Click on the menu button next to a team to access the options for a specific team

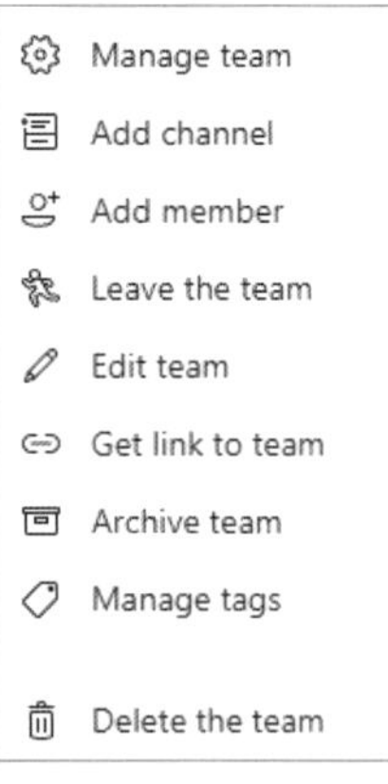

Click on the **Create a team** button at the top of the window in Step 3 to create a new team from here.

Accessing analytics

To access analytics for all teams:

1. Click on the **Analytics** tab on the top toolbar in Step 2 on the previous page

2. The analytics for each team are displayed, including the numbers of team members and guests, the number of posts and replies, and the type of team

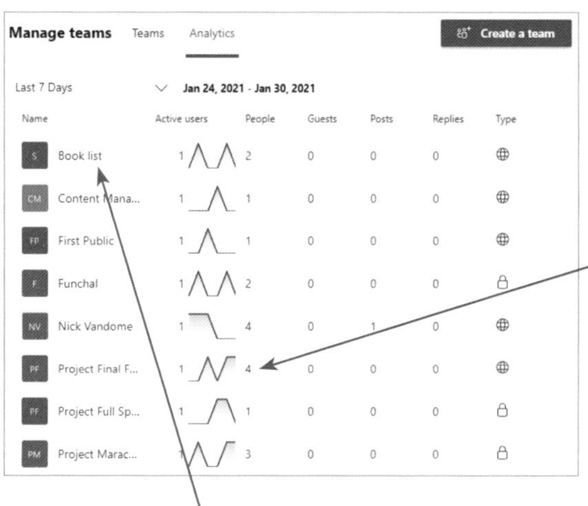

Click on an item within a team in Step 2 to access the full range of team management options for that team.

3. Click on a team name to view its analytical details, as shown in Step 2 on page 77

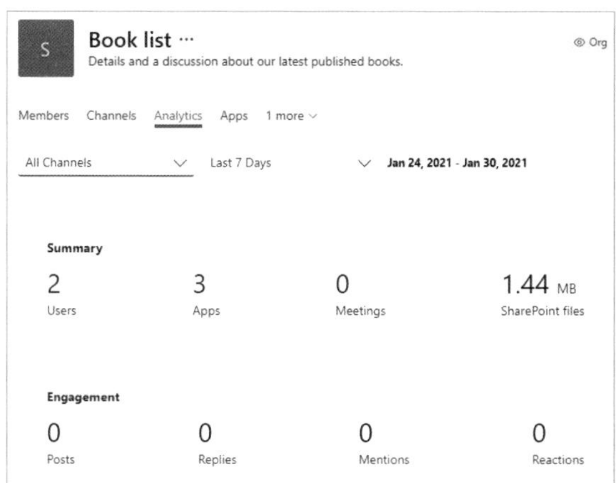

Teams Settings

A range of settings can be applied for individual teams so that they can be customized to the needs of users and the subject matter of the team. To use settings for a team:

1. Click on a team name, click on the menu button, and click on the **Manage team** button

2. Click the **Settings** tab, or click on the down-pointing arrow on the toolbar and click on the **Settings** option

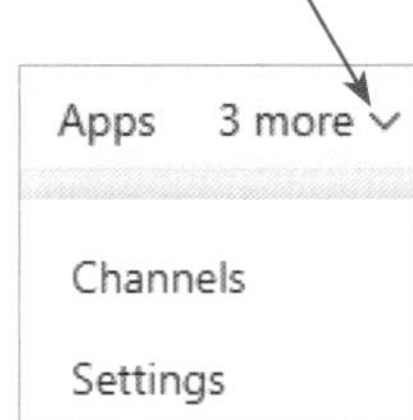

3. The **Settings** categories for the team are listed

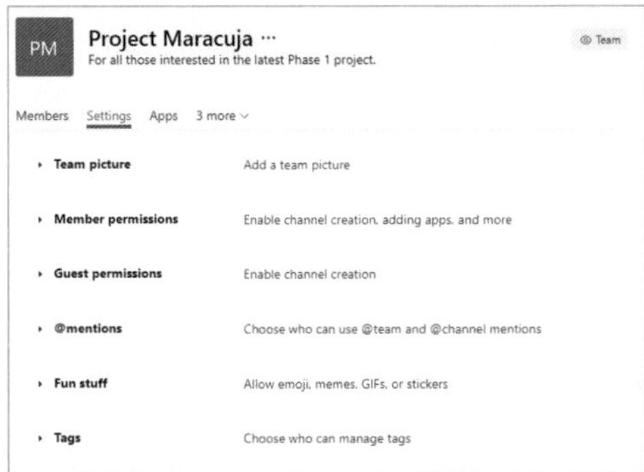

4. Click on the **Team picture** option and click on the **Add a team picture** button

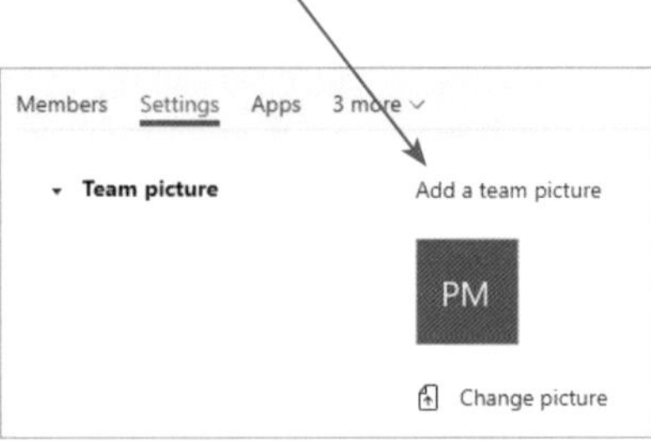

If a picture has already been added for the team, click on the **Change picture** button in Step 4 to update it.

5 Click on the **Upload picture** button, select a picture for the team, and click on the **Save** button

6 Click on the **Member permissions** option and make the required selections for what team members can do within the team, such as whether members can create channels, add and remove apps, create and manage tabs, and manage messages

Member permissions	Enable channel creation, adding apps, and more	
	Allow members to create and update channels	☑
	Allow members to create private channels	☑
	Allow members to delete and restore channels	☑
	Allow members to add and remove apps	☑
	Allow members to upload custom apps	☑
	Allow members to create, update, and remove tabs	☑
	Allow members to create, update, and remove connectors	☑
	Give members the option to delete their messages	☑
	Give members the option to edit their messages	☑

7 Click on the **Guest permissions** option and make selections for what guests can do in terms of working with channels

Guest permissions	Enable channel creation	
	Allow guests to create and update channels	☐
	Allow guests to delete channels	☐

If you want a guest to be enabled to make more changes within a team, add them as a full team member.

...cont'd

8. Click on the **@mentions** option and select options for what happens when mentions are used within your team and by other teams

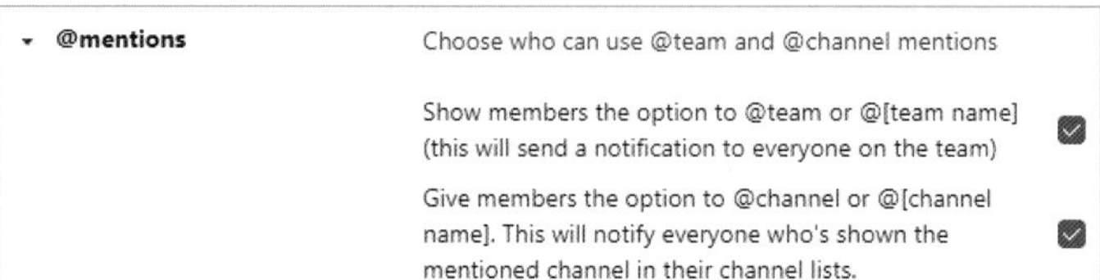

Items such as emojis, GIFs, stickers and memes should be used sparingly within a workplace Teams environment, as they are not to everyone's taste.

9. Click on the **Fun stuff** option and select which items are allowed to be used within the team, including emojis, GIFs, stickers and memes

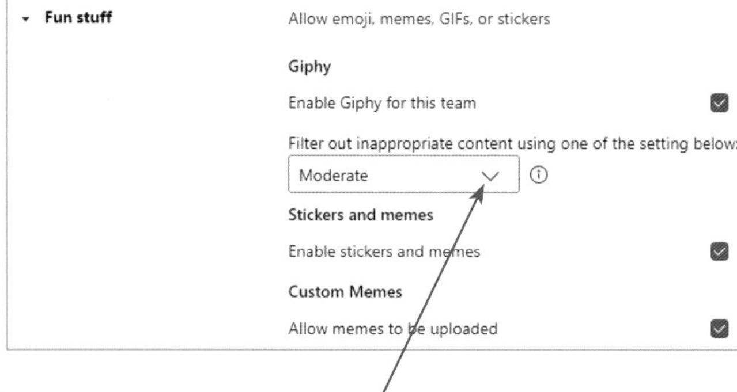

10. In the **Fun stuff** window, click here to select the security level for allowing inappropriate content, from **Strict** or **Moderate**

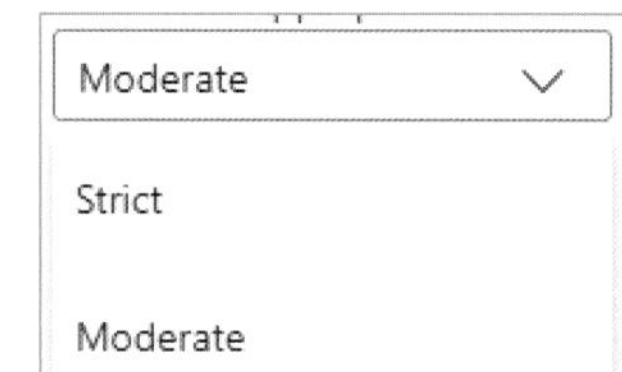

Tags can be used to contact a group of people at once, based on categories such as role, project name or location. For example, if a **Project Manager** tag is used, this will notify everyone in the team with this title.

11. Click on the **Tags** option to select how tags are managed within the team

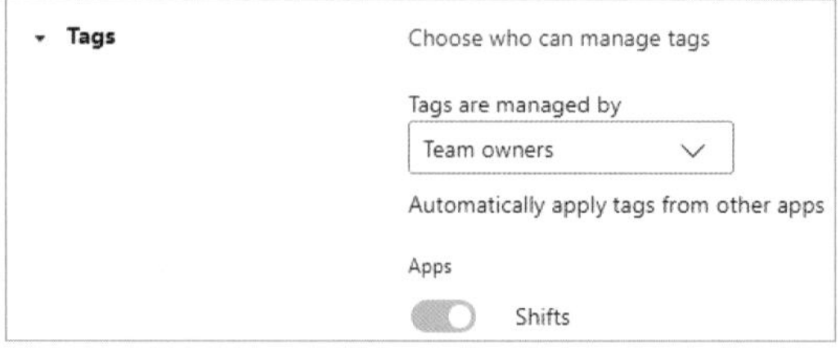

5 Channels and Tabs

Teams that are created have considerable flexibility for their members, and this chapter looks at creating channels within a team and adding tabs for more content.

Viewing Channels

Within the Teams section is an option for adding channels to teams that have been created. These are sub-categories that can be used to create a hierarchy of information within the team's format, and make it more manageable to view subjects within the team. To view channels:

The **General** channel is created automatically when a new team is created.

1. The channels are located below the team name

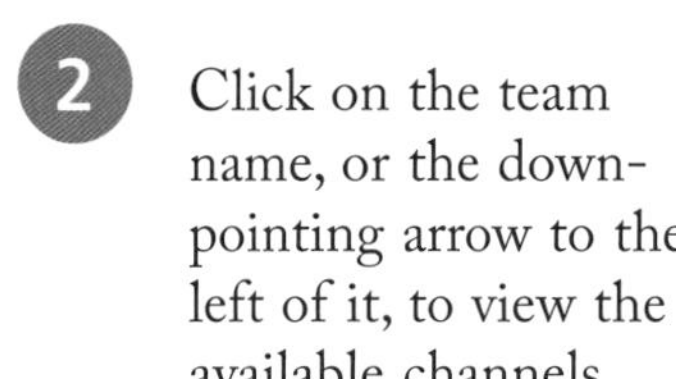

2. Click on the team name, or the down-pointing arrow to the left of it, to view the available channels

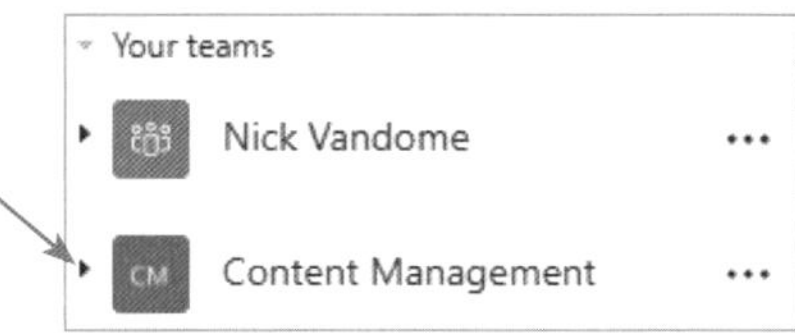

3. Click on a channel to view its contents in the main window

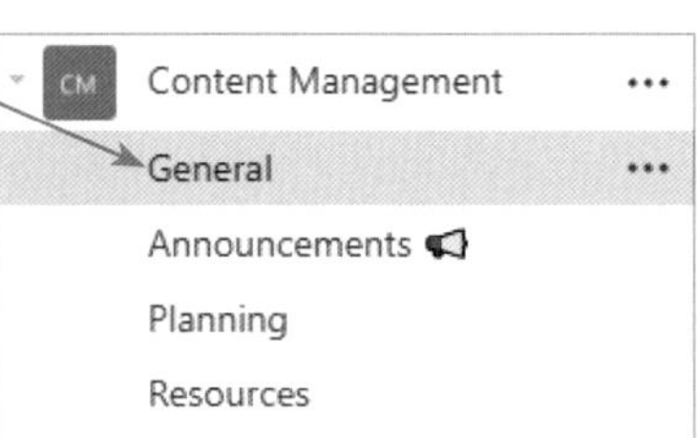

To hide a channel on the channel list, click on the menu button next to it and select **Hide**.

4. The name of the channel is displayed here

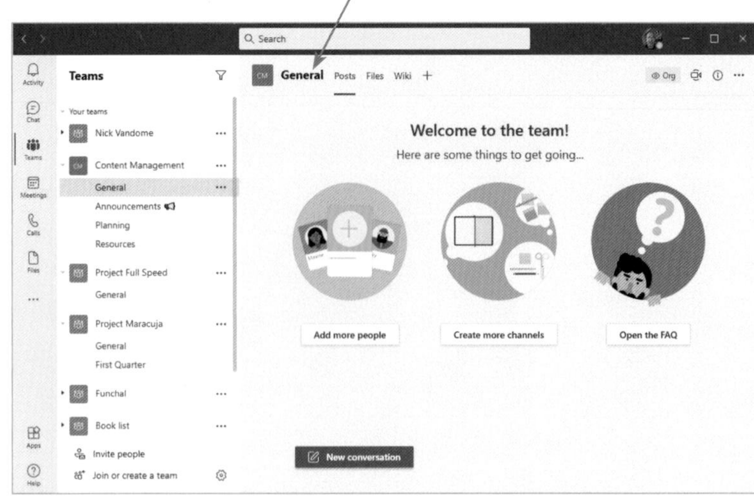

5 Click on another channel. The main window will display this channel's content

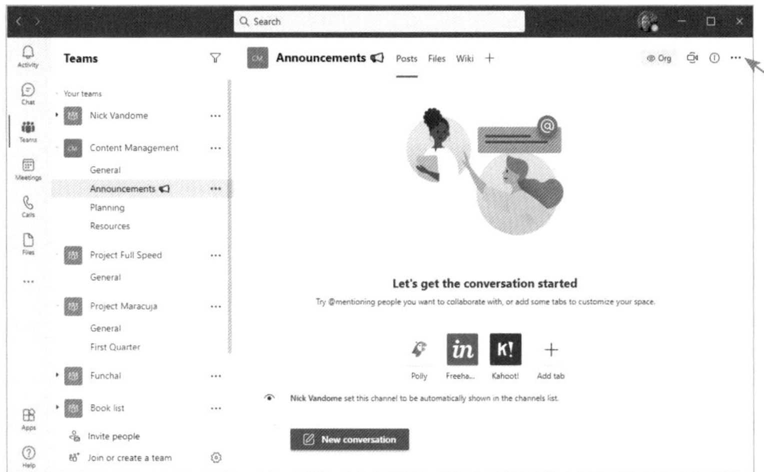

Click on this menu button in the top right-hand corner of the main window to access options for managing channels. This menu can also be accessed from the menu button next to a channel in the left-hand panel. See pages 90-91 for details about managing channels.

6 Each individual channel will display its own content. As the selection in the left-hand panel changes, so does the content in the main window, and the channel name listed on the top toolbar

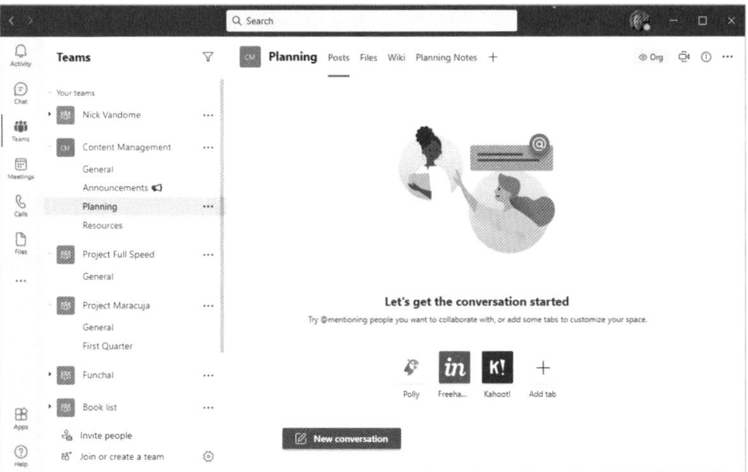

Adding Channels

The General channel is automatically available when a team is first created. It is also possible to add more channels to a team, to create a structure related to the content matter of the team. This is an effective way to ensure that the content within the team is organized appropriately. Channels can be added directly from the team menu, or from within the Manage team option.

Creating a channel from the team menu

To create a channel directly from the team menu:

Channels should follow a logical structure, rather than just adding them for the sake of it.

1. Select one of the teams in the **Teams** section and click on the menu button

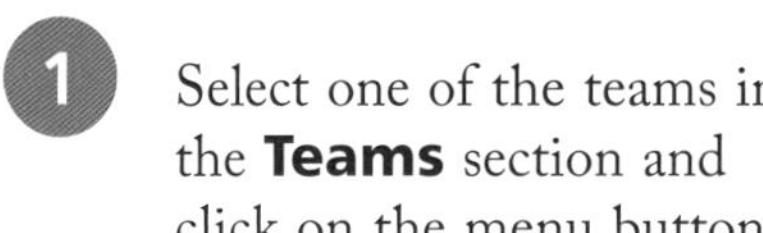

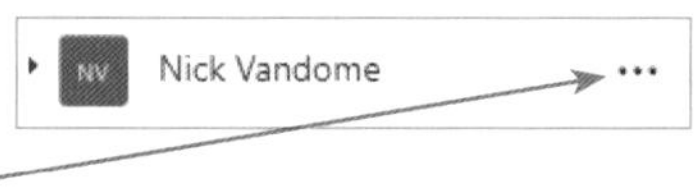

2. Click on the **Add channel** option

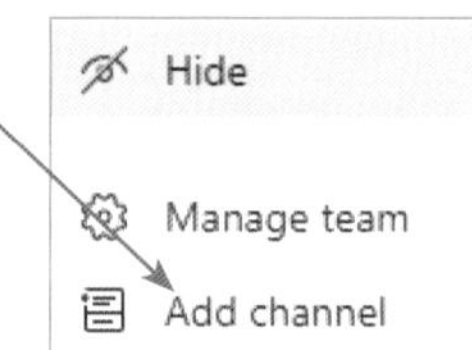

3. Enter a name for the channel and add any settings, as required, such as privacy settings for who can see the channel, and whether it is automatically displayed

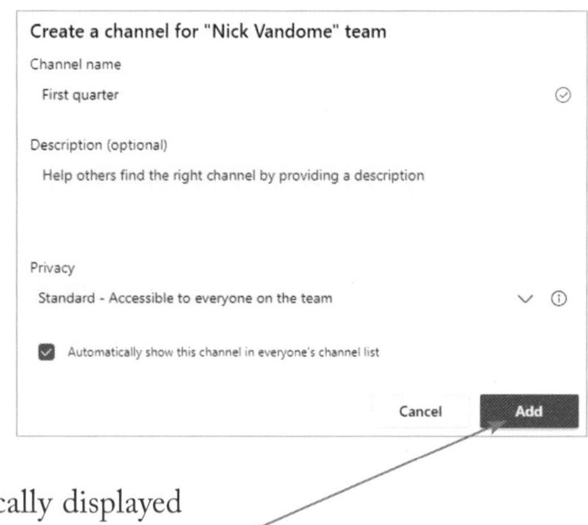

4. Click on the **Add** button to create the channel

5. Click here next to the main team name to display the available channels

6. The available channels are shown below the main team name. Click on a channel name to view its contents

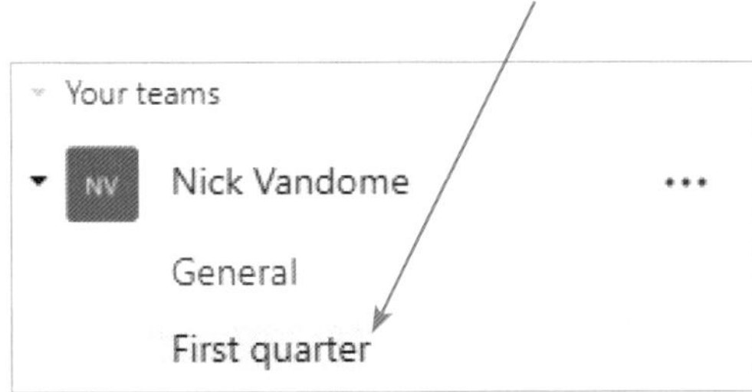

7. The name of the channel is displayed on the top toolbar, and the main window displays the content in the channel

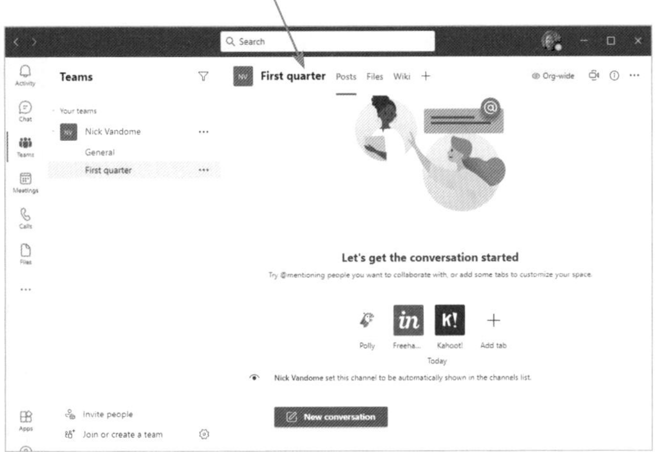

8. Click on the Channels menu button in the left-hand panel to access options for managing the channel

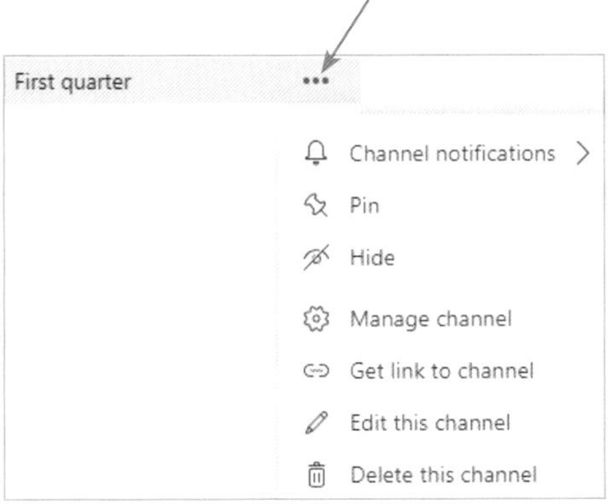

See pages 90-91 for details about managing channels within a team.

...cont'd

Adding a channel from the Manage team option

New channels can also be created using the Manage team option from the team menu. This is a similar process to that shown on pages 86-87, but it also provides an overview of the channels within a team, rather than just creating a single new channel. To create a new channel from the Manage team option:

If the Channels tab (or any other tab) is not available, click on the **More** button on the top toolbar and click on one of the required options.

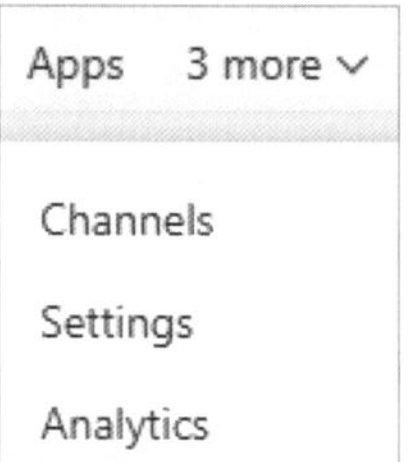

1. Select one of the teams in the Teams section and click on the menu button

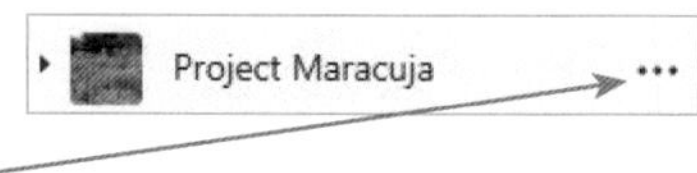

2. Click on the **Manage team** button

3. Click on the **Channels** tab on the top toolbar

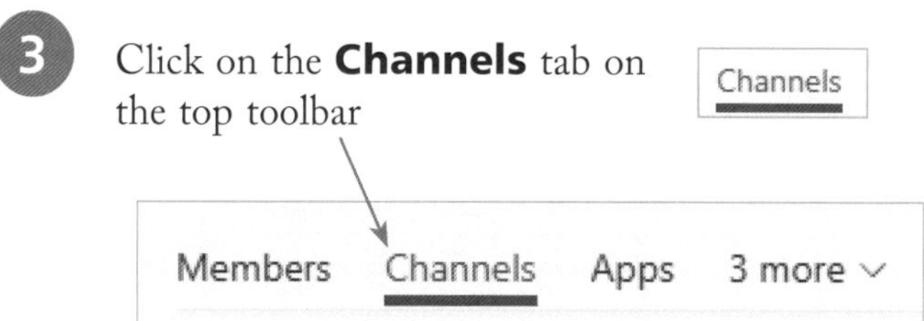

4. The current channels are listed in the window. Click on the **Active** heading to view the current channels

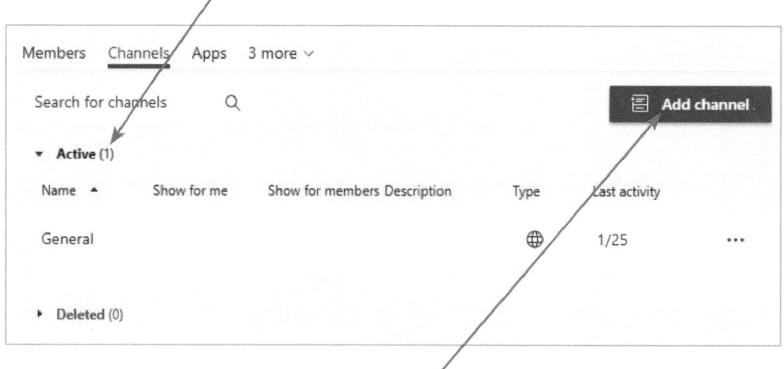

5. Click on the **Add channel** button to create a new channel for the team

6 Enter the details for the team, including name, description, who can see the channel, and whether it is visible automatically. Click on the **Add** button

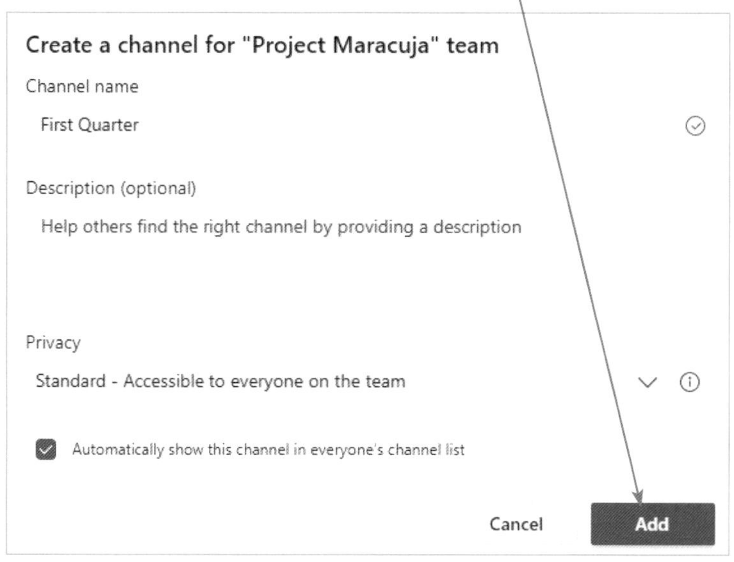

If a channel name has already been taken, you will be alerted to this when you enter it in Step 6.

7 The new channel is added to the Channels list, with the settings that were applied in Step 6 above

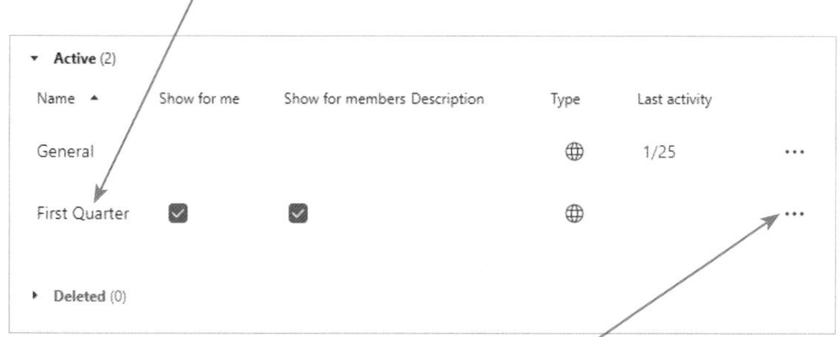

After a channel has been created, click on its name below the team name to start adding content to the channel.

8 Click on the menu button next to the new channel to view its options (see pages 90-91)

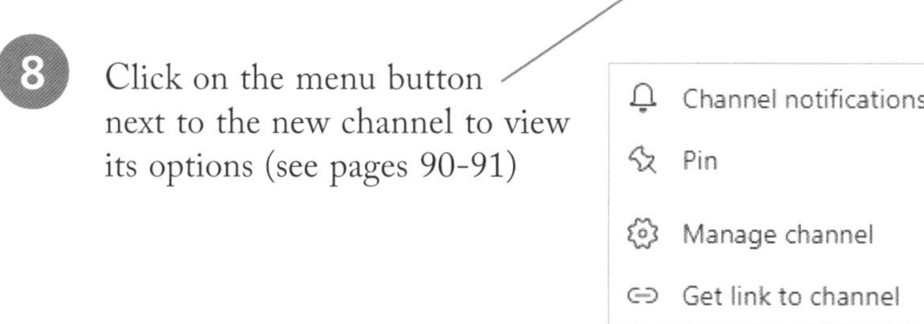

Managing Channels

There is a range of settings that can be applied for channels, including notifications and settings. To do this:

1. Select a team channel in the left-hand panel and click on its menu button

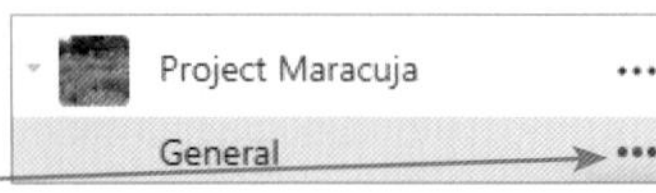

2. Click on the **Channel notifications** option to select how notifications appear in the channel

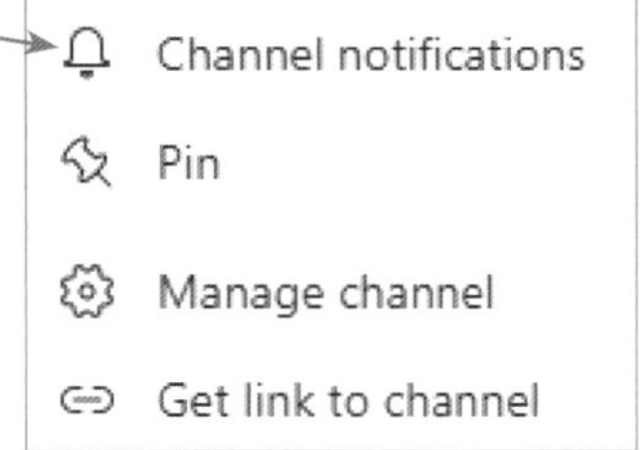

In general, it is best to start with as many notifications in place as possible so that items do not get missed. If the number of notifications becomes annoying, this can be amended at a later date.

3. Apply settings for how notifications work with all posts, and when the channel name is mentioned somewhere else within Teams

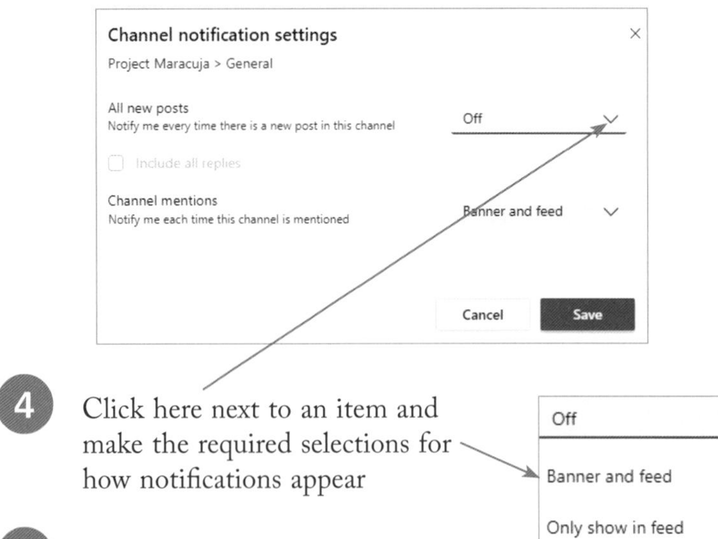

4. Click here next to an item and make the required selections for how notifications appear

Off
Banner and feed
Only show in feed
Off

5. Click on the **Save** button to save the settings for notifications

Save

6. Click on the **Manage channel** option in Step 2 on the previous page and click on the **Channel settings** tab to view options for settings permissions within the channel, such as what can be included and who can post messages to the channel

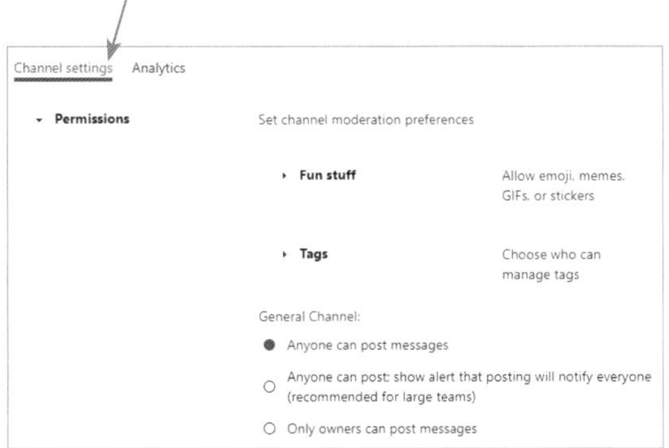

7. Click on the **Analytics** tab to view details about the engagement that has taken place in the channel

Channel settings Analytics
Last 7 Days Jan 21, 2021 - Jan 27, 2021
Summary
3 Users
3 Apps
Engagement
0 Posts
0 Replies
0 Mentions
0 Reactions

8. Click on the **Get link to channel** option in Step 2 on the previous page and click on the **Copy** button to copy the link to the channel, and send it to someone else

Depending on the subject matter of a channel, you may want to limit the amount of **Fun stuff** in Step 6 that users can include in their posts.

Hot tip

Links can be emailed to other people, even if they are not in your organization, provided the Teams guidelines allow this. In this instance, the person will join the team as a guest.

Deleting Channels

Channels can be deleted from within a team, and there are also some settings that can be applied to determine who in a team is allowed to do this. To delete a channel:

1. Depending on your permissions, some channels may not be available for deletion by you. Select a channel and click on its menu. If there is no **Delete this channel** option, the channel cannot be deleted

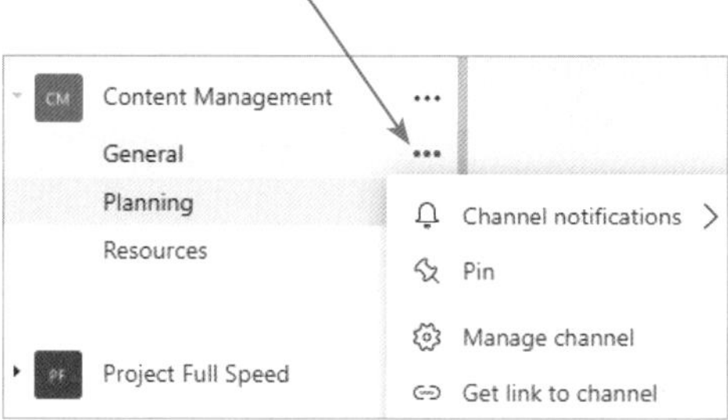

2. Click on the **Delete this channel** option, if it is available

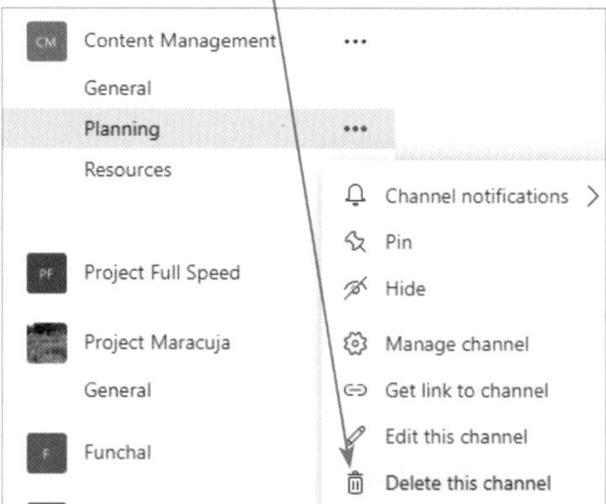

3. Click on the **Delete** button to confirm the operation

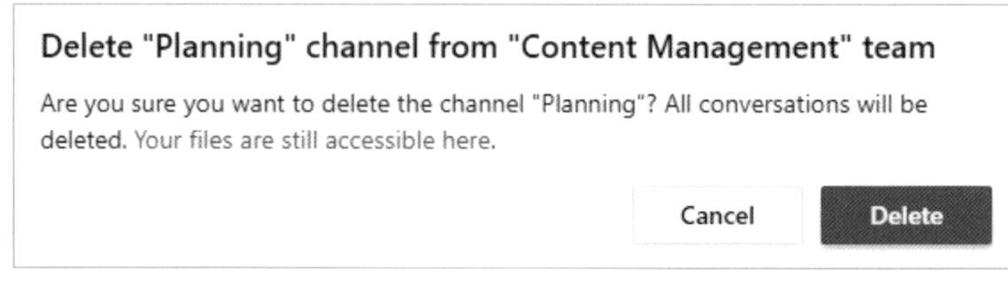

If everyone in a team has permission to delete teams, you may find that they disappear without your knowledge. See the next page for details about preventing channel deletion.

Preventing channel deletion

If you are the owner of a team you may not want other team members to delete channels without your approval, which is possible unless this is specified within the channel settings. To prevent other users deleting channels:

1. Click on the menu button next to a team name in the left-hand panel

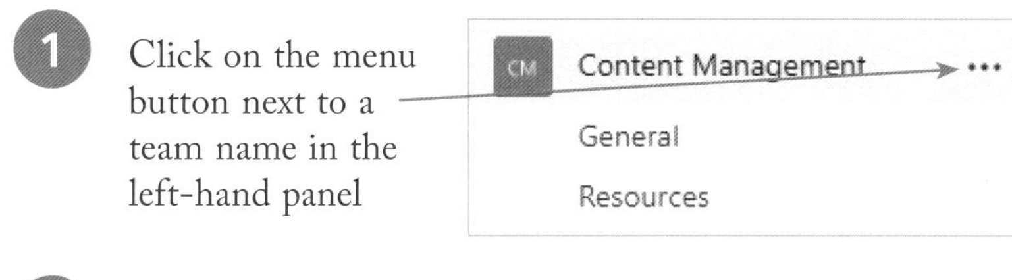

2. Click on the **Manage team** button

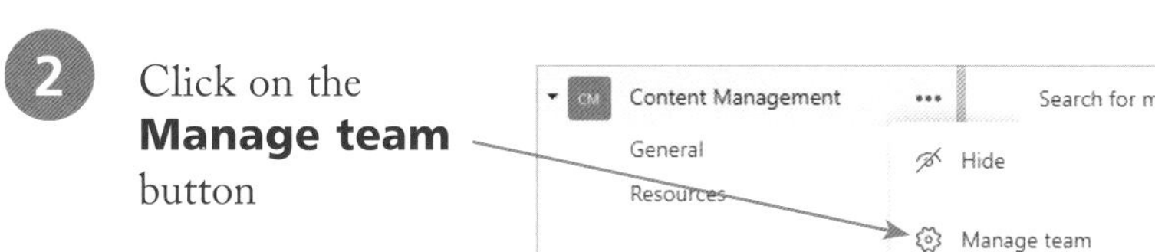

3. Click on the **Settings** tab

4. Click on the right-pointing arrow next to the **Member permissions** heading to expand it

5. Check **Off** the **Allow members to delete and restore channels** option

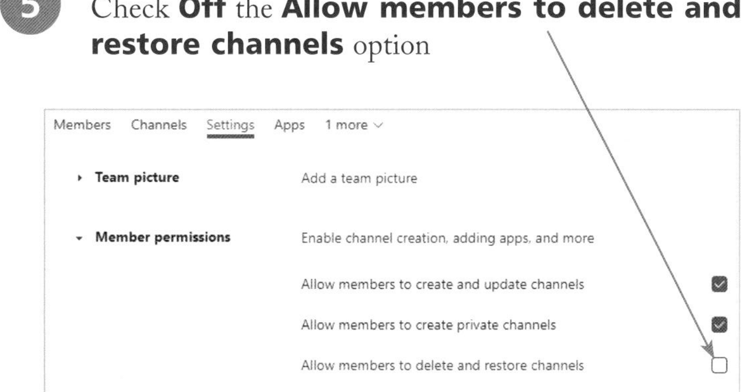

If someone has permission to delete channels, make sure you tell them if you are going to remove this access, and explain why.

Viewing Tabs

Each team has a range of tabs that can be used to access a variety of functions for the team, such as posts within the team, files that have been shared, and knowledge Wikis that have been added. To view the available tabs:

1. Click on a team name in the left-hand panel
2. The tabs appear at the top of the main window

3. Click on the **Posts** tab to view text communications that have been undertaken within the team

4. Conversations are listed in the main window

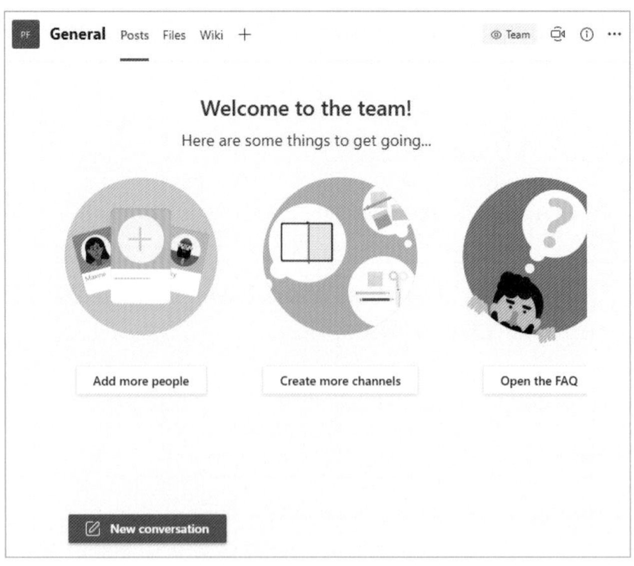

5. Click on a conversation to add to it, or click on the **New conversation** button to start a new one

Tabs are an excellent way to organize the content within a team, particularly as this starts to grow with more and more team members.

6. Click on the **Files** tab to view files that have been uploaded to the team for sharing

7. The available files are shown in the main window. Click on one to open it

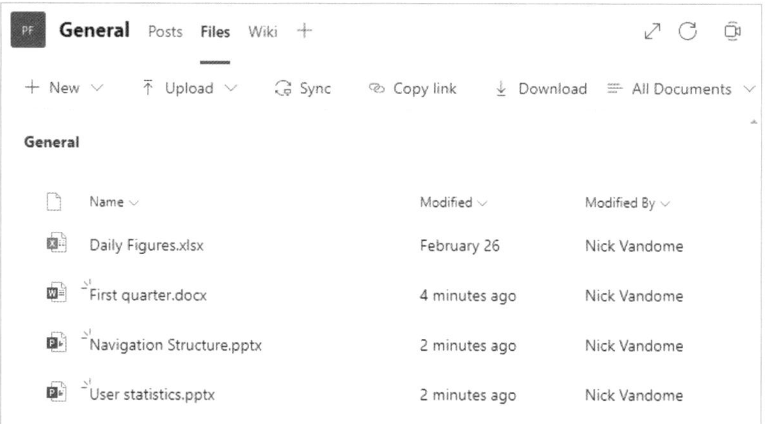

8. Click on the **Wiki** tab to view knowledge Wikis that have been created within the team

9. The available Wikis are displayed in the main window. Click in a text box to add or edit content

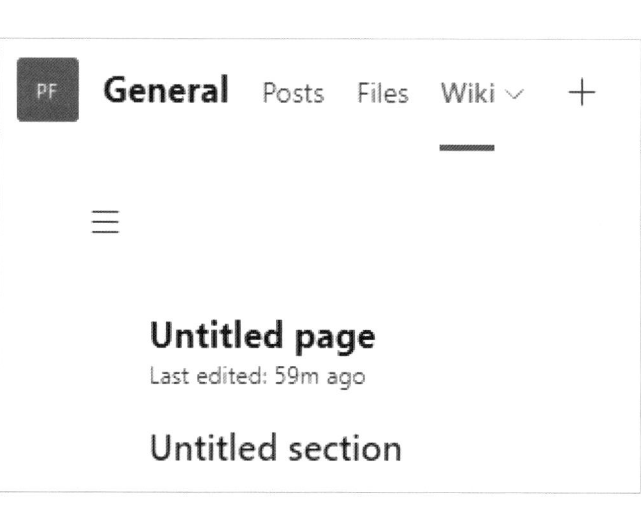

If an item on the Tabs toolbar has a down-pointing arrow next to it, click on this to access options for renaming or removing the item.

Adding Tabs

In addition to the default tabs that appear when a new channel is created, there is a range of options for adding new tabs, from apps from within Teams. To do this:

The Tabs toolbar expands as more apps are added as tabs.

1. Click the **+** button on the Tabs toolbar +

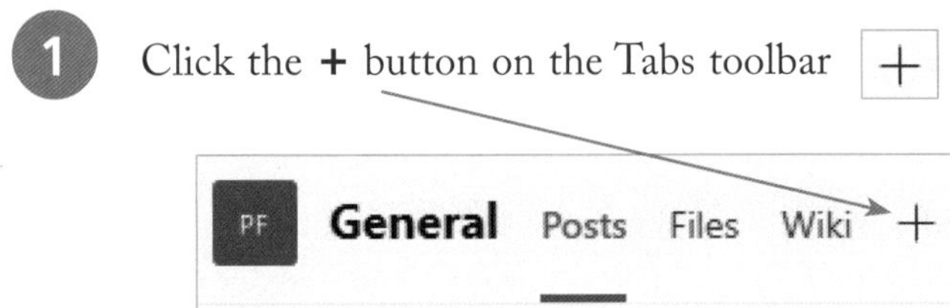

2. The available apps are displayed. Click on one to view its details

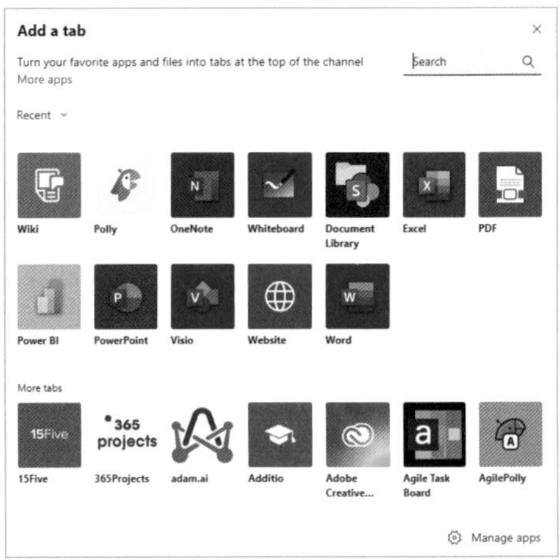

Use the Search box in the top right-hand corner in Step 2 to search for specific apps, or functions, within the Teams app.

3. Enter a name for the app. This will appear as the tab name, once the app has been added as a tab

4. Click on the **About** button at the top of the window in Step 3 on the previous page to view details about the app

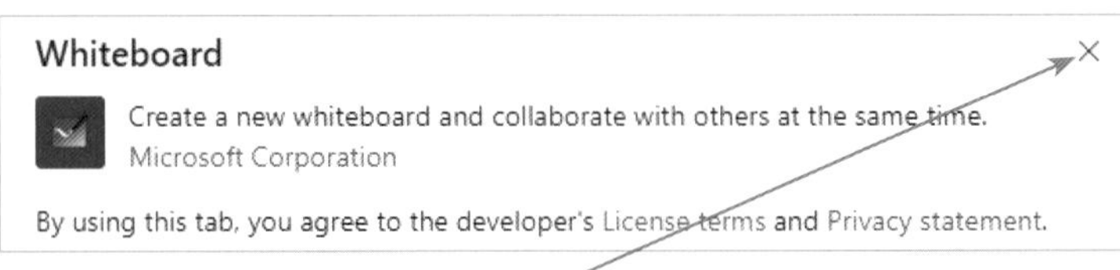

5. Click on the cross in the top right-hand corner to close the **About** window

6. Click on the **Save** button at the bottom of the window in Step 3 on the previous page to add the app as a new tab

7. The app is added as a tab on the Tabs toolbar. Click on its name to view its functionality in the main window

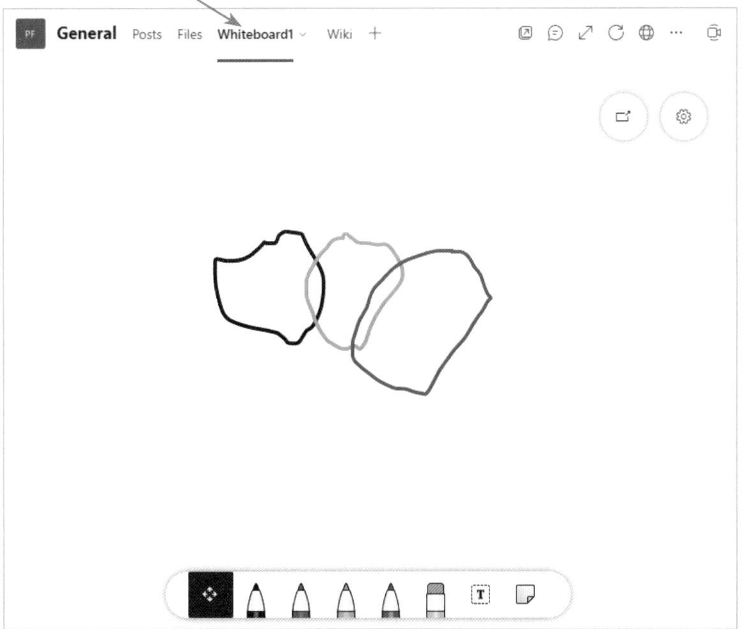

Once an app has been added as a new tab, it will be available to everyone in the team; team members will not have to download it individually.

Renaming and Removing Tabs

Existing and new tabs can be renamed and also removed, as required. To do this:

Renaming a tab

To rename an existing tab:

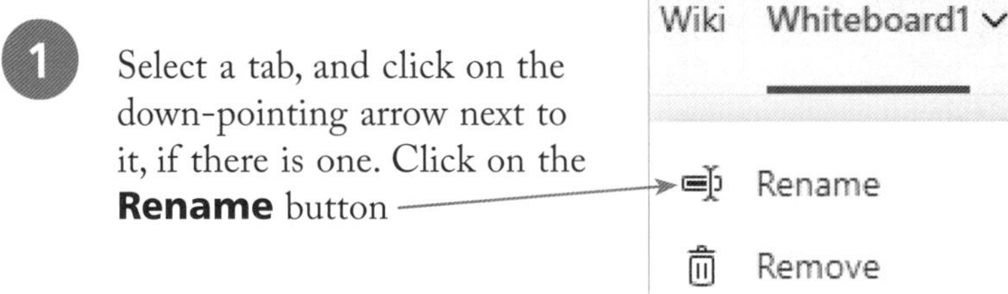

1. Select a tab, and click on the down-pointing arrow next to it, if there is one. Click on the **Rename** button

2. Enter a new name for the tab in the **Tab name** text box and click on the **Save** button

To exit the **Rename** or **Remove** windows without making any changes, click on the cross in the top right-hand corner.

Beware

Only new tabs that have been added can then be renamed or removed. The default tabs **Posts**, **Files** and **Wiki** cannot be changed.

Removing a tab

To remove an existing tab:

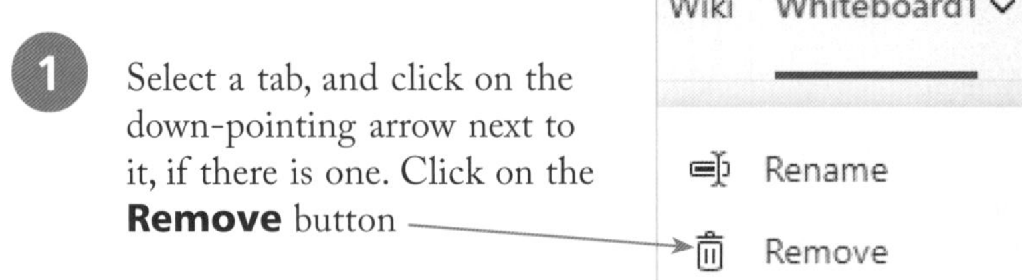

1. Select a tab, and click on the down-pointing arrow next to it, if there is one. Click on the **Remove** button

2. Click on the **Remove** button to delete the tab

6 Text Chatting

Text chatting is a quick and efficient way for work colleagues to communicate with each other. This chapter details the options for text chatting in Teams, including formatting text in a chat and also adding content such as images and emojis.

Accessing Chats

Sending text messages to individuals or groups is one of the most popular uses of the Teams app. It is a quick and effective way to keep in touch with colleagues and workmates and can be used for formal or informal subjects.

Chats within the Teams app can be done in a team environment, or directly with individuals or groups, without the need to first create a team.

Accessing chats within a team

To use text chatting within a Teams environment:

1. Click on the **Teams** button in the sidebar

2. Select a channel within a team, in the left-hand panel

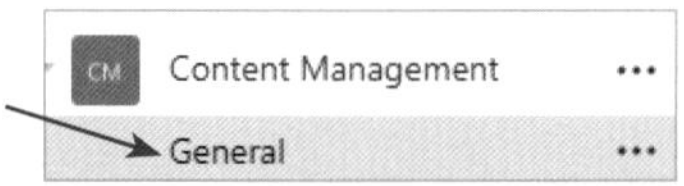

3. Click on the **New conversation** button in the main window

4. Enter the required text in the text box

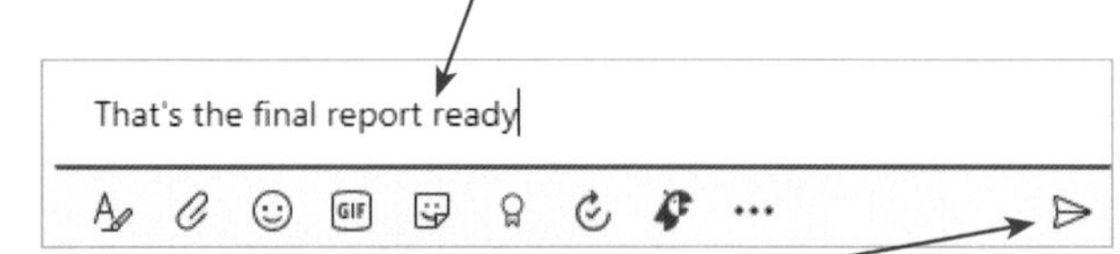

5. Click on the **Send** button to the right of the text box

6. The message is available on the team page, for all team members to see – or reply to – below the original message

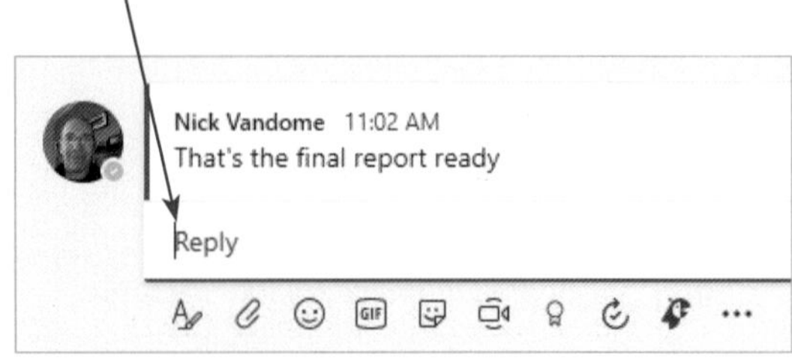

Use the toolbar below the text box in Step 4 to add more content, such as emojis and photos. See pages 108-109 for more details about adding content from this toolbar.

Accessing chat from the Chat section

If you do not want to have a text chat that is visible to everyone in a team, it is possible to have private chats that are only seen by the individuals involved. To do this:

1. Click on the **Chat** button in the sidebar

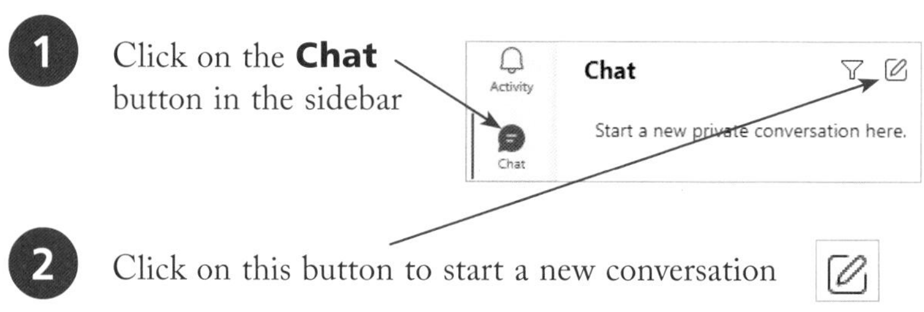

2. Click on this button to start a new conversation

3. Click in the **To:** text box to enter recipients

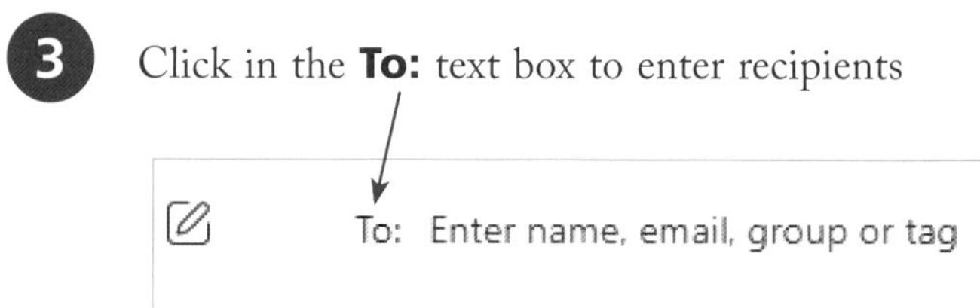

4. Start typing a name and click on one of the options that appear, to select it

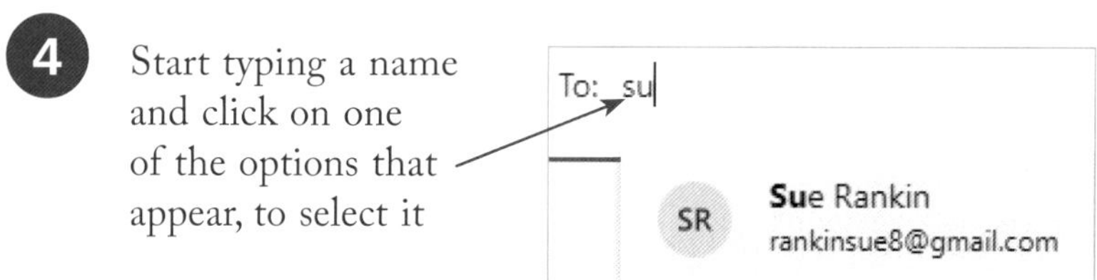

5. The selected person is added as a participant in the conversation

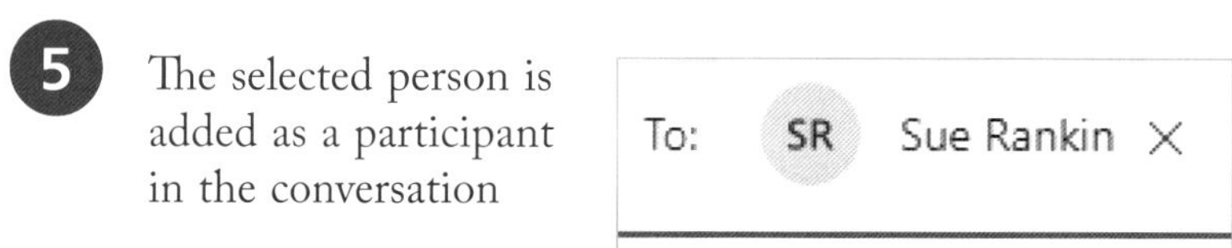

6. Enter text for the message

7. Click on the **Send** button to send the message

The more that you type in the **To:** text box in Step 4, the more defined the name will be.

One-to-One Chats

When an individual, one-to-one chat is taking place there are various options that can be used:

1. The chat is displayed in the main window

2. Move the cursor over the person's name at the top of the chat window to access options for chatting with them, emailing them, viewing their position in the organizational structure, starting a video call, or starting a voice call

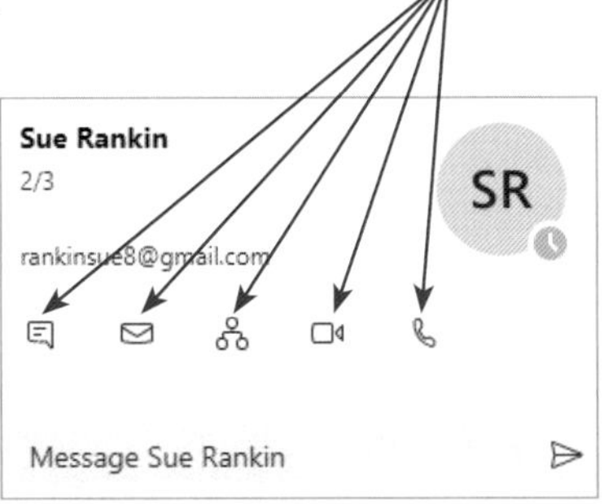

3. Click on these buttons at the top of the chat window to, from left to right: start a video call; start a voice call; share your screen; add people to the chat; or create a pop-out chat

4. Move the cursor over an item in the conversation and click on one of the emoji icons to add it as a comment in the message

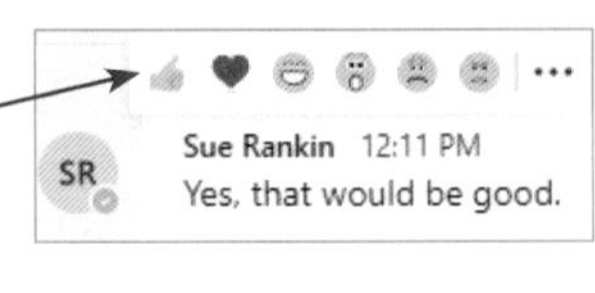

Click on the menu button next to the emoji icons in Step 4 to access options that can be applied to the message, including saving it, marking it as unread, translating it, or having it spoken in a special reader designed for this.

The emoji selected in Step 4 appears above the message.

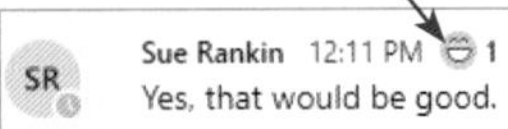

Group Chats

It is possible to have text chats with multiple people at the same time, in which case a group can be created for the chat so that all of the members can participate. To do this:

1. Click on this button at the top of the left-hand Chat panel to start the chat 

2. Click in the **To**: text box at the top of the main window

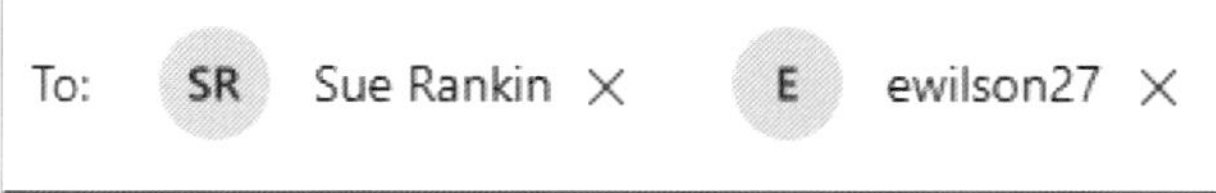

3. Enter the details of all of the people that you want to include in the group chat

4. Click on this button to create a group with the selected recipients, and give it a name

5. Enter a name for the group and press the **Enter** button on the keyboard

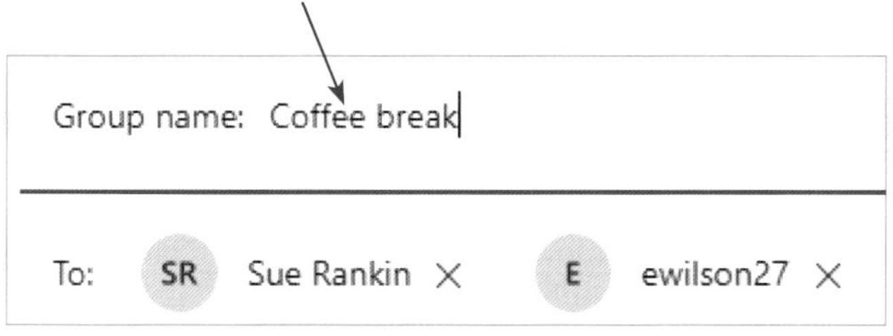

More people can be added to a group chat at a later date, by clicking on this button on the toolbar in Step 3 on the previous page and selecting the **Add people** option:

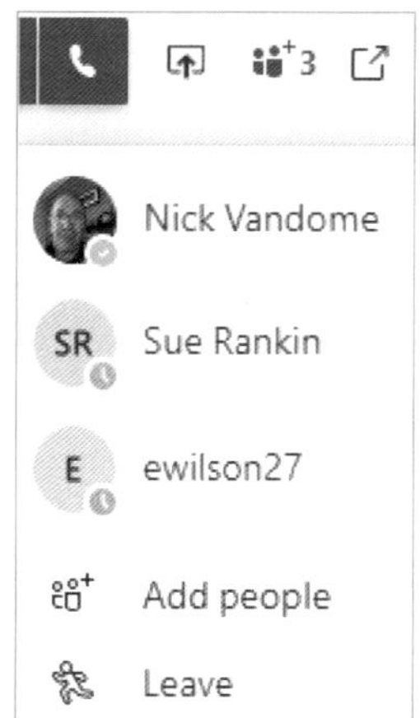

...cont'd

6. The group name appears in the left-hand panel and at the top of the main text conversation window, when selected

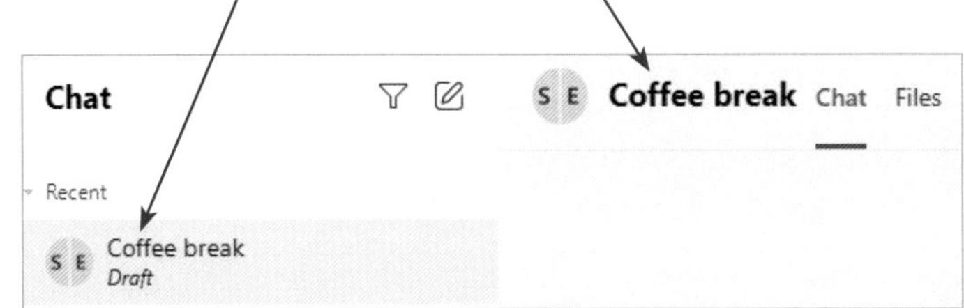

7. Click in the text box at the bottom of the main window, enter a message, and click on the **Send** button

8. The message appears in the main window of the group conversation, with the group name at the top of the window

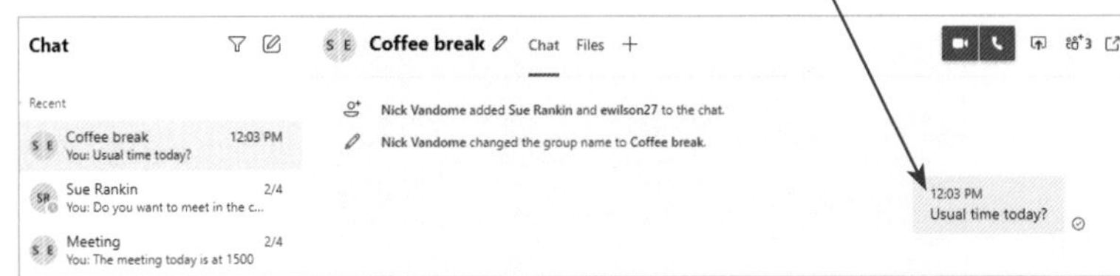

9. The group conversation continues down the main window as more comments are added

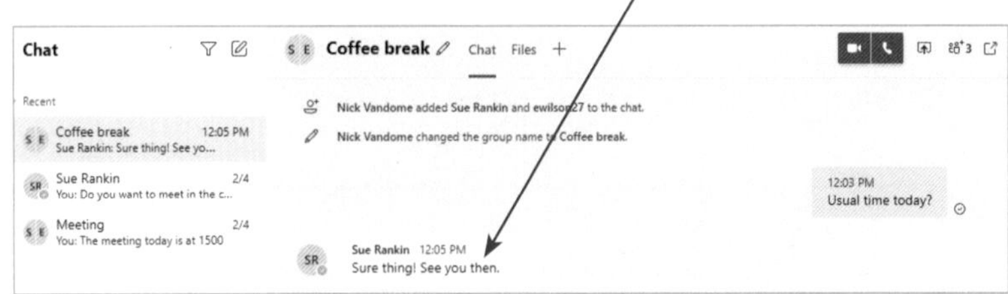

Don't forget

The group conversation toolbar in the main window in Step 6 has options for more functionality, such as adding files for the group to see. See pages 156-158 for more details.

10 Click on the menu button next to the group name in the left-hand panel to access a menu of options for the group conversation

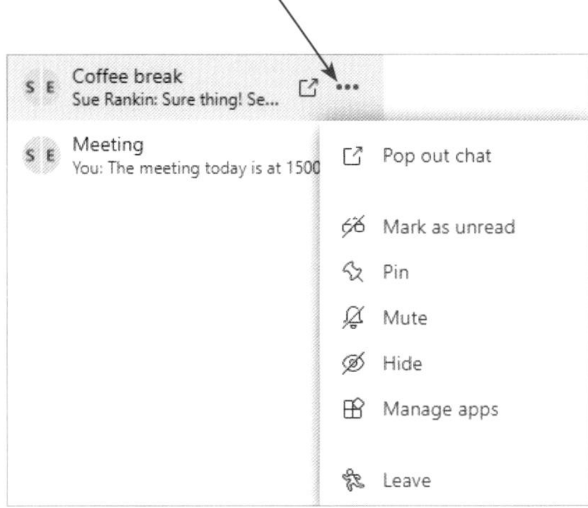

Click on the **Pin** option in Step 10 to pin the conversation at the top of the left-hand panel in the Chat section.

11 Click on the pencil icon next to the group name at the top of the main window to edit the group name

Coffee break

12 Double-click on the group name and overtype it with a new name, as required. Click on the **Save** button

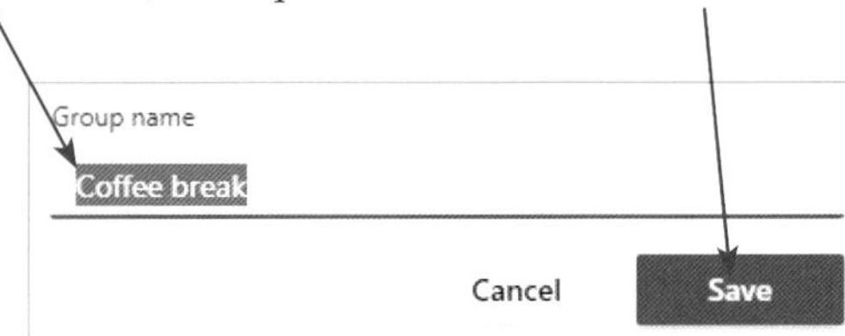

13 Once a group has been created, it can be accessed from the Chat **To**: box, by entering the first letters of the group

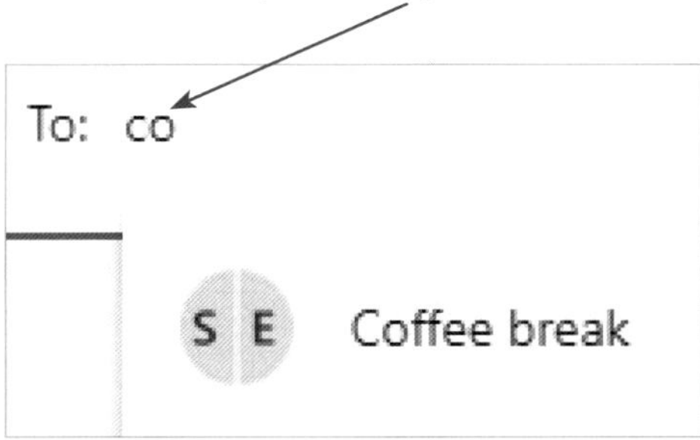

Formatting Text Chats

Text in text chat messages can be formatted in a number of ways, rather than with just the plain default text. To do this:

Text formatting in a text message is not as important as for more official documents, such as those produced with a word processing app, but it can be a good way to make your messages – or elements within them – stand out.

1. Enter text in the text box and, before the message is sent, click on the text formatting button on the toolbar below the text box

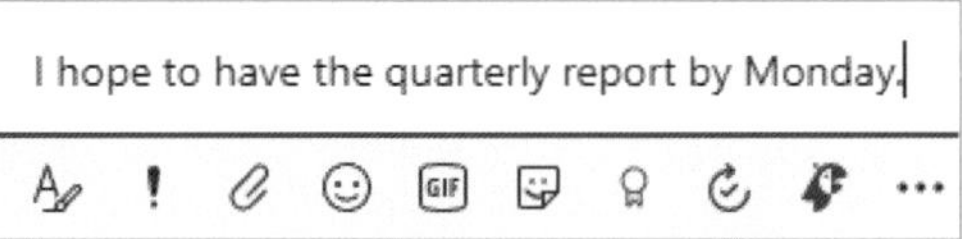

2. The text formatting toolbar contains options for formatting the text in the text box

Double-click on a word to select it. Triple-click within a paragraph to select all of the text in the paragraph.

3. Select an item of text and use these buttons to, from left to right: apply bold, italics, underlining or strikethrough

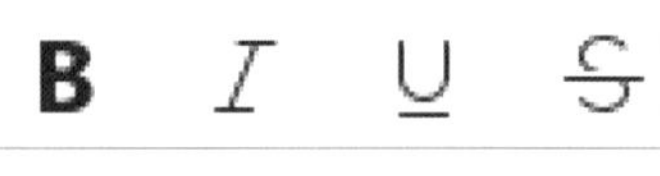

4. Select an item of text and click on this button to apply a text highlight color, which appears behind the text

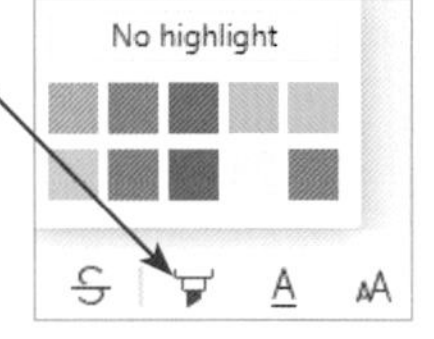

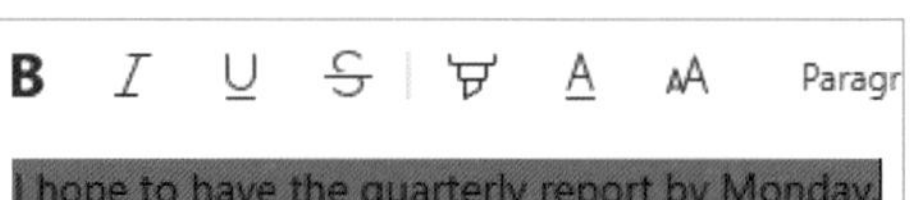

5. Select an item of text and click on this button to apply a text color, which is applied to the text itself

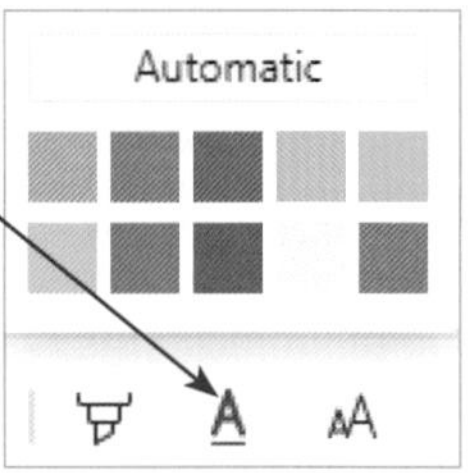

6 Select an item of text and click on this button to access options for the size of the text, from **Small**, **Medium** or **Large**

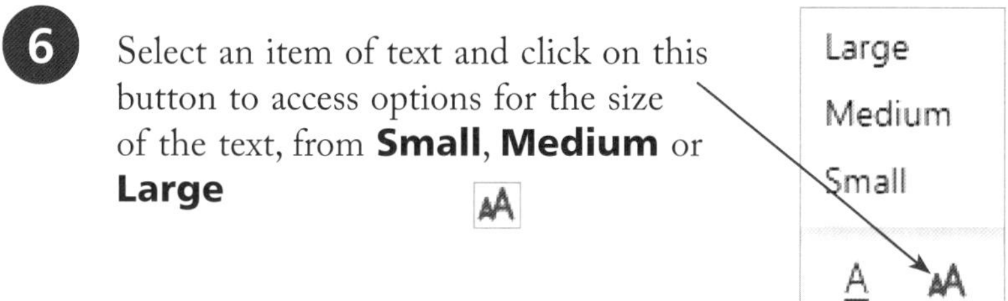

7 Select an item of text and click on the **Paragraph** button to access preset styles to apply to the text

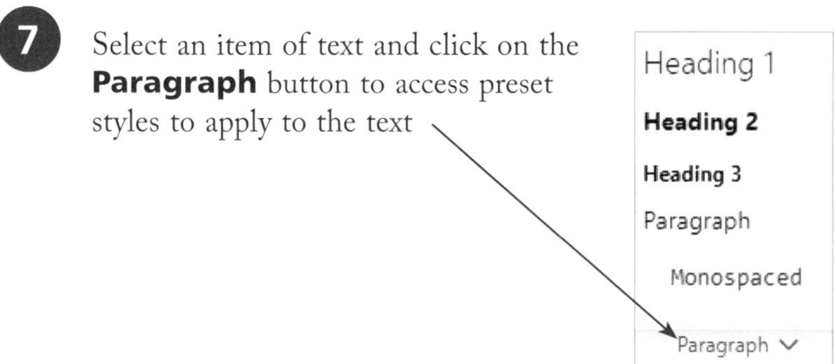

8 Select the formatted text and click on this button to delete all of the formatting that has been applied

9 Use these buttons to, from left to right: decrease the indent of text, increase the indent of text, or create a bulleted list

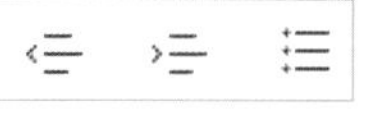

10 Click on the menu button at the right-hand side of the text formatting toolbar to access more options, including adding a numbered list, inserting a horizontal rule, or inserting a table

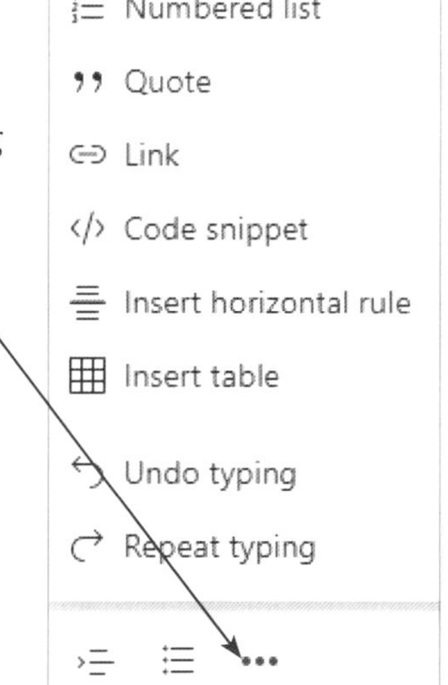

Click on the **Trash** icon at the right-hand side of the text formatting toolbar to delete the current draft message before it is sent.

Adding Attachments

Text chatting can be used as a quick way to share documents with individuals or groups. To do this:

1. Create a text message and click on this icon on the toolbar below the text box

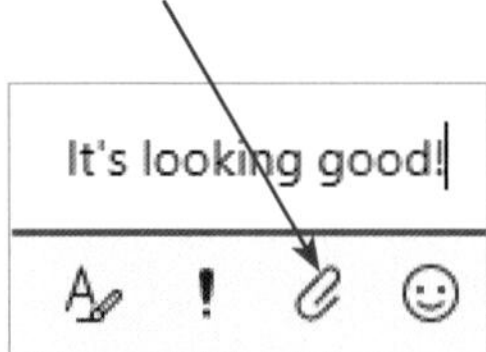

2. Select a location for uploading the required file

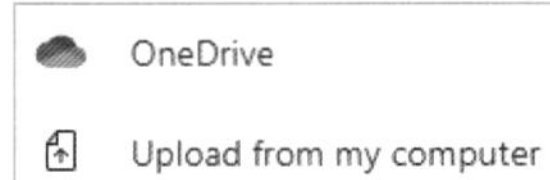

3. Navigate to the file, select it and click on the **Open** button

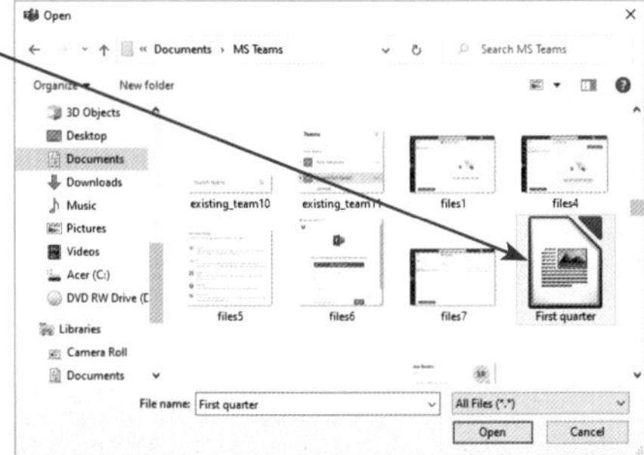

4. The attachment is added to the message

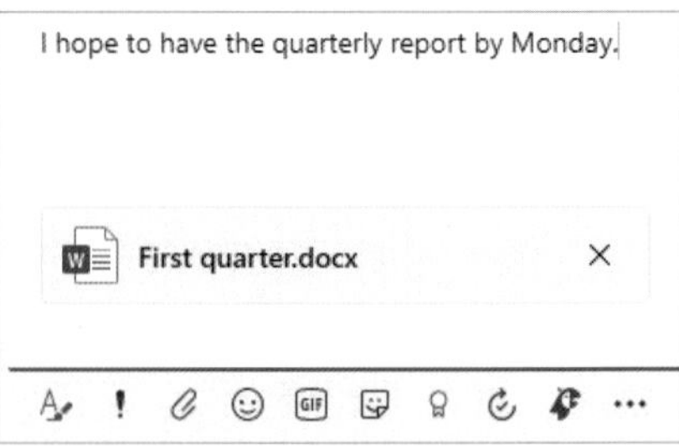

5. Once the message has been sent, the attachment is available for anyone in the conversation

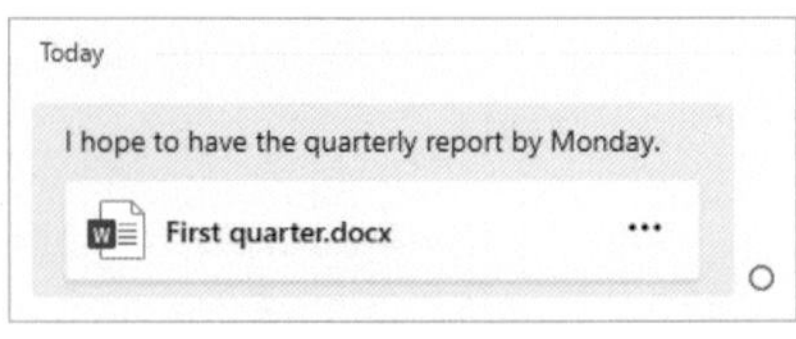

Files can be shared within Teams using the **Files** option in the main sidebar. See pages 166-167 for details about this.

Adding Emojis

Emojis can be added to text chats, in a similar way to adding them to a text message on a smartphone. To do this:

1. Create a text message and click on this icon on the toolbar below the text box

   It's looking good!

2. A list of emojis is displayed. Swipe down the page to view all of the emojis, or click in the **Search** box and enter a keyword to look for a specific emoji

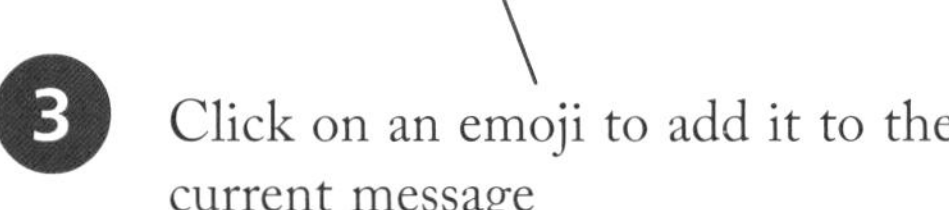

3. Click on an emoji to add it to the current message

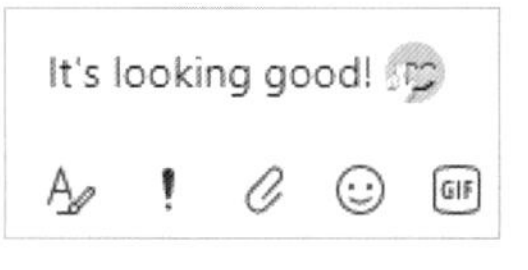

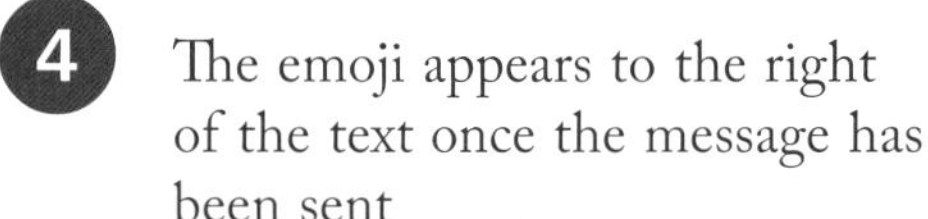

4. The emoji appears to the right of the text once the message has been sent

The range of emojis in Teams is not as extensive as those available on a smartphone.

Animated GIFs and stickers can be added in a similar way to emojis. To do this, click on these icons on the toolbar:

Popping Out Chats

When a regular text conversation is taking place, any other action will result in moving from the Chat interface. However, by popping out a chat, it can be continued while other chats can be undertaken in the main chat window. To do this:

Don't forget

A conversation can also be popped out by clicking on this button in the top right-hand corner of the main conversation window:

1. Select a chat in the left-hand panel and click on this button, or click on the menu button and select the **Pop out chat** option

2. The chat is displayed within its own "popped-out" panel

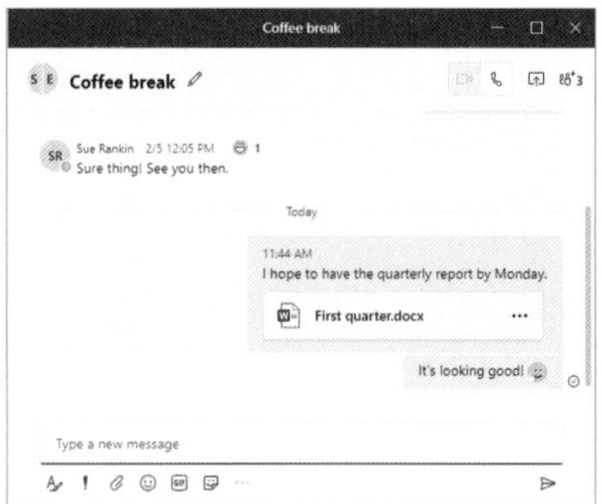

The popped-out conversation is treated as a new, separate window within Teams.

3. The popped-out conversation sits above the main chat window. Click in the main window to make it active and conduct another conversation, while the popped-out window remains open

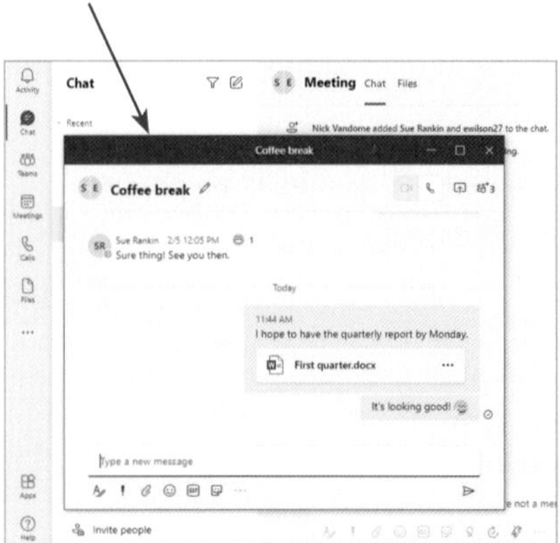

Pinning Chats

Conversations that you have most frequently can be pinned at the top of the left-hand panel, for easy access. To do this:

1. Select a chat in the left-hand panel and click on the menu button

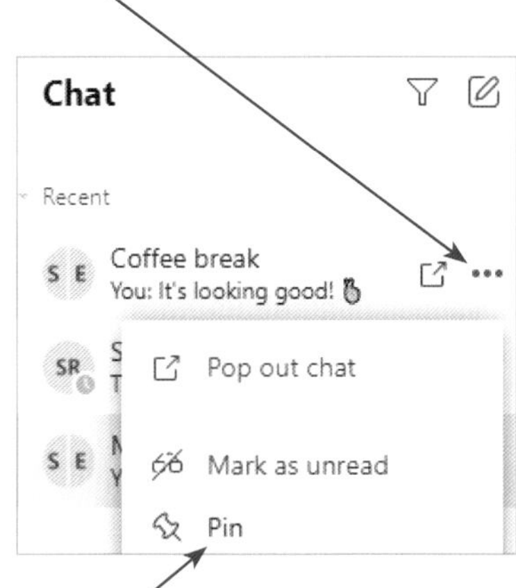

2. Click on the **Pin** option

3. The conversation is pinned at the top of the left-hand panel, below the **Pinned** heading

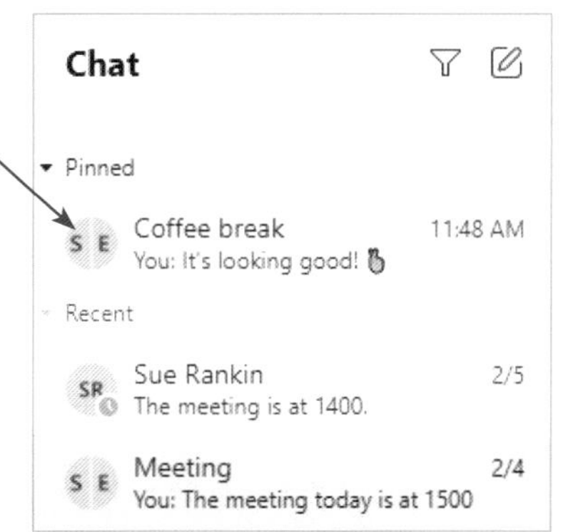

4. Click on the arrow next to the **Pinned** heading to show, or hide, the pinned conversations

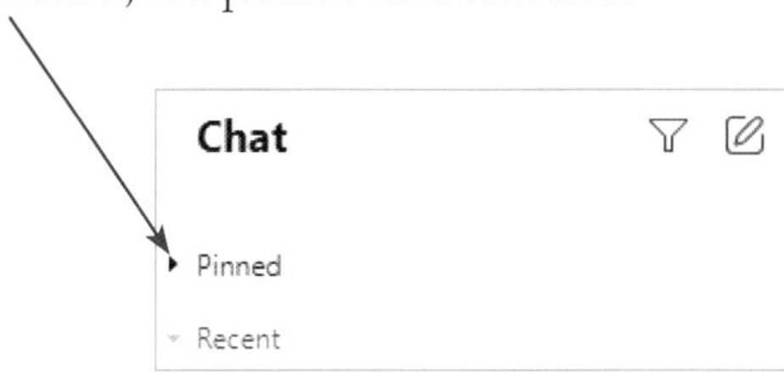

To unpin a conversation, click on its menu in the left-hand panel and click on the **Unpin** option.

Escalating to Audio or Video

Text conversations are a great way to quickly get in touch with an individual or a group. However, there may be times during a conversation when something comes up that requires a voice call or even a video call. From within the Chat section, text chats can quickly be converted into audio or video calls. To do this:

When you make or receive a video call, make sure that the video button is not disabled – e.g. it does not have a line through it.

The duration for the current call is shown in the top left-hand corner of the window.

1. During a chat with an individual or a group, click on these buttons to start a video call or an audio call

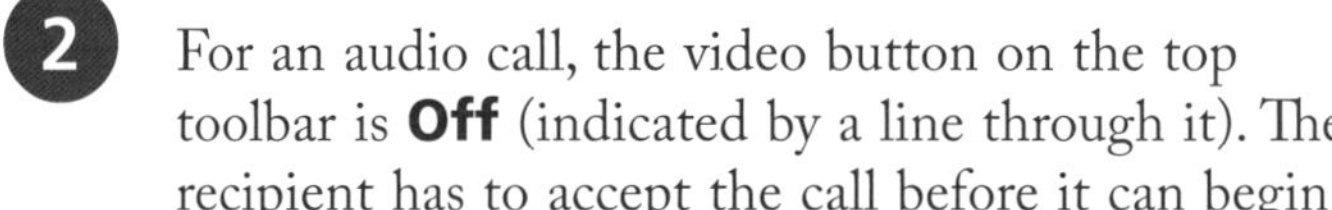

2. For an audio call, the video button on the top toolbar is **Off** (indicated by a line through it). The recipient has to accept the call before it can begin

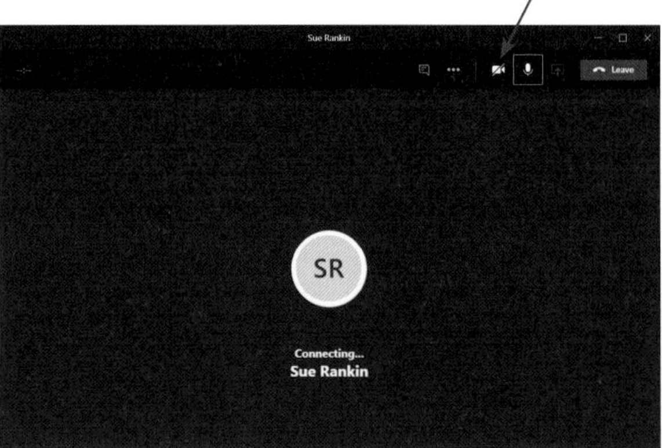

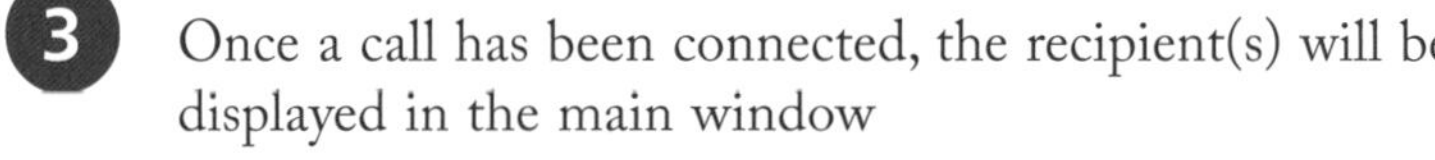

3. Once a call has been connected, the recipient(s) will be displayed in the main window

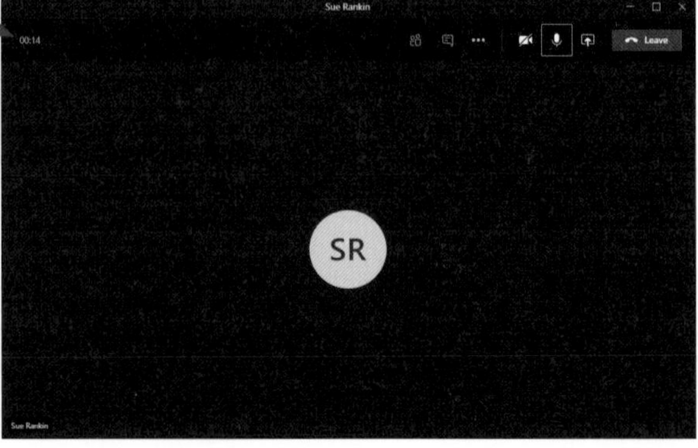

4. The top toolbar, at the right-hand side of the main window, can be used to manage the call

5. If you receive a call, click on the blue video or audio buttons to accept it, or click on the red button to decline the call

6. During a call, click on this button on the top toolbar to access the Chat panel, to include text conversations while you are talking

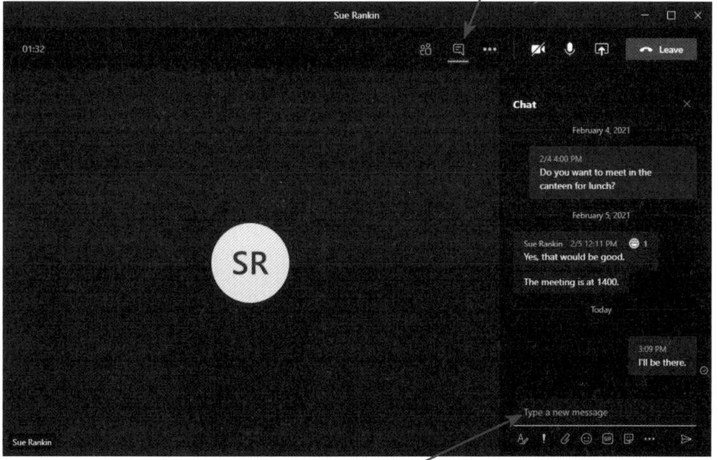

7. Type in the text box and click on the **Send** button to create a text conversation, or continue with an existing one, if there is already one in place for the recipient(s) of the call

If no-one answers a call you will be able to leave a voicemail message.

If the call has been made to a group, all of the group members will be able to include text comments during the duration of the call.

...cont'd

8 Click on this button on the top toolbar to view all of the participants in the call

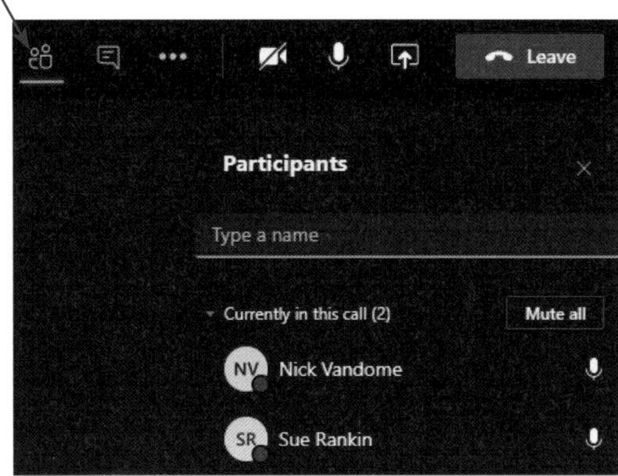

More participants can be added to a call by entering their name in the **Type a name** box in Step 8 and selecting their name from the subsequent list.

9 Click on this button on the top toolbar to share your screen with the people in the call. Click on a screen option to share it

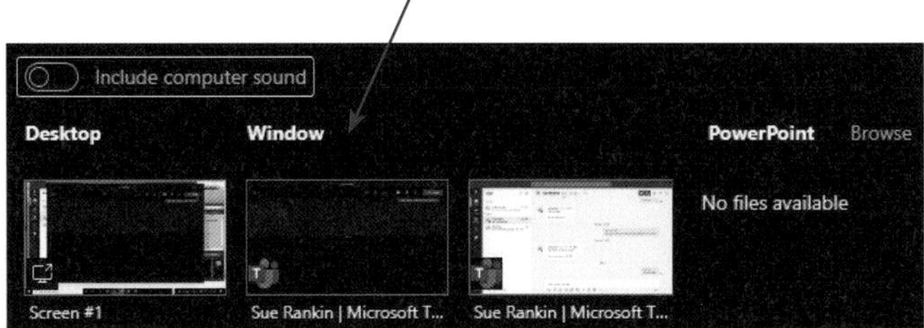

For more details about screen sharing, see pages 152-154.

10 Click on the menu button on the top toolbar to access more options for managing the call

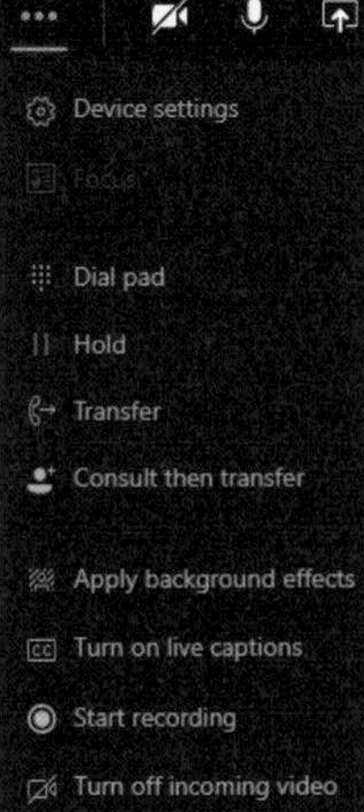

Viewing a video call

If a call is made using the video button on page 112, the recipient's video feed appears in the main window, with your own feed as a thumbnail at the bottom of the screen.

For more details about making and receiving video calls, see Chapter 8.

Viewing call history

To see a list of the audio and video calls that you have made:

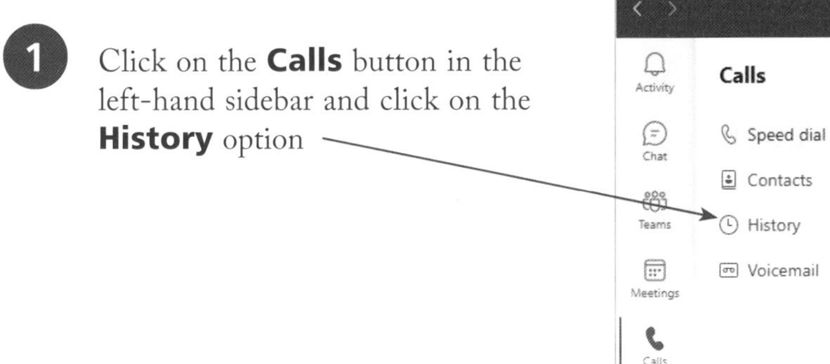

1. Click on the **Calls** button in the left-hand sidebar and click on the **History** option

2. A list of the calls made and received is displayed in the main window

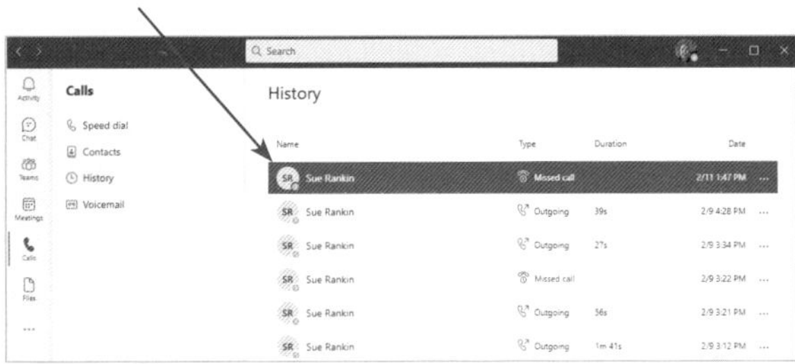

Translating Text

The Chat function in Teams recognizes that there may be users whose first language is not the default one being used. If this is the case, messages can be translated. The default language that messages are translated into is usually the one for the location in which Teams is being used. To translate a message:

Hot tip

Individual users can change the default language for their own version of Teams. To do this, click on your own account icon and click on **Settings**. Below the **Language** > **App language** heading, click on the current language and select a new one. Click on the **Save and restart** button to apply the change. This changes the system text in Teams (i.e. windows, menus and buttons) to the newly selected language.

Hot tip

The **Language** section in Settings can also be used to enable the spell checker for when text is entered. To do this, check **On** the **Enable spell check** box.

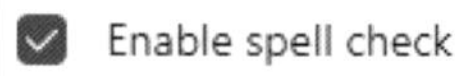

1. Messages can be sent in any language, regardless of the default language being used by Teams

1:24 PM
Hola. Puedo verte después de comer mañana. Entonces podemos organizar una reunión de equipo.

2. Move the cursor over the message and click on the menu button

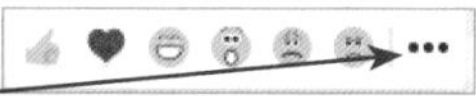

3. Click on the **Translate** button

Save this message
Edit
Delete
Mark as unread
Translate

4. The message is translated into the default language being used by Teams, or the one specified by the user (if they have selected a different default language; see first Hot tip)

1:24 PM
Hello. I can see you after lunch tomorrow. Then we can arrange a team meeting.

5. This icon at the top of the text box indicates that a message has been translated

7 Organizing Meetings

Holding virtual meetings is one of the main functions of Teams. This chapter shows how to harness this functionality for audio and video meetings, to share information, ideas and documents. It also explains how to create breakout rooms and take notes.

Settings for a Meeting

One of the main functions of the Teams app is to enable two or more people to conduct online meetings, using either audio only or video and audio. Before other users are invited to a meeting there are various settings that each person can apply. To do this:

1. Click on the **Meetings** button in the left-hand sidebar

2. Any meetings that have already been scheduled will be listed in the main window

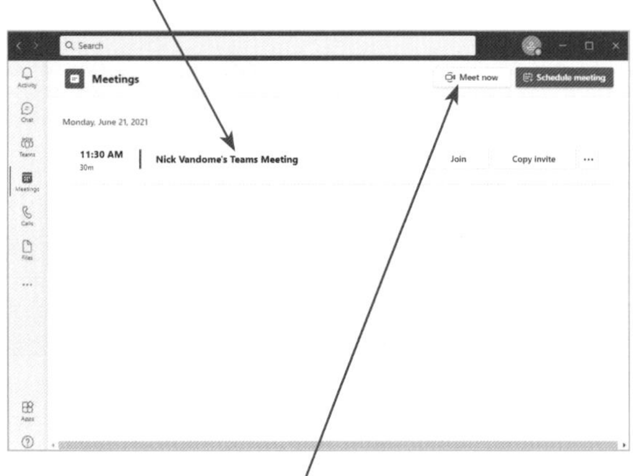

3. Click on the **Meet now** button to start a new meeting immediately

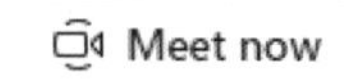

4. The Meeting window is displayed. This contains options that can be selected before the meeting starts

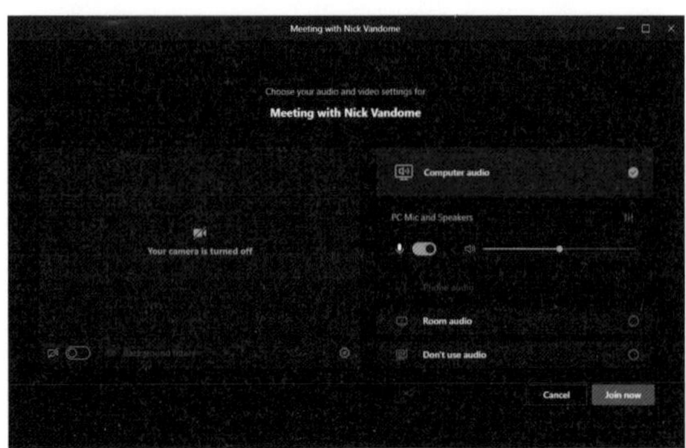

The **Meet now** button in Step 3 accesses the settings for the meeting; it does not create the meeting itself at this point. This is done with the **Join now** button – see Step 8 on the next page.

5. Triple-click on the meeting title at the top of the Meeting window and type a new one, as required

Choose your audio and video settings for

Client presentation

Double-click on a word in Step 5 to select it; a triple-click selects the whole title.

6. Click on the **Computer audio** option to select options for how the audio on your device will be used for the meeting, including muting/unmuting the microphone and setting the volume by dragging this slider

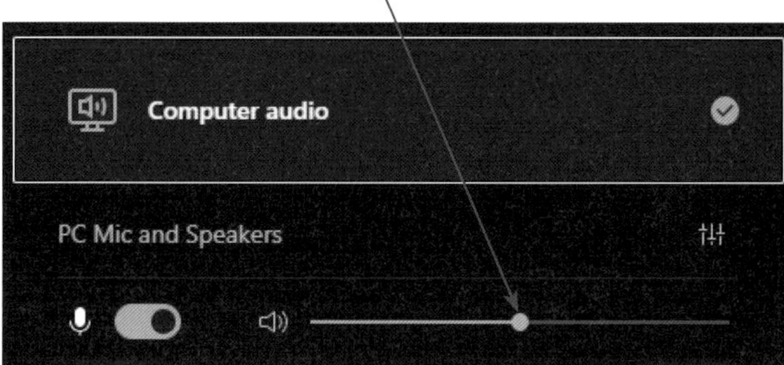

Make sure that your microphone is turned on before a meeting starts, otherwise no-one in the meeting will be able to hear you. There may be times during the meeting that you may want to mute your microphone, or be asked to do so, which can be done by clicking on the microphone icon on the top toolbar so that it has a line through it. Click on the icon again to unmute the microphone.

7. Drag this button to the right to activate the camera on your device, to make a video call

8. Click on the **Join now** button to start a meeting

Join now

Starting a Meeting

There is no point in having a meeting on your own, so once you have applied the required settings and joined the meeting, you will be able to invite other people to the meeting. To do this:

If someone from outside your organization is invited to a meeting, they do so as a guest.

1. In the Meeting window, click on either of these options to invite someone who is not in your organization to join the meeting. If you do not want to do this, click on the cross in the top right-hand corner to close this dialog box

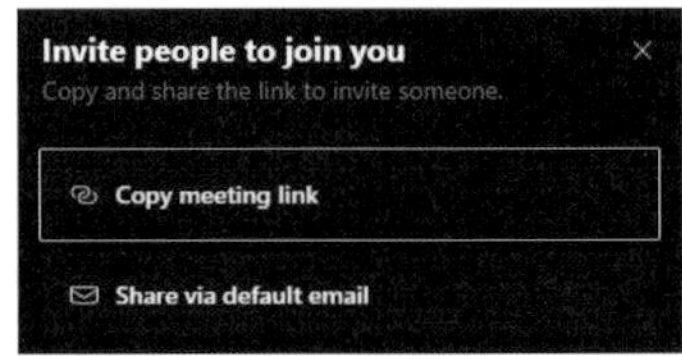

2. Your own account icon is shown in the Meeting window, as the sole current participant of the meeting

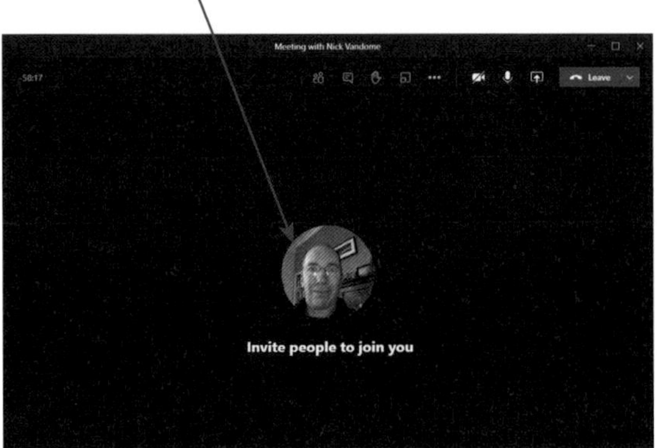

3. Click on this icon on the top toolbar to view the meeting's participants, and add new ones

4. The current participants are shown below the **In this meeting** heading

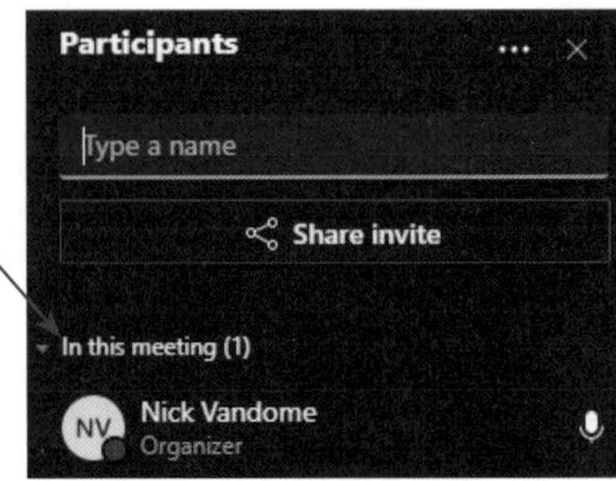

5. Start typing the name of the recipient here and click on one of the options to invite that person to the meeting

6. While the connection is being made, the invitee's icon pulses in the Meeting window

7. Once the invitee has accepted the invitation they are added to the meeting

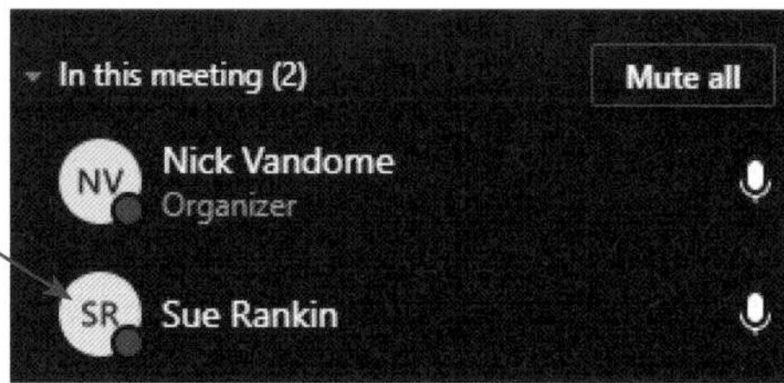

8. Move the cursor over a participant's name and click on the menu button to access options for their participation in the meeting

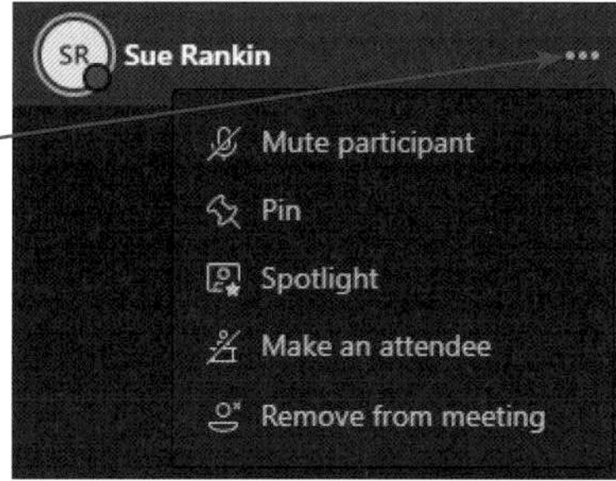

9. To finish a meeting, click on the **Leave** button in the top right-hand corner of the Meeting window. Click on **Leave** to just leave the meeting, or **End meeting** to end it for everyone

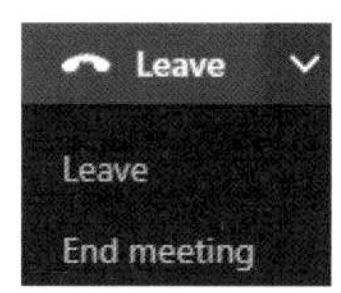

10. To end a meeting, click on the **End** button to confirm the action

Click on the menu button next to the Participants heading in Step 4 on the previous page, to access options for managing the people in the meeting, including stopping participants from unmuting their microphones.

Scheduling a Meeting

Meetings can also be scheduled in advance and the Meetings section enables you to view all of the meetings that have been scheduled. To schedule a new meeting:

1. In the Meetings window, click the **Schedule meeting** button in the top right-hand corner

2. Default details of the meeting are displayed. Click here to enter a title for the meeting

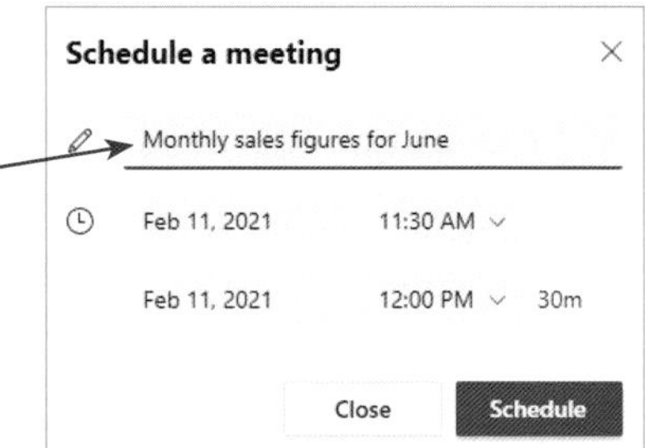

3. Click on the date in Step 2 and select a new start date for the meeting from the calendar

Feb 11, 2021					11:30 AM	
June 2021						
S	M	T	W	T	F	S
30	31	1	2	3	4	5
6	7	8	9	10	11	12

4. The end date of the meeting is automatically updated to match the start date

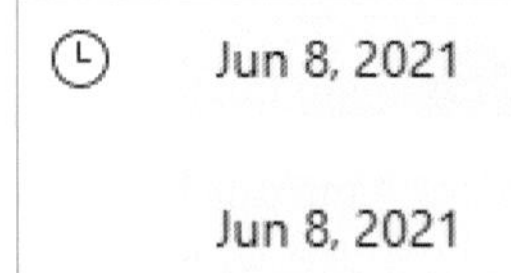

5. Click on the start time in Step 2 and select a new start time for the meeting, as required

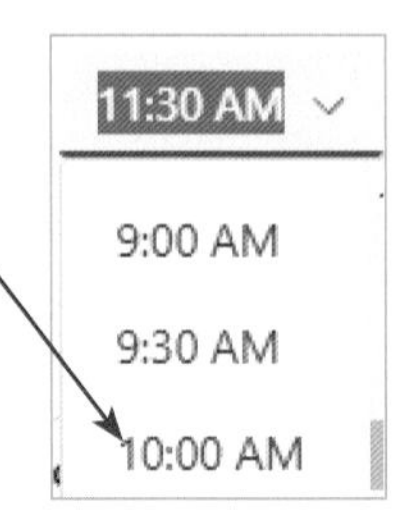

In general, the shorter the meeting duration the better: if a meeting is scheduled for an hour, the participants may feel the need to use up the allotted time, whether anything productive is being done or not.

6. Click on the start time and select a new time, as required. The end time is adjusted automatically, 30 minutes later. Click on the end time and select a new one, as required

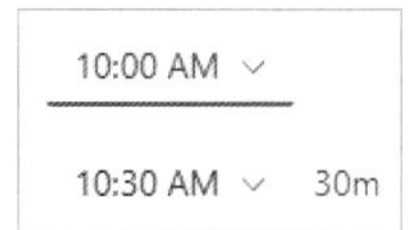

7. Click on the **Schedule** button

8. Click on an option for sharing the meeting details

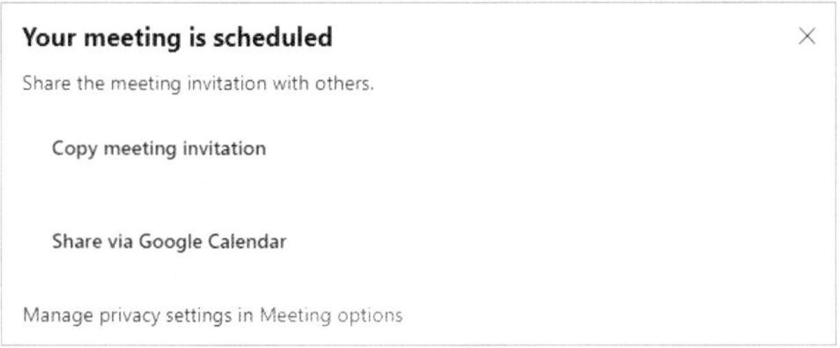

9. If the **Copy meeting invitation** option is selected in Step 8, the meeting request can be pasted into an email and sent to a recipient

10. Once a meeting has been scheduled, it appears in the main Meetings window. Details of the meeting can be edited before it takes place; see Hot tip

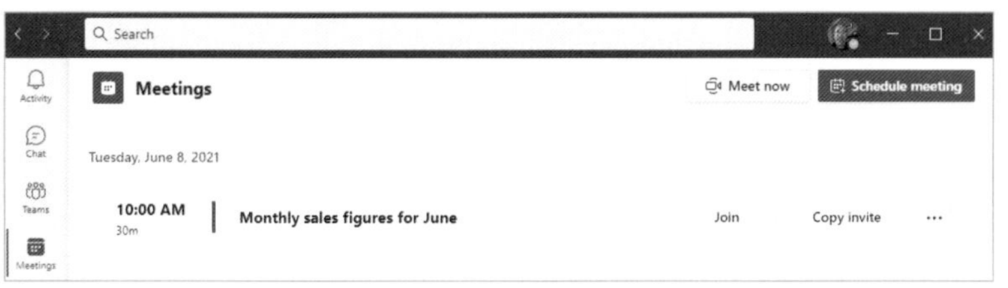

The Meetings section is mainly a planner for upcoming meetings. The meetings are not activated at the specified time and you have to physically join a scheduled meeting by clicking on the **Join** button in Step 10. Also, participants can only join once the scheduled meeting has started.

Move the cursor over the **Copy invite** option in Step 10 and click on the menu button to access options for editing the meeting or deleting it.

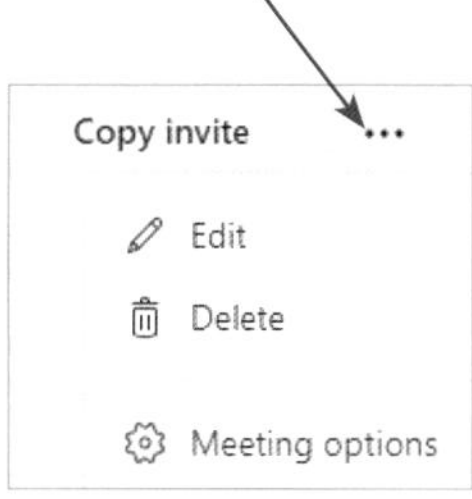

Joining a Meeting

If someone invites you to a meeting there are different options for joining it, depending on how you have been invited:

1. If someone instigates an instant meeting and calls you, as shown on pages 120-121, click on the video or audio button to accept the call and start the meeting

2. If someone sends you a link to the meeting, either in a Teams chat or in an email, click on the link in the message

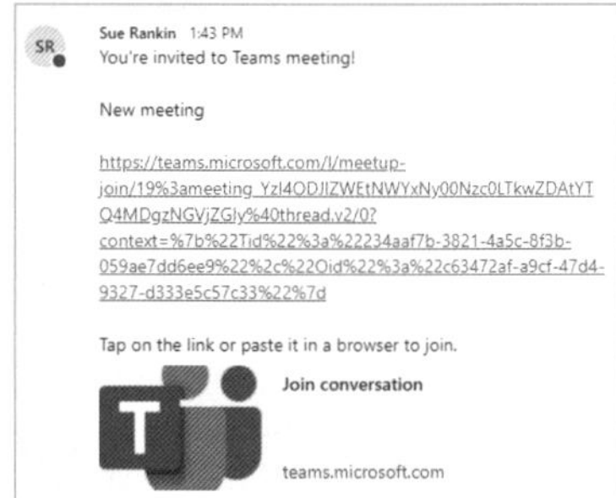

3. Make your selections for the meeting, as shown on pages 118-119

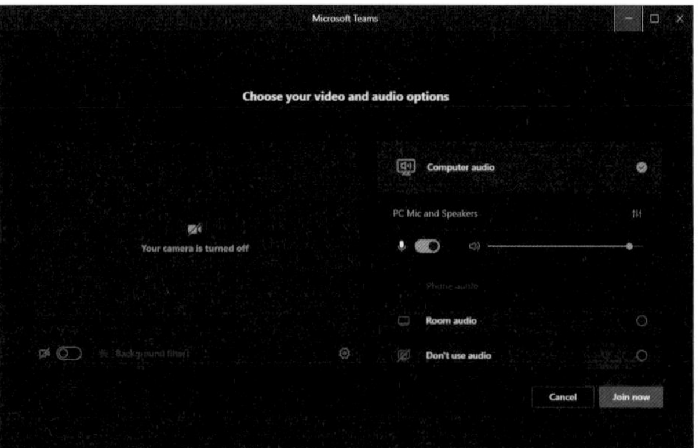
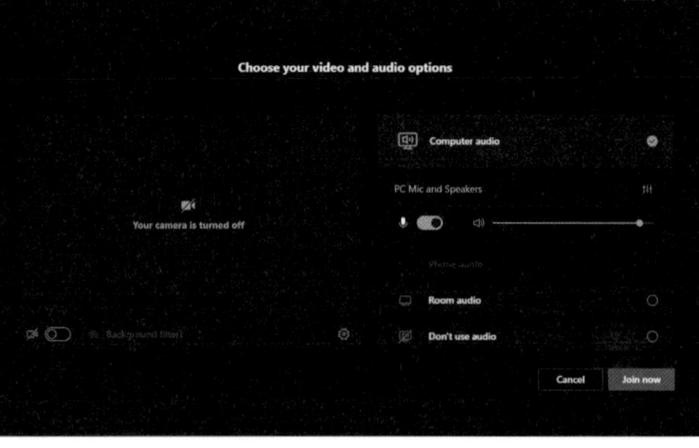

4. Click on the **Join now** button to join the meeting

Join now

Don't forget

The process for joining a meeting from an invitation in an email is the same as in Step 2 for an invitation in a chat message – i.e. click on the link in the email to access the window in Step 3.

Raising a Hand

Managing online meetings – particularly those with a large number of participants – can be difficult at times, in terms of who speaks and when. One way to overcome this is through the use of raising a virtual hand, so that everyone in the meeting knows that you have something you want to say. This can be particularly useful if people are muted during a meeting, to prevent everyone speaking at the same time. To raise a hand for attention:

1. During a meeting, click on this icon on the top toolbar and click on one of the options 

2. The selected item is displayed next to the person in the Participants list

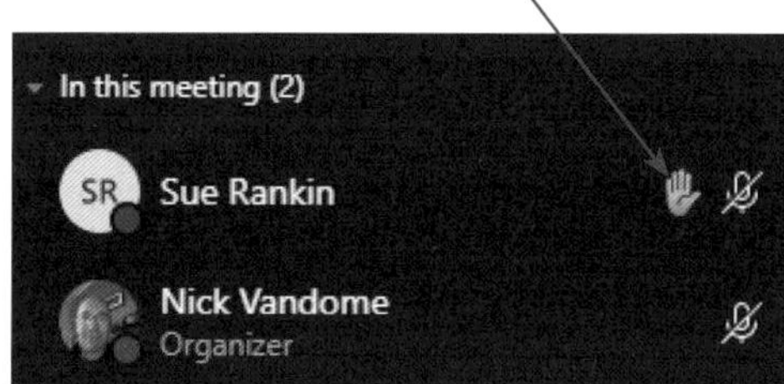

3. If no hands are raised, the next person to raise one will be moved to the top of the Participants list

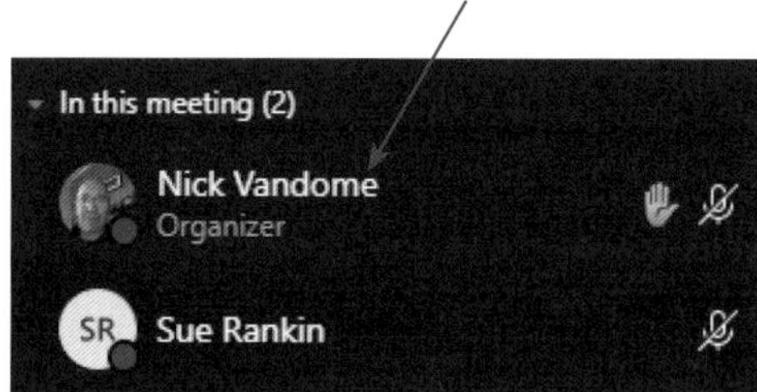

4. If there is a raised hand, the **Participants** button on the top toolbar indicates this with a label on the icon

The organizer of the meeting should be responsible for unmuting people's microphones and asking them to speak once they have raised their hand. If it is not the organizer, someone else should be nominated so that everyone knows who is in charge of the meeting.

If someone has raised a hand, this is also displayed next to their icon in the main Meetings window.

Click on the hand icon again to lower a raised hand.

Using Breakout Rooms

When a meeting is being conducted with a large number of people there may be times when a subset of the main meeting wants to have a separate meeting, without leaving the meeting itself. This is done through the use of breakout rooms, where a group from the meeting can create another, virtual, room in which they can discuss issues that are specific to them, but not necessarily relevant to the whole meeting. To use a breakout room during a meeting:

If breakout rooms are used, this should be discussed with all members of the meeting first so that everyone knows what is going to happen.

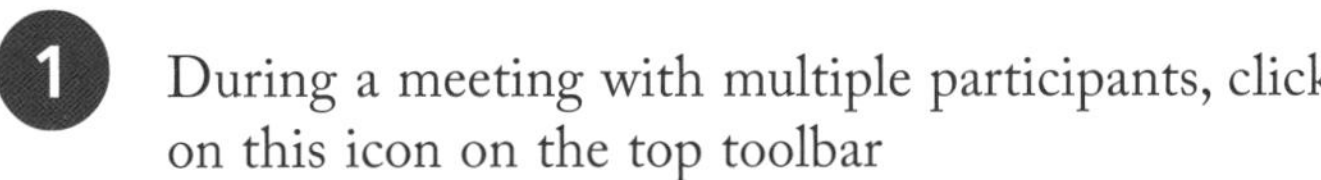

1. During a meeting with multiple participants, click on this icon on the top toolbar

2. Select how you would like to create the breakout rooms. Click on the **Automatically** option to enable the Teams app to assign users to a room

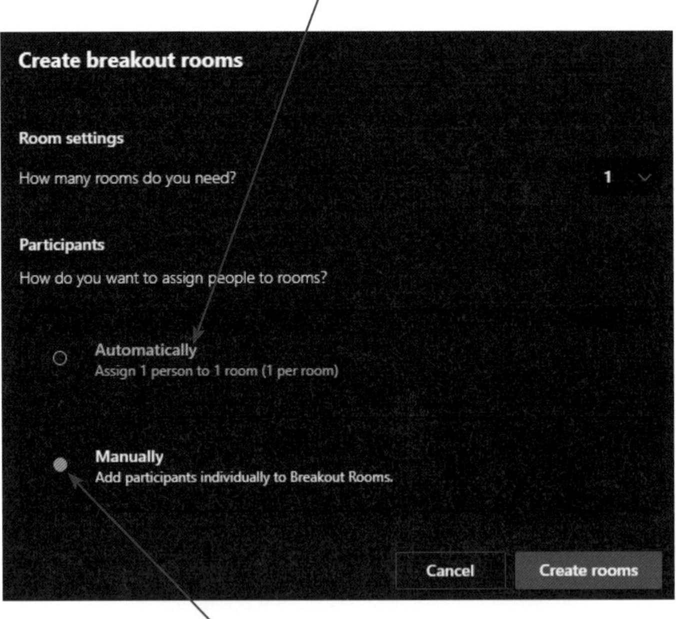

3. Click on the **Manually** option to create rooms and assign people to them manually

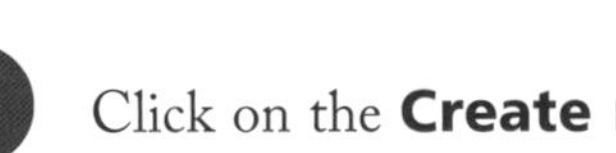

4. Click on the **Create rooms** button

5. For the **Manually** option, click on **Assign participants**, to assign people to breakout rooms

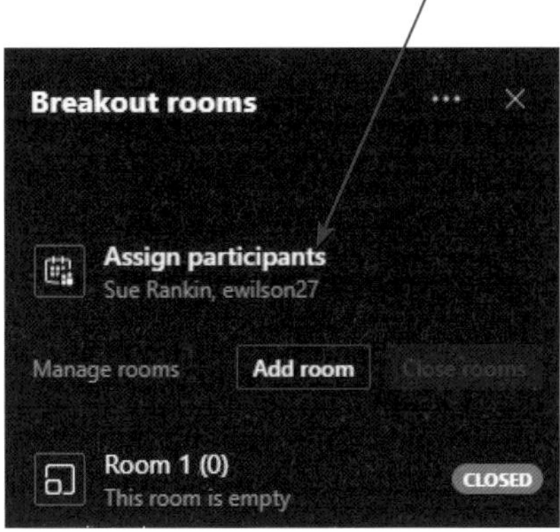

6. Check **On** the checkbox next to the participant(s) you want to include in the breakout room and click on the **Assign** button

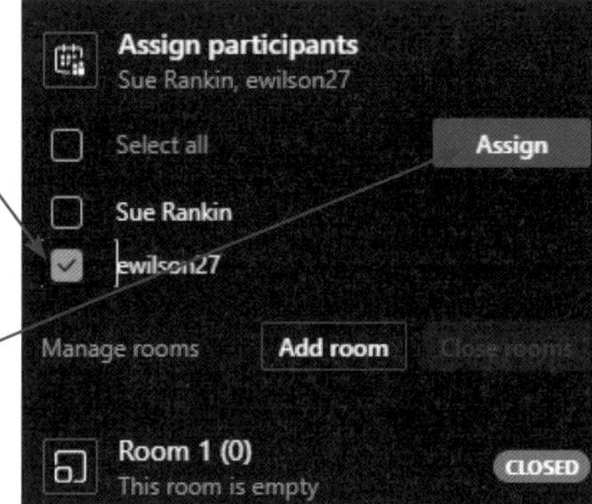

Click on the **Add room** button in Step 6 to add another breakout room, if required.

7. Click on a room name to assign the selected participant(s) to it

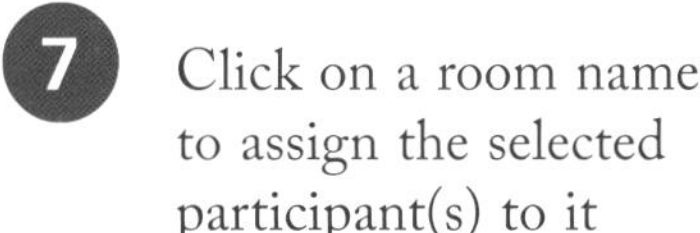

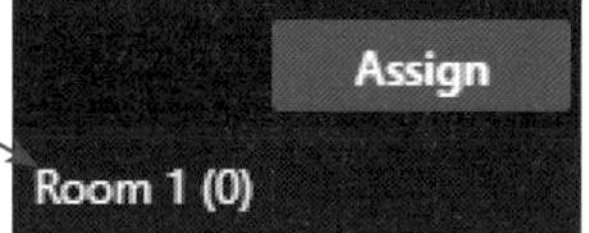

8. The participant(s) is listed below the selected room

...cont'd

9 Once someone has been added to a room, it can be opened as a breakout room, by clicking on the **Start rooms** button

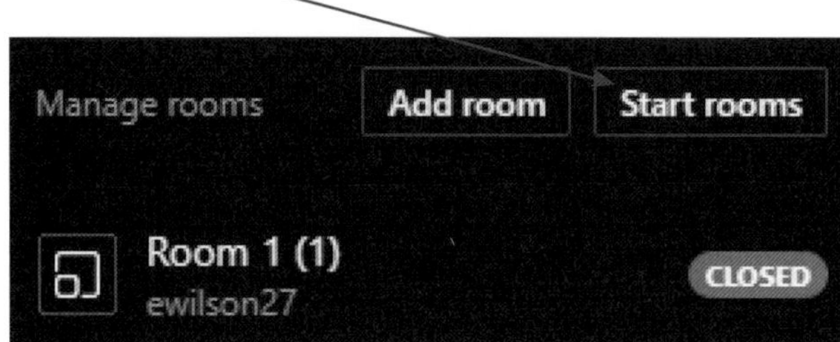

10 Move the cursor over the **OPEN** button

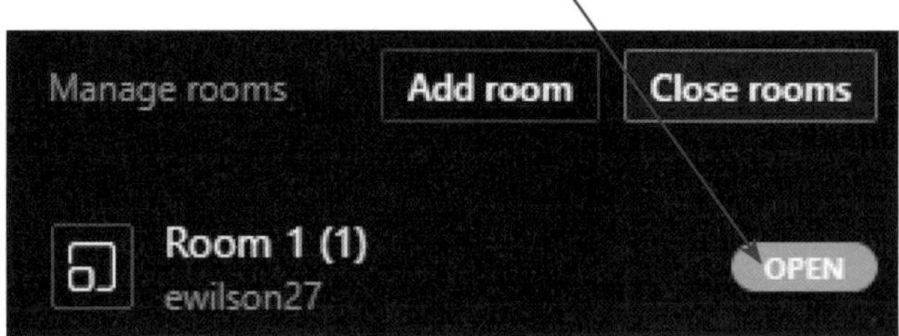

11 Click in the menu button next to the room name and click on the **Join room** option

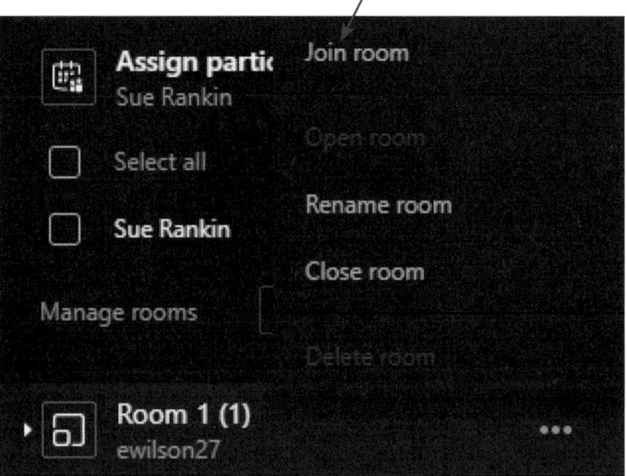

Click on the **Rename room** option in Step 11 to give the room another name, rather than Room 1, Room 2, etc.

Rename room

12 The breakout room is created, containing the participants who have been assigned to it. The name is at the top of the window

Room 1

13 Click on the **Leave** button to leave the breakout room

Leave

Don't forget

If you leave a breakout room you can rejoin it again, by clicking on the **Breakout rooms** button on the top toolbar and rejoining the room, as shown in Step 11 on the previous page.

Breakout rooms settings

Some settings can be applied for breakout rooms. To access these:

1 Click on the menu button next to the **Breakout rooms** heading, as shown in Step 5 on page 127

2 Click on the **Rooms settings** option

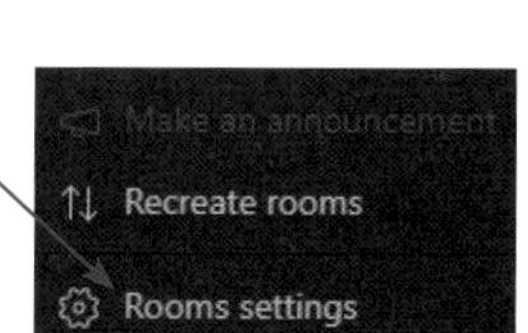

3 Drag the buttons **On** or **Off** to apply, or remove, specific settings for how participants can use breakout rooms

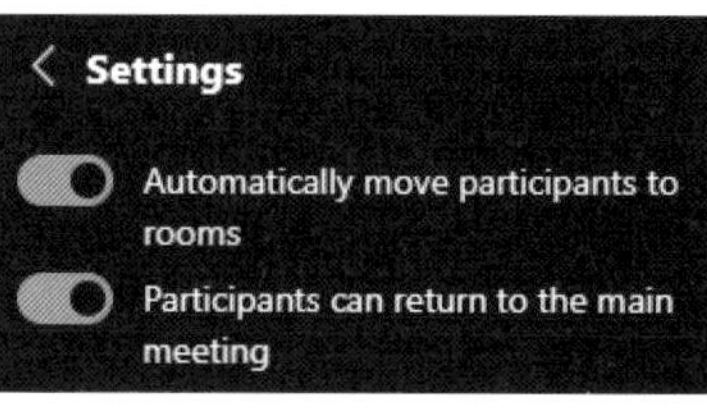

When you join a breakout room, your participation in the main meeting is paused. When you leave the breakout room, click on the **Resume** button on the top toolbar to continue in the main meeting.

Resume

Meeting Settings

Settings can be applied to meetings before anyone has been invited, or while a meeting is taking place. To do this:

1. Join a meeting and click on the menu button on the top toolbar

2. The available options are listed. These can be used for settings for people in the meeting; the appearance of the interface for the meeting; applying background effects; using live captions; recording the meeting; and also turning off incoming video from the participants in the meeting

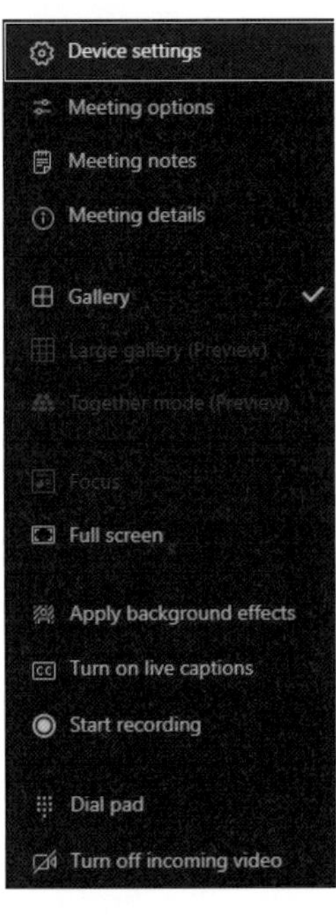

3. Click on the **Meeting options** button to apply settings for whether people can bypass the lobby when joining a meeting and who can display presentations in the meeting

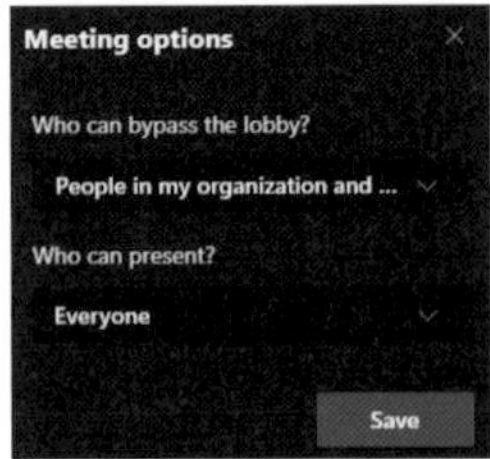

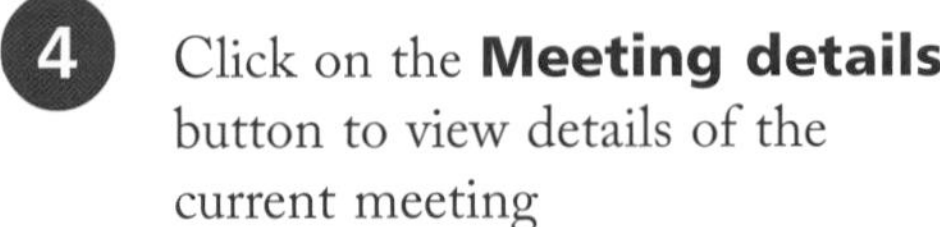

4. Click on the **Meeting details** button to view details of the current meeting

For more details about applying background effects during a meeting, see pages 142-145.

For more details about applying live captions during a meeting, see next page.

The lobby is the waiting area where you are placed before a meeting organizer accepts you into a meeting, if you have asked to join it.

Meeting Accessibility

For anyone with hearing issues, an audio or video meeting can be a challenge. This is particularly true for an audio-only meeting, as it can be much harder to understand people if there are no visual clues with facial expressions and the chance to lip-read what is being said. One option within Teams to overcome this is live captions, which provide a text display of what is being said. This includes everyone in the meeting, including yourself. To use live captions during a meeting:

The live captions function only displays two lines of text at a time and you cannot scroll through it to see what was previously said in the conversation.

1. Access the meeting settings, as shown on the previous page, and click on the **Turn on live captions** button

   Turn on live captions

2. A text display of what is being said appears at the bottom of the Meeting window

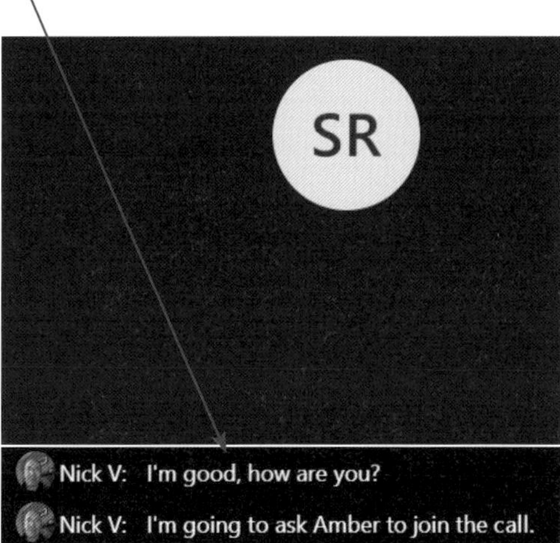

3. When another meeting participant says something, the text display is updated

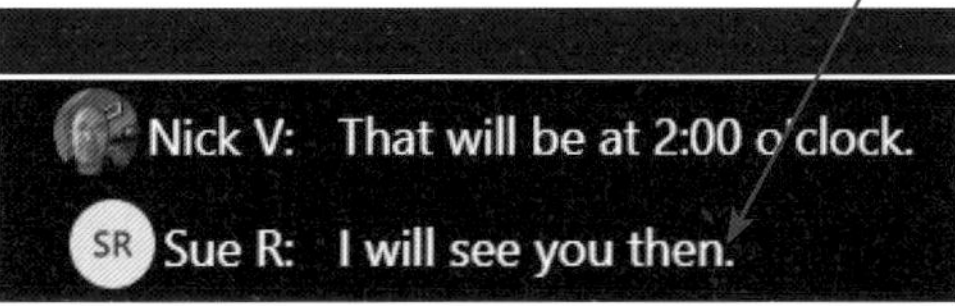

Using live captions in Teams is not always an exact science and there may be times when the text message is different from what was said.

Taking Notes

Within the Meeting settings there is an option to take notes during a meeting. To do this:

1. Access the Meeting settings as shown on page 130 and click on the **Meeting notes** option

2. In the **Meeting Notes** panel, click on the **Take notes** button at the bottom of the panel

Only make notes in a meeting when your attention is not required in the meeting itself.

3. The Meeting Notes option opens up in the **Chat** section of the Teams interface

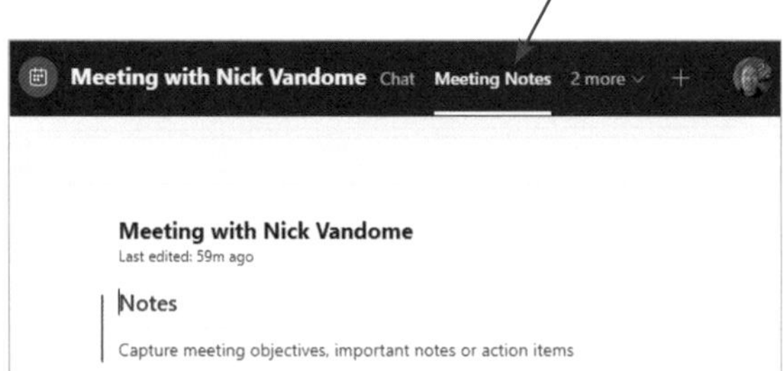

4. Enter a note as required. This will be able to be viewed by the other people in the meeting

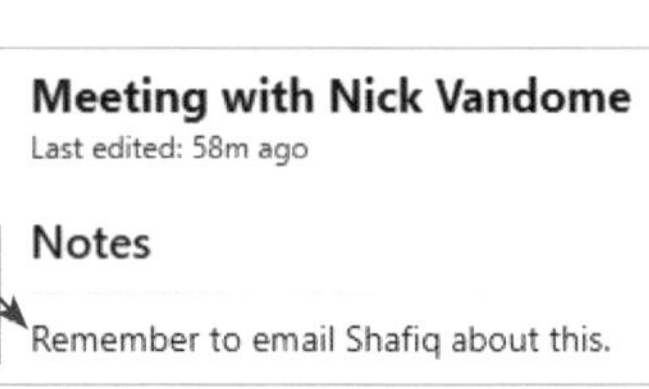

Recording a Meeting

If you want to keep a record of a meeting, or any part of it, this can be done by recording it. To do this:

1. Access the Meeting settings, as shown on page 130, and click on the **Start recording** option

2. The recording function is indicated by a red icon next to the meeting duration

3. To finish recording a meeting, access the Meeting settings and click on the **Stop recording** option

4. Click on the **Stop recording** button to confirm the action

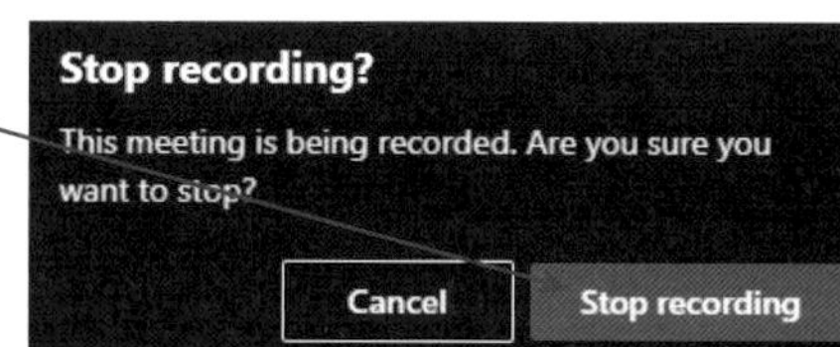

5. To access a recording of a meeting, click on the **Chat** button in the left-hand sidebar and click on the relevant meeting

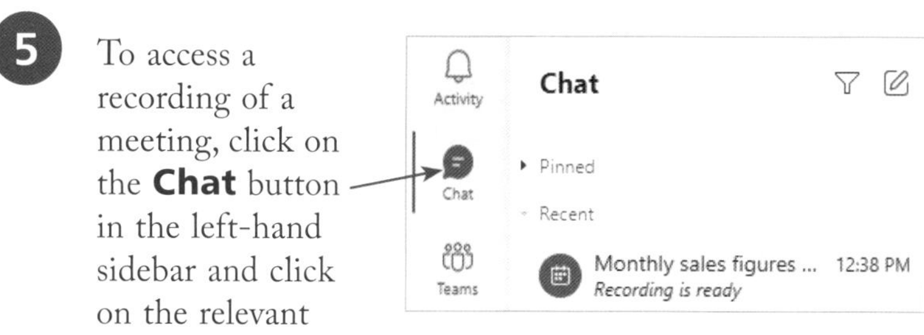

6. Click on the video thumbnail to play the recording of the meeting

Always tell other participants in a meeting if you are planning to record it.

Meetings Etiquette

There are a number of pitfalls to try to avoid when taking part in online meetings. Some things to consider are:

- Try not to talk over other people during a meeting. This can be harder to achieve than during a face-to-face meeting, partly due to the reduced amount of body language that is available. It can be particularly problematic if everyone in the meeting is unmuted and trying to talk at the same time. A good way to overcome this is for the organizer of the meeting to mute all of the participants and then unmute them as required. This can be done by the organizer asking individual people to speak, or by people using the raise-hand function as shown on page 125, and the organizer can then call on them.

Beware

When using the raise-hand function, the organizer of a meeting has to pay attention to ensure that people are called to speak in the order in which they raised their hands.

- Tell people around you that you are going to be in an online meeting. This will, hopefully, prevent them from interrupting you during the meeting. This is particularly important if you are working from home with other people there, especially children. There have been numerous examples that have found their way onto social media sites of online meetings that have been interrupted by children, pets, or other people in the household. If possible, hold your Teams meetings somewhere where you will not be disturbed.

For more details about applying background effects during a meeting, see pages 142-145.

- Never use derogatory or offensive language: if it's not acceptable in a face-to-face meeting, it's not acceptable in an online one either.
- Don't shout at other participants. It's not something that should be done in a face-to-face meeting, and it can seem exaggerated in an online environment.
- Never say anything that you would not be happy to have played back to you. Even if a meeting is not being recorded, someone could still film it on a smartphone and so have a permanent record of it.
- If you are taking part in a video meeting, be aware of your background and ensure that it is not distracting, and does not contain any inappropriate items.
- Check your audio and video settings before the meeting starts, paying particular attention to your microphone to ensure it is muted or unmuted, as required.

8 Video Meetings

Being able to see colleagues in a meeting makes it much more similar to an in-person meeting. This chapter tells you everything you need to know to perform informative and productive video meetings.

Starting a Video Meeting

Video meetings can be created from within a team (in which case all team members can be involved) or from the Meetings section, where individuals can be invited to a video meeting.

Video meetings from within a Teams environment

To start a video meeting from within the Teams environment:

1. Click on the **Teams** button in the left-hand sidebar

2. Click on a team in the left-hand panel. All members of this team will be able to access the subsequent video meeting

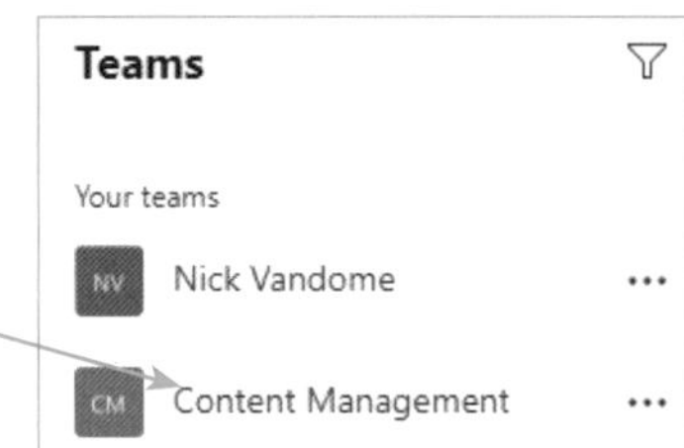

3. Click on this button in the top right-hand side of the main Teams window

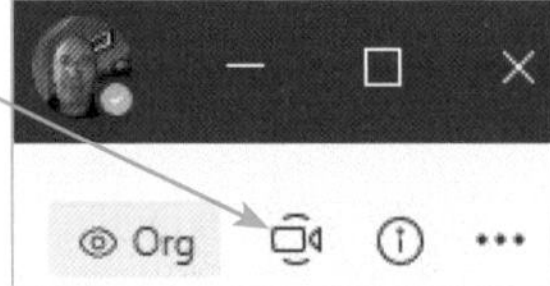

4. The window for applying settings for the video meeting is displayed

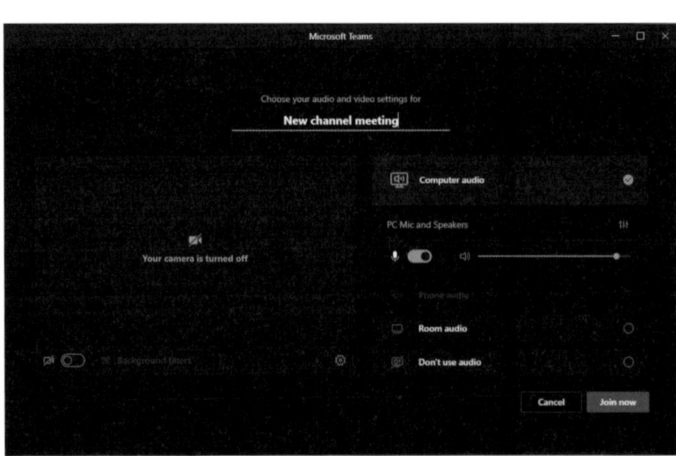

The window in Step 4 is the same for starting a video or an audio meeting.

5. Triple-click on the text at the top of the window and enter a name for the video meeting

6. Drag this button **On** to display your own video feed

7. Click on the **Join now** button in the bottom right-hand corner of the settings window in Step 4 on the previous page

8. Once you have joined the meeting, other members of the team will receive a notification and an option to join the meeting, by clicking on the **Join** button in the main channel window of the relevant team

Once a meeting has been joined using the **Meet now** button in Step 2, participants can be invited to the meeting by clicking on this button on the top toolbar of the Meetings window:

Video calls to individuals

To make a video call that is not from the Teams environment:

1. Click on the **Meetings** button in the left-hand sidebar

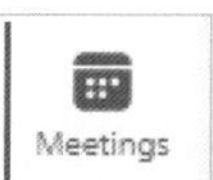

2. Click on the **Meet now** button to start the video call

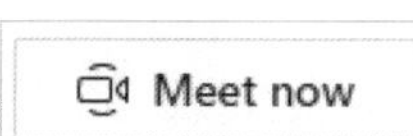

Adding Team Participants

Starting a meeting from within a team is similar to the process from within the Meetings section. However, when you start a meeting for an established team, the team members are available as suggested participants when you join the meeting:

Participants can also be located, and invited to a meeting, by typing their name in the **Type a name** box at the top of the Participants window.

1. From within a team, join a meeting, as shown on page 137. In the **Participants** panel, the members of the team are listed below the **Suggestions** heading

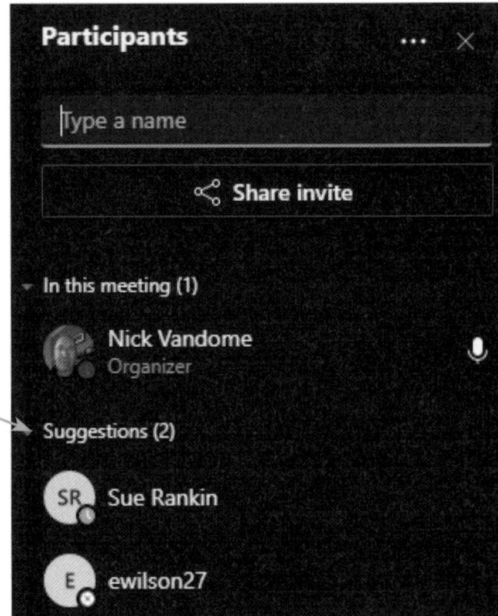

2. Move the cursor over someone's name and click on the **Request to join** button

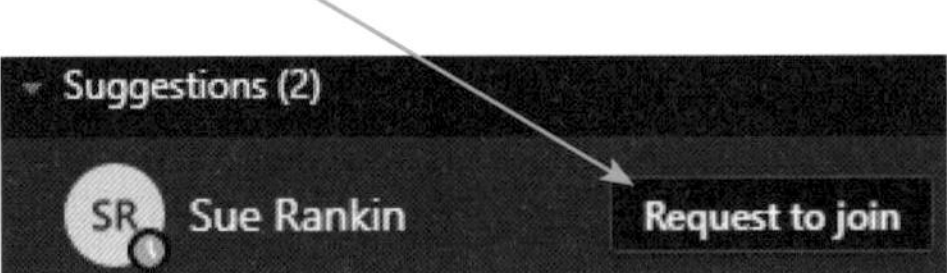

3. A call is made to the selected recipient and they will join the meeting once they accept the call

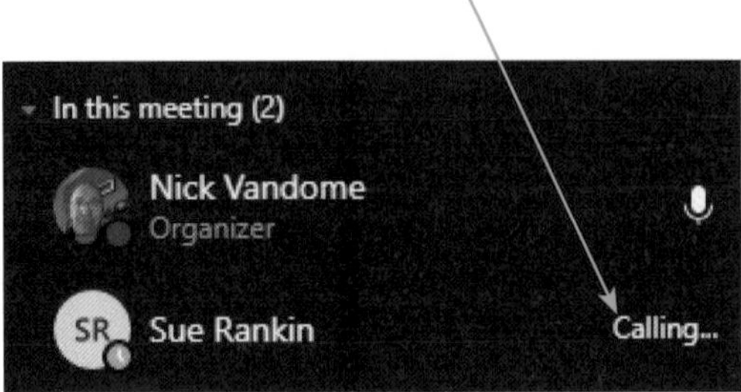

Sharing an Invite

In addition to inviting participants from within your own Teams environment, it is also possible to invite other people to a meeting, for maximum flexibility when deciding who to include. To do this:

1. Once you have joined a meeting, click on the **Share invite** button in the right-hand **Participants** panel

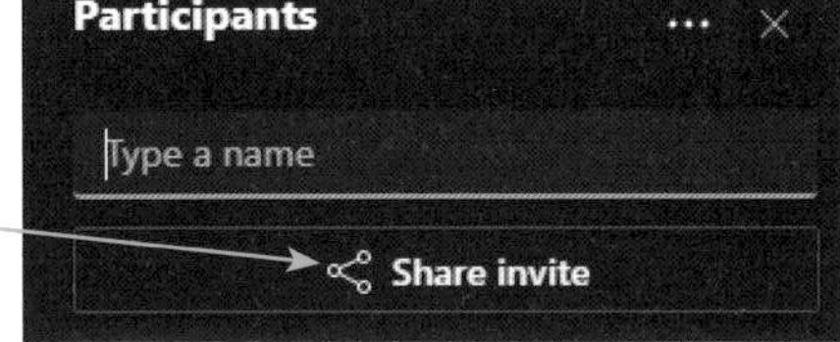

2. Click on either **Copy meeting link** (to copy the link and paste it into another app for sending it to someone) or on the **Share via default email** option

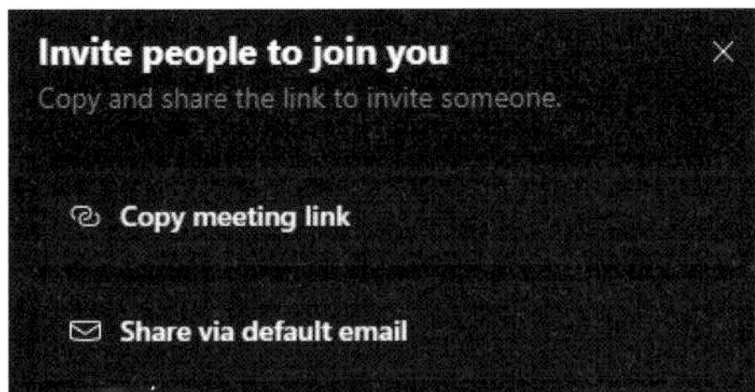

3. If **Share via default email** is selected, the default email app will open automatically, with the link to the meeting already inserted. Select a recipient for the email and send it. The recipient will then be able to join the meeting by clicking on the link

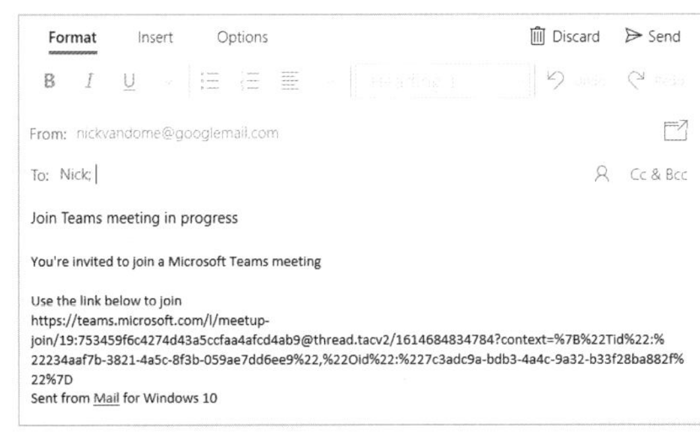

Check with your organization's policy regarding inviting external people to Teams meetings, as in some cases this may not be allowed.

When an external participant is invited to a meeting, they do so as a guest. Once they have activated the link in their email, they will be held in the lobby until the organizer of the meeting admits them, by clicking on the tick symbol.

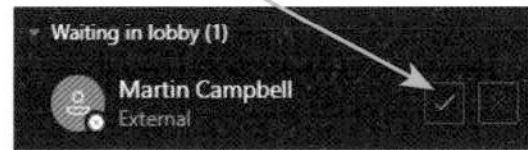

Once a guest has joined a meeting, they are identified as an external participant.

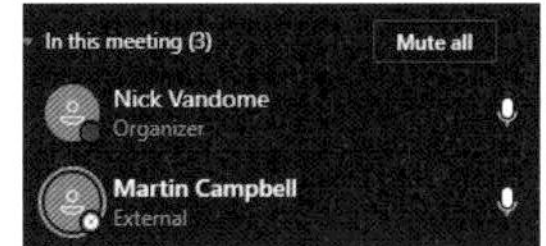

One-to-One Video Meetings

Video meetings offer slightly different functionality, depending on whether they are with one other person or a group of people. When conducting a one-to-one video meeting there are more limited options than when having a group meeting.

1 When the meeting is connected, your own video feed is shown as a thumbnail and the other person's video feed is displayed in the main window

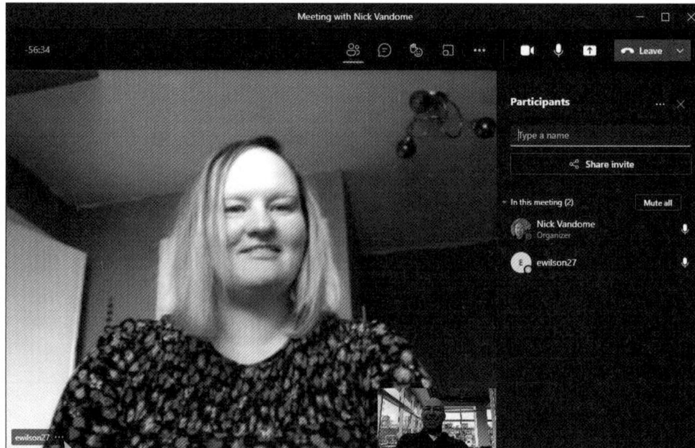

In a one-to-one meeting, the **Spotlight** option in Step 2 highlights the participant's video feed. This feature comes into its own more when a group meeting is taking place. See page 147 for details.

2 Move the cursor over the participant's name, click on the menu button and click on the **Mute participant** option, as required

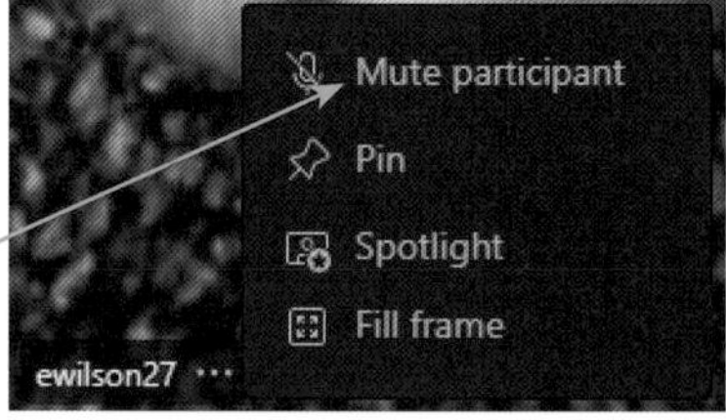

3 Details of the actions applied to a participant are displayed next to their name in the right-hand panel

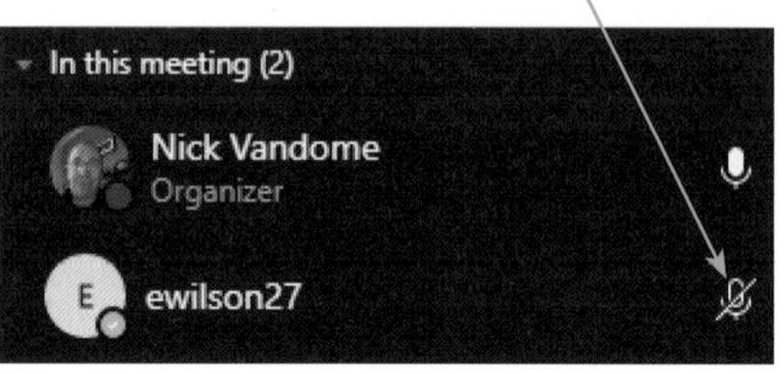

4. From the menu in Step 2 on the previous page, click on the **Pin** option

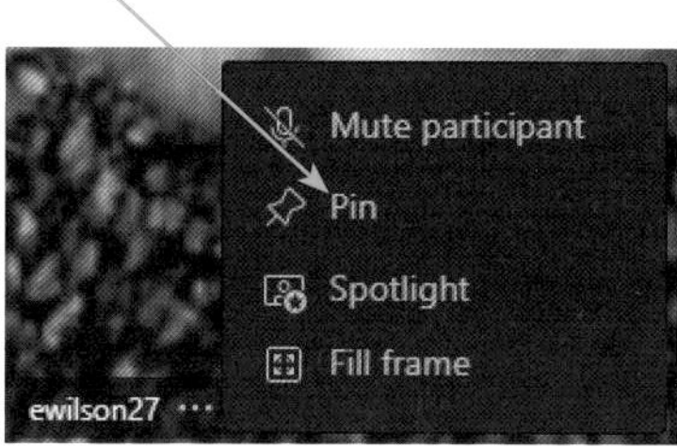

5. The participant's video feed is pinned at the top of the Meeting window, clear of your own video feed

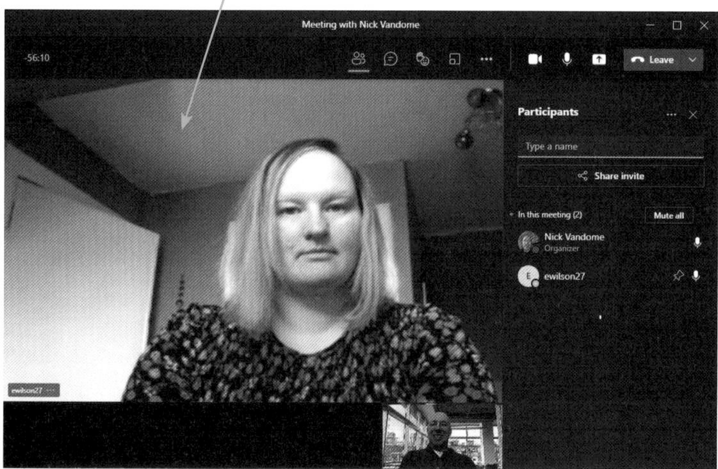

6. Click on the menu button at the top of the **Participants** panel to access more options for managing the meeting

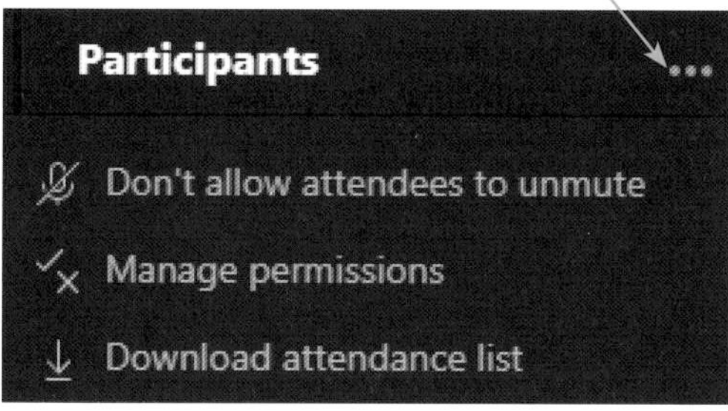

In a one-to-one video meeting, the **Pin** option does not change the appearance of the call greatly, except that it enables you to see the whole of the participant's video feed, without your own thumbnail over it.

Adding Background Effects

As video communication has become more widespread, so the options for video calls have increased. One area in which this has developed significantly is in terms of the backgrounds that can be used behind people during a video call. This can be done to blur out distracting objects or add a variety of professional or fun backgrounds. To do this during a Teams video meeting:

1. In the video window in Step 6 on page 137, click on the **Background filters** button below the video preview window

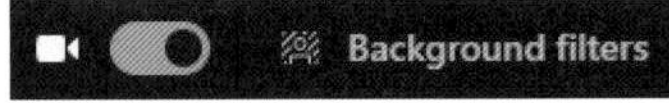

2. The **Background settings** panel is available at the right-hand side of the window

3. Click on the **Blur** button in the Background settings window to blur the background in the video window

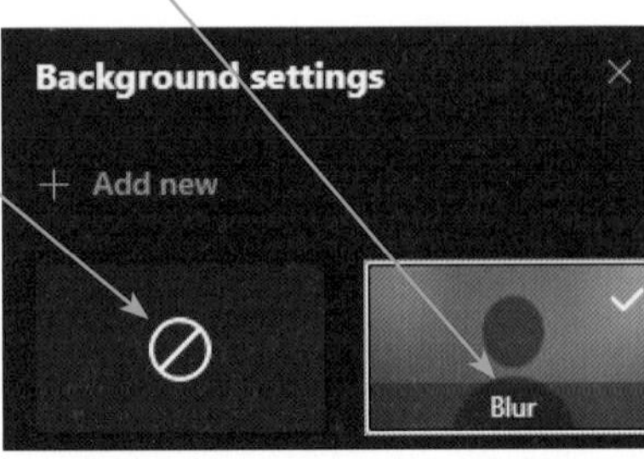

Click on this button in the **Background settings** panel to remove any background effects that have been applied:

4 The blurred background effect can be used to lessen distracting backgrounds and give the participant in a video meeting greater prominence

5 Click on one of the background image thumbnails in the **Background settings** panel

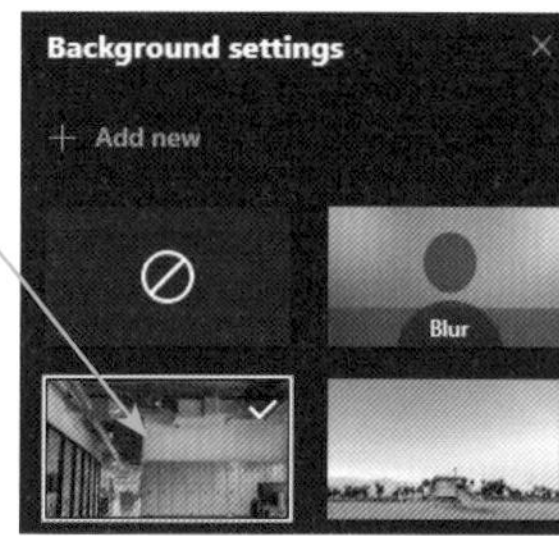

6 The background is applied behind the participant in the video meeting

Background images are shown as a mirror image when they appear in the video-feed window.

...cont'd

7 Background options in Teams range from the professional office-type scene...

8 To the more outlandish...

9 To the fantastical...

Someone's location during a video call may not be the one that appears on screen.

Adding Your Own Backgrounds

Backgrounds for video meetings can also be created from your own photos or images. To do this:

1. Access the **Background settings** panel, as shown on page 142, and click on the **Add new** button

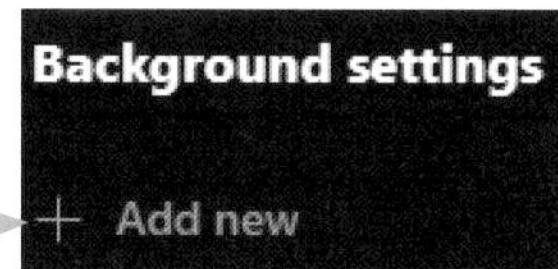

2. Navigate to an image on your computer, select it, and click on the **Open** button

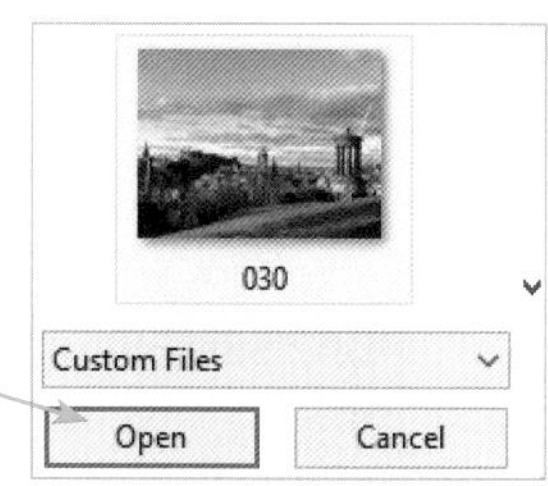

3. The image is applied as the video background

4. The image is added at the bottom of the **Background settings** panel so that it can be selected at any time

Beware

Some organizations may limit the use of backgrounds in video meetings so that only those applicable to the workplace are available.

Group Video Meetings

When conducting a group meeting of three or more people, there are a number of options for managing the meeting.

Fitting video feeds

To ensure all video feeds appear at the same size during a group video meeting:

The menu options for each participant in a meeting can be accessed from this button next to their username, which is located below their video feed.

ewilson27 ···

1. When a group meeting is started, the participant's video feeds appear in the main window, with your own feed as a thumbnail below them. They may appear at different sizes

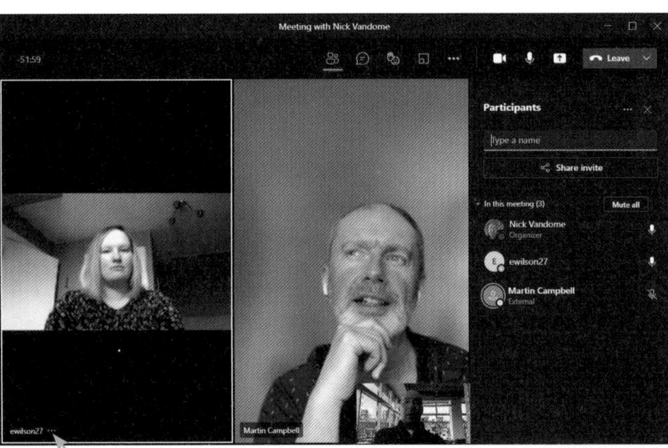

2. To change the appearance of a participant's video feed, move the cursor over here, and click on the **Fit to frame** option

The default mode for a video meeting is **Gallery** view. However, if there are more than nine people in a meeting, **Large gallery** view can be used. This is accessed from the menu button on the top toolbar of the Meeting window.

3. The video feed is resized within the Meeting window so that all of the feeds are the same size

Spotlighting participants

During a video meeting with multiple participants, there will probably be times when you want to give someone more prominence in the meeting, usually when they are talking. In Teams this can be done using the Spotlight feature:

1. Move the cursor over a participant's name and click on the menu button

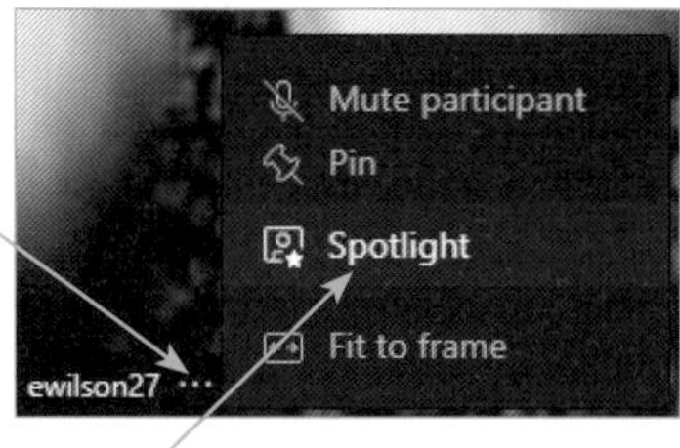

2. Click on the **Spotlight** option

3. The participant's video feed becomes the dominant one in the window, with other users appearing as thumbnails below the spotlighted user

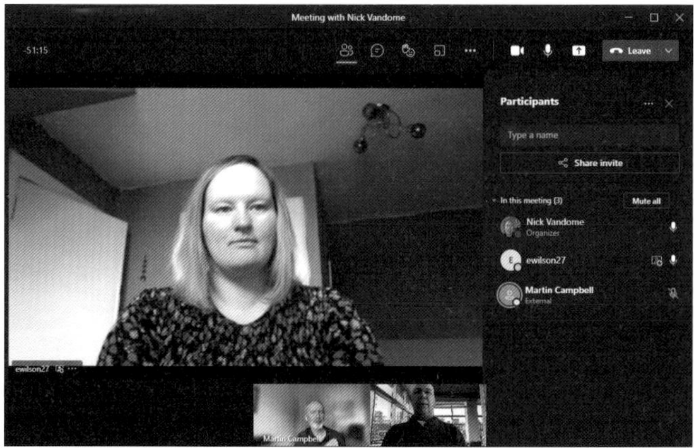

4. To stop someone being spotlighted, move the cursor over their name, click on the menu button, and click on the **Stop spotlighting** option

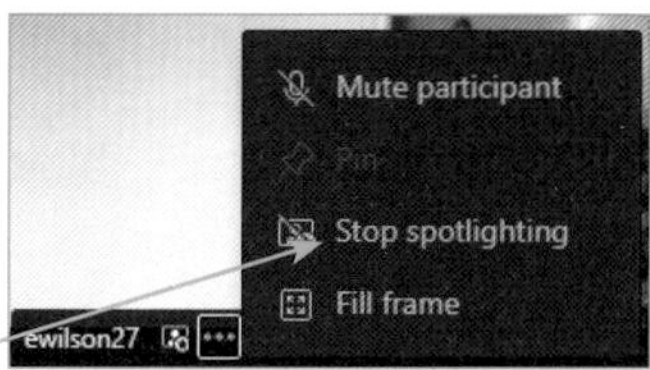

If you are going to spotlight some in a group meeting, tell them first so that they know their video feed will be the main one.

...cont'd

Pinning participants

Another option for highlighting people in a group video meeting is to pin their video feed within the meeting. To do this:

1. During a group video meeting, move the cursor over a participant's name, click on the menu button, and click on the **Pin** option

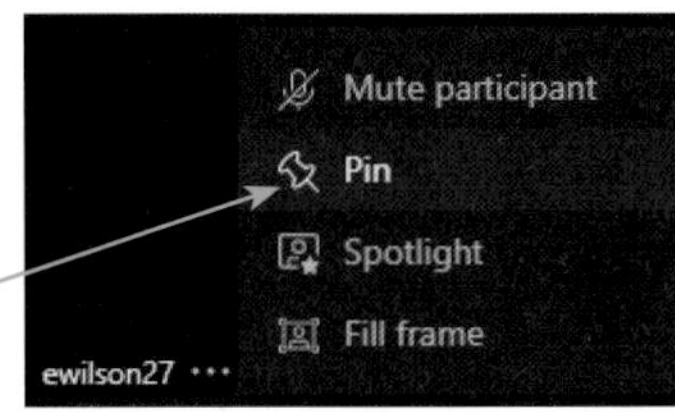

2. The user's video feed is pinned at the top of the window

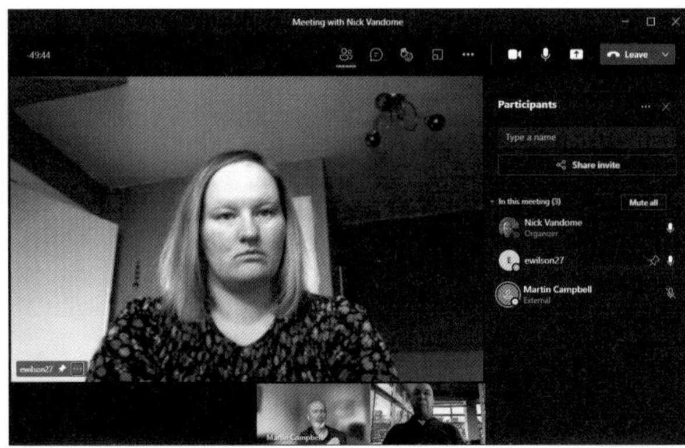

Pinning differs from spotlighting in that several participants can be pinned in a meeting, while only one person can be spotlighted at the same time.

3. If other users are pinned, their video feed will also be pinned at the top of the window

Changing a participant's role

By default, the organizer of a meeting is the presenter, which gives them the authority to perform a range of actions, such as muting other participants and sharing content. However, it is possible for the presenter to change the role of other participants in a group meeting so that they too can act as presenters. To do this:

1. During a group video meeting, move the cursor over a participant's name, click on the menu button, and click on the **Make a presenter** option

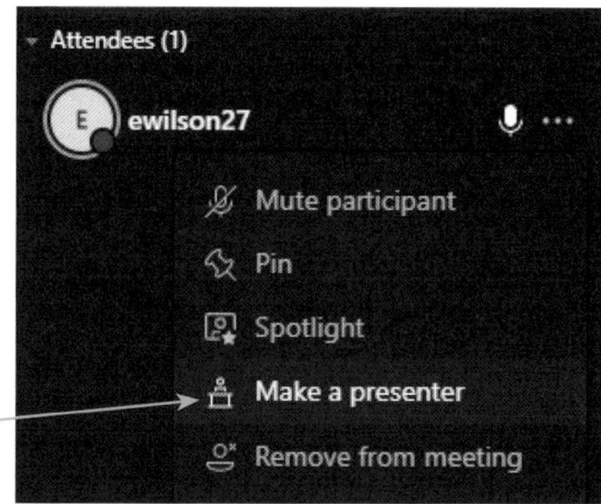

2. Click on the **Change** button to confirm the action

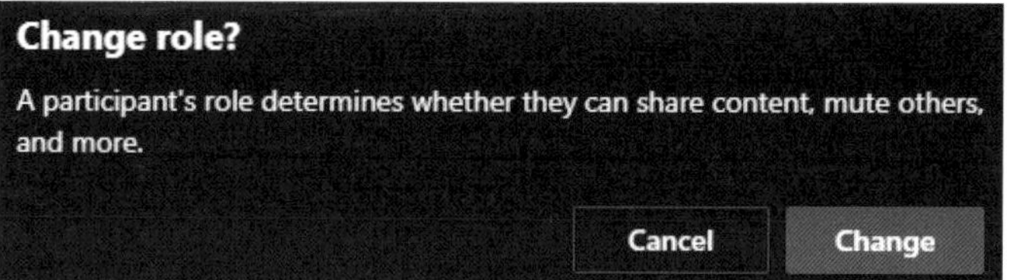

3. To change the role of a presenter, move the cursor over a participant's name, click on the menu button, and click on the **Make an attendee** option

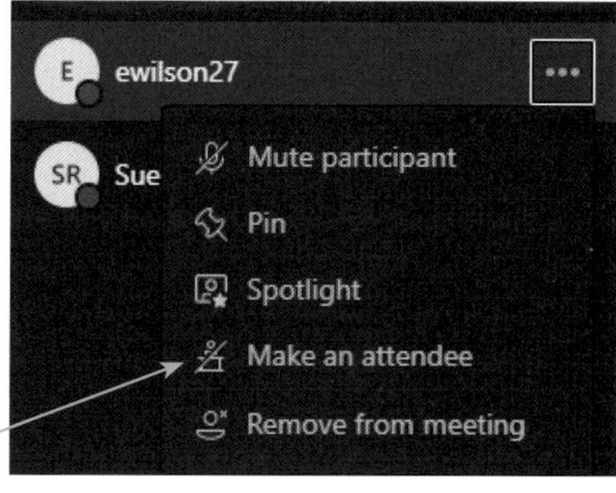

The **Participants** panel displays whether someone is an Organizer, an Attendee, or a Presenter in a meeting.

...cont'd

Removing participants

If you are the organizer of a meeting, then you will be able to remove people from a meeting. To do this:

1. During a group video meeting, move the cursor over a participant's name in the **Participants** panel and click on the menu button

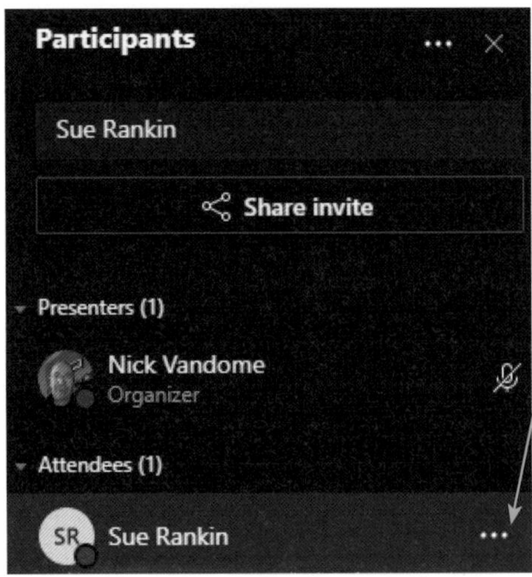

2. Click on the **Remove from meeting** option to remove the participant from the meeting. There is no confirmation window for this; the participant is just removed from the meeting immediately

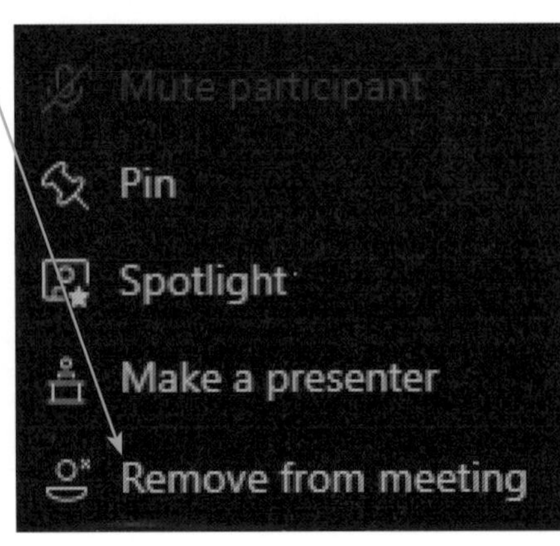

Always tell someone before you remove them from a meeting so that it is not unexpected.

Video Settings

Before a meeting has been joined, there are some settings that can be applied in terms of audio and video. To access these:

1. In the main video window right-hand panel, click on the **PC Mic and Speakers** heading to select settings for the device's microphone and speakers. Drag this slider to adjust the volume

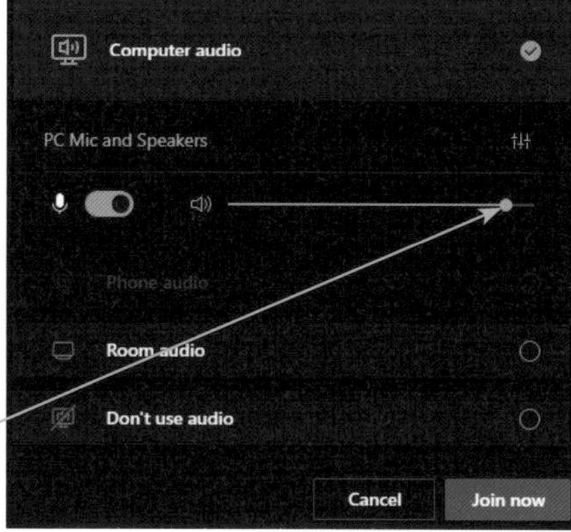

Audio and video settings can also be changed while a meeting is taking place.

2. Below the video window, click on this icon to access device settings for audio and video

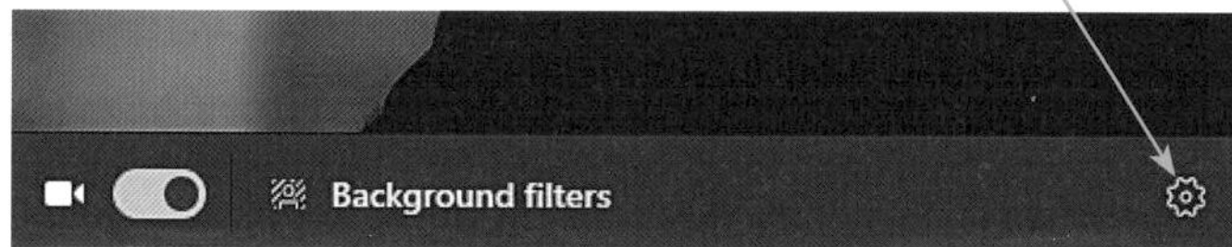

3. Select the required options for **Audio devices**, **Speaker**, **Microphone** and **Camera**

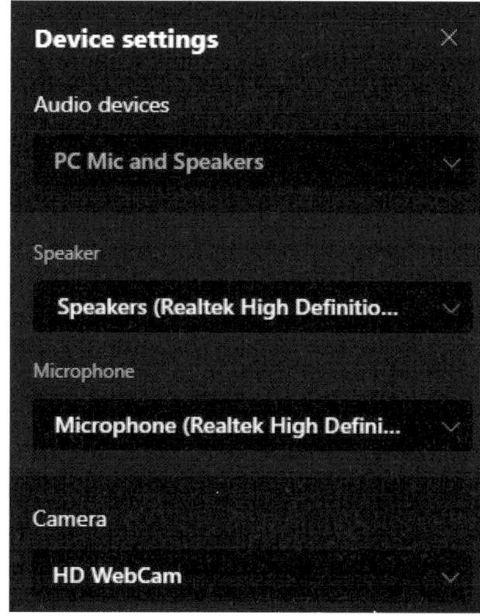

Screen Sharing in a Meeting

Being able to share what you see on your own screen during a meeting is a valuable feature of Teams so that participants can view files that have been created, or are being edited, in real time:

1. During an audio or a video meeting with one person or a group, click on this button on the top toolbar

2. The bottom half of the Meeting window contains options that can be shared. Click on one of the items to make this the active shared window

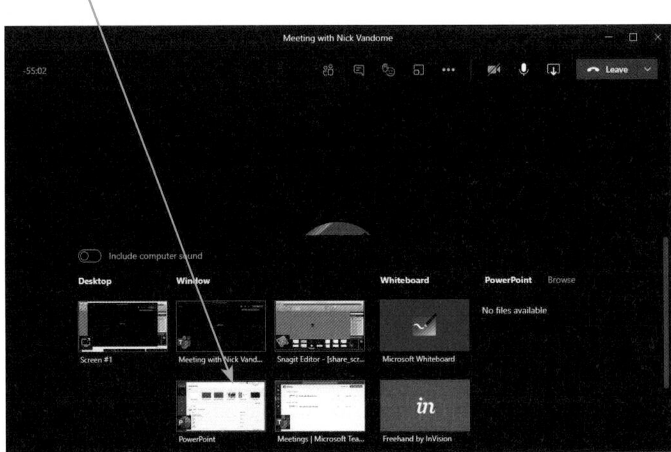

3. The selected item is then visible to all of the participants of the meeting

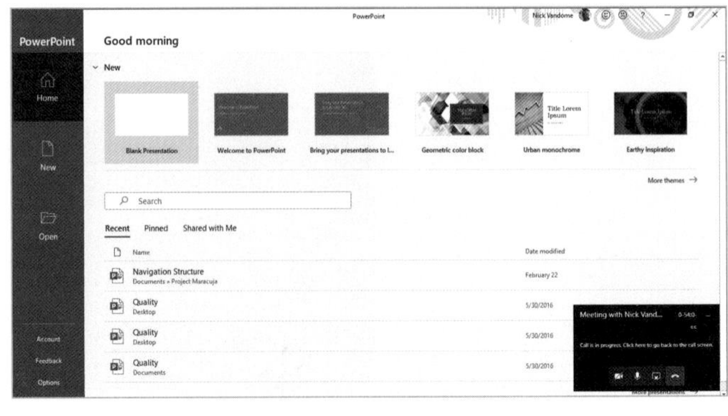

Although you can work on and edit a document while it is being shared, it is best to have as much of it as ready as possible before it is shared. This will give more time for discussing the contents of the document, rather than editing it.

4. If you change what is being viewed on your own screen, this will also be visible to everyone in the meeting

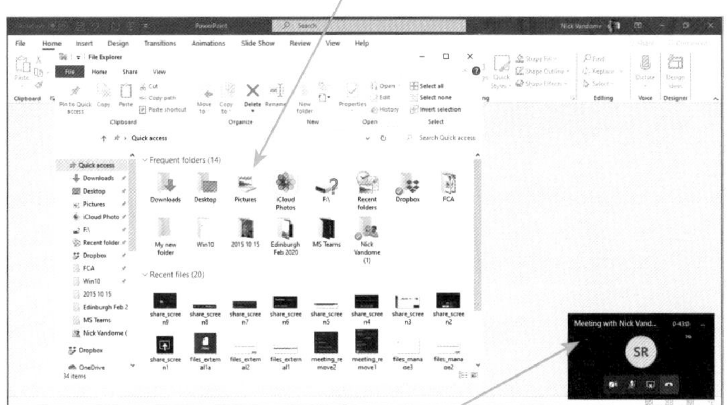

Make sure you know which files you have open before you start sharing your screen, in case you inadvertently share something by mistake.

5. A thumbnail version of the meeting controls is displayed in the bottom right-hand corner of your own screen

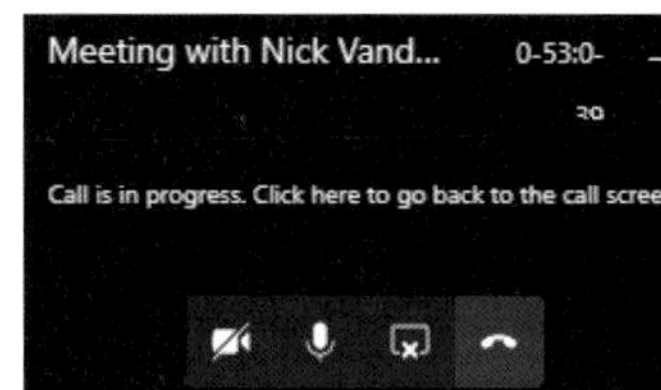

The controls in Step 5 can be used to, from left to right: turn your own video feed on or off; mute or unmute yourself; stop sharing your screen; or leave the meeting.

6. Click anywhere within the thumbnail controls to return to the main Meeting window. The other participants will continue to see the shared window, but you can use the Meeting window for other tasks, such as inviting more participants or sending text messages within the meeting

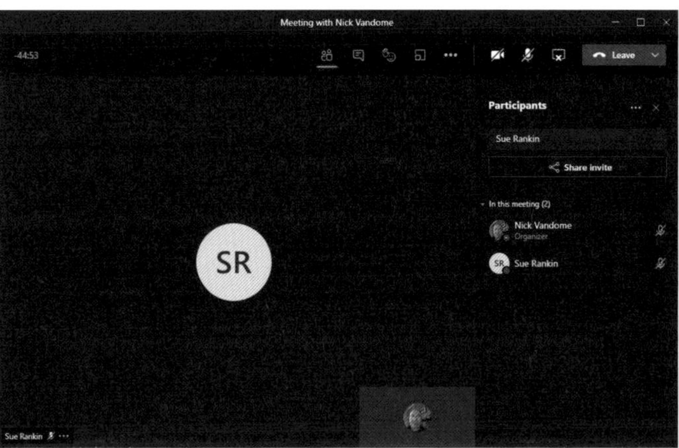

...cont'd

7. Move the cursor over the top of a window that is being shared, to access the sharing controls. Click on the **Give control** option to select participants in the meeting who can control the shared screen

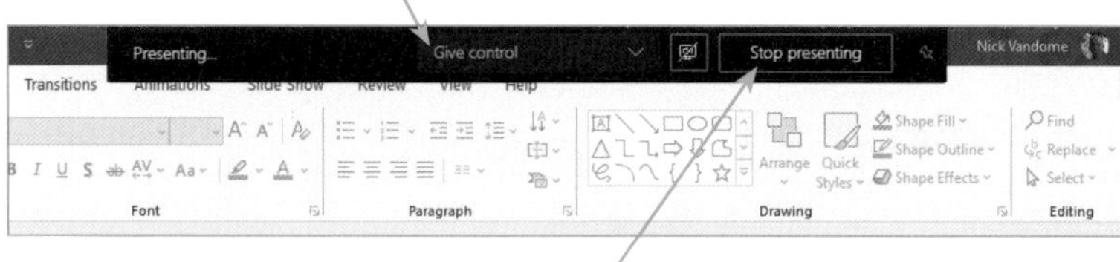

8. Click on the **Stop presenting** button to stop sharing the current screen

9. In the main sharing section in Step 2 on page 152, click on the **Browse** button to find more files to share

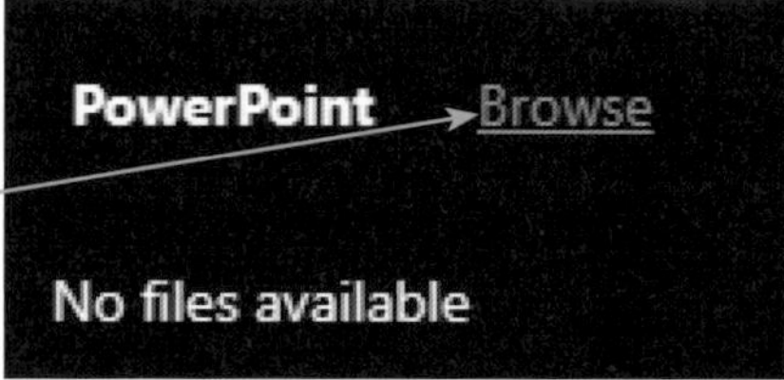

10. Select a location from where you want to share files during the meeting

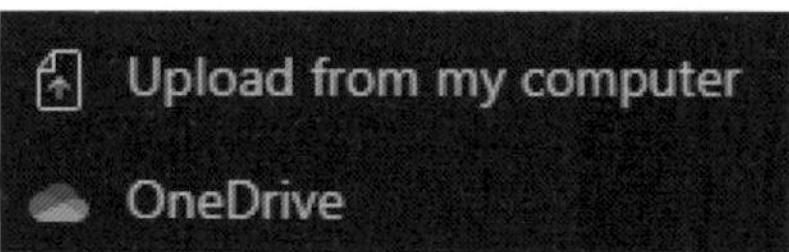

11. To stop sharing your screen, click on this button, in either the thumbnail of the meeting controls in a shared screen or on the top toolbar of the Meeting window

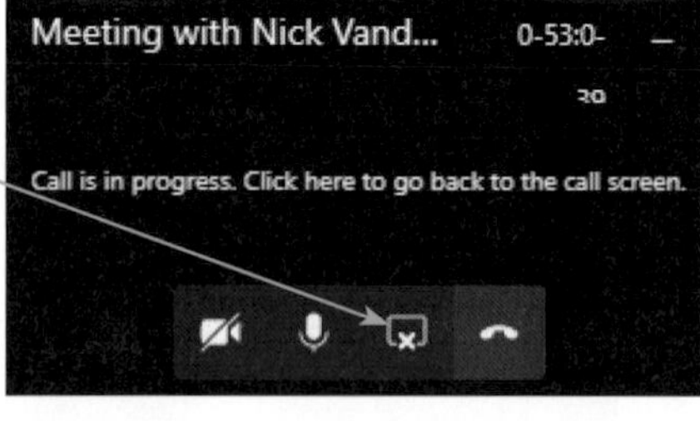

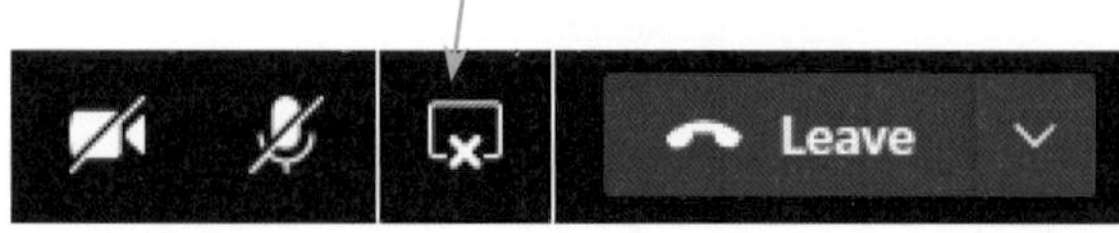

If you stop sharing your screen, you can continue the meeting in the same way as before. You can also share your screen again, if required.

9 Sharing Files

The collaboration element of Teams is done through sharing files. This chapter details how to do this, within a specific team and also between individuals.

Adding Files in a Team

Teams is a powerful tool for sharing files throughout an organization. This can be done within the Teams environment, and also during individual meetings. When adding files to a team there are various options.

Adding files by dragging

Files can be dragged into the Teams environment, from File Explorer in Windows. To do this:

1. Click on the **Teams** button in the left-hand sidebar

2. Select a team, and click on a channel within it

3. Click on the **Files** tab on the toolbar at the top of the main window

4. Open File Explorer and locate the required file

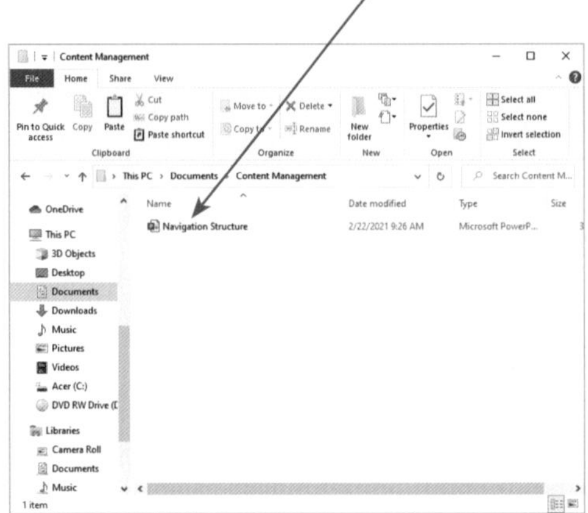

For the Mac version of Teams, files can be dragged from the Finder.

5. The main window in the Teams app has an area into which files can be added

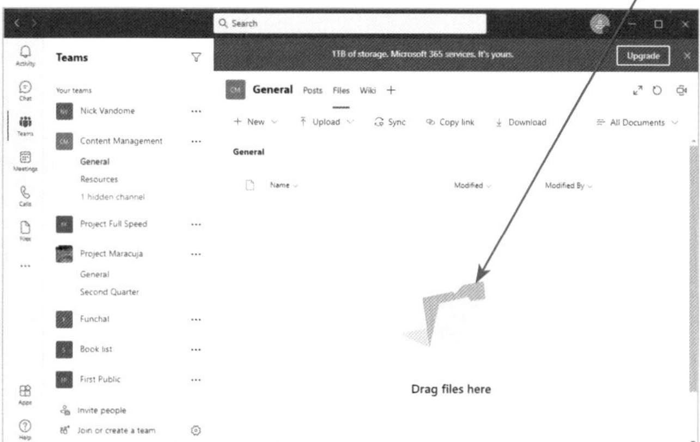

6. Position File Explorer and the Teams app so that File Explorer is on top of the Teams window. Click and hold on the file in the File Explorer window and drag it over the **Drag files here** icon

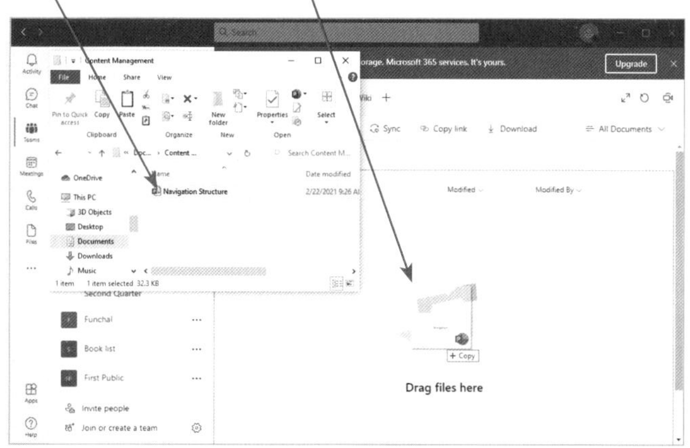

7. The file is added to the selected team, and all other team members will be able to access it

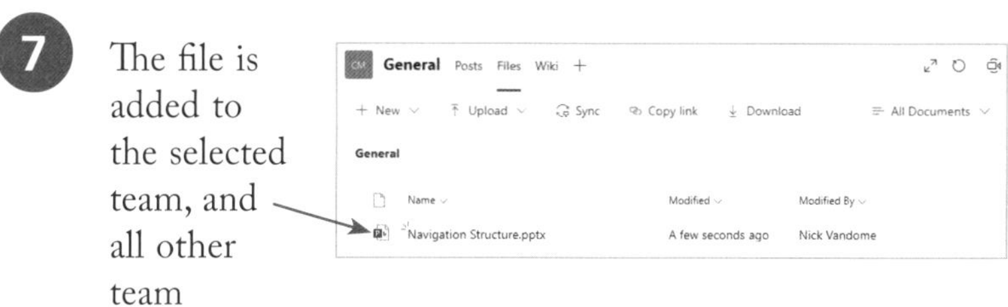

The file is copied into the Teams environment and remains in place in its original location.

Team members require the appropriate apps to open different types of files that have been shared with the team.

...cont'd

Adding files by uploading

To upload a file to a team:

1. Click on the **Files** tab of a team channel, as shown on page 156

2. Click on the **Upload** button

If a folder is uploaded in Step 3, all of the files within it will be included.

3. Select whether to upload **Files** or a **Folder**

4. Click on the required item and click on this button

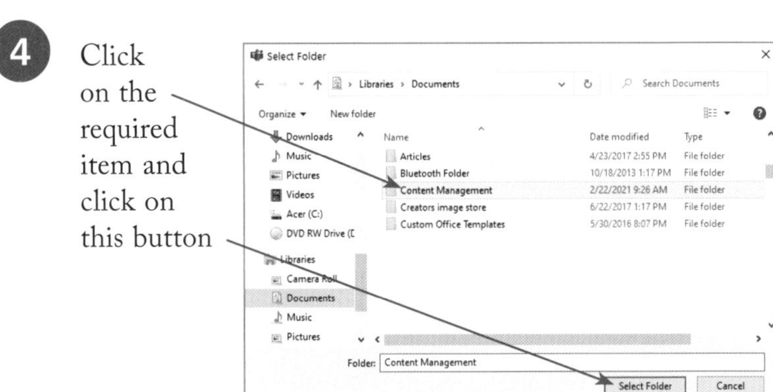

The button in Step 4 will say **Select Folder** if a folder has been selected in Step 3, or **Open** if a file has been selected.

5. The selected item is added to the **Files** tab window, and is available to all other team members

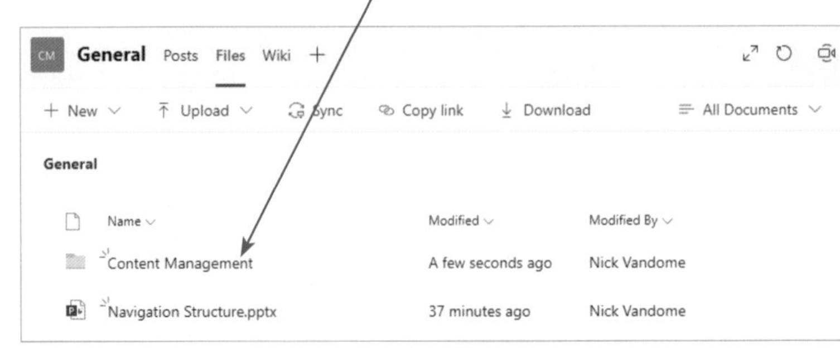

Creating Files in a Team

Files can also be created from scratch from within a team:

1. Click on the **Files** tab of a team channel, as shown on page 156

2. Click on the **New** button on the Files toolbar

3. Click on the type of file to be created

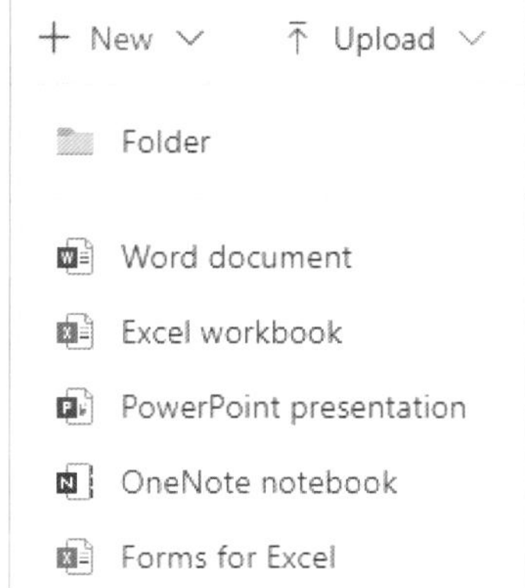

4. Enter a name for the new file and click on the **Create** button

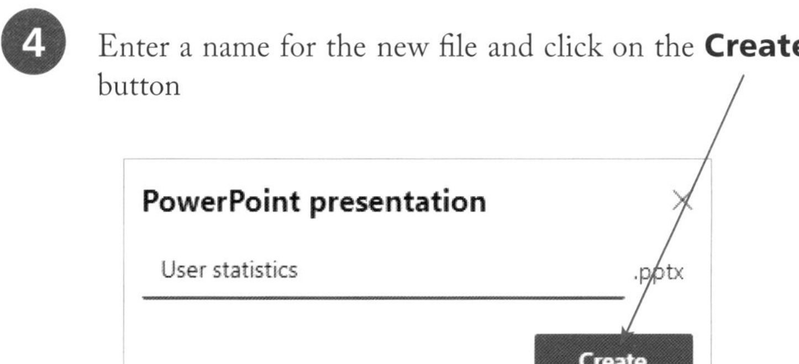

Click on the **Folder** button in Step 3 to create a new folder within the Files section of the team's channel, rather than creating a new file.

The Microsoft 365 suite of apps must have a valid subscription in order to use them with the Teams app.

...cont'd

5. The selected app in Step 3 on page 159 opens within the Teams interface. For instance, for a PowerPoint file, the PowerPoint Ribbon and the main window appear within the **Teams** section of the Teams app. Add content in the usual way for the selected app

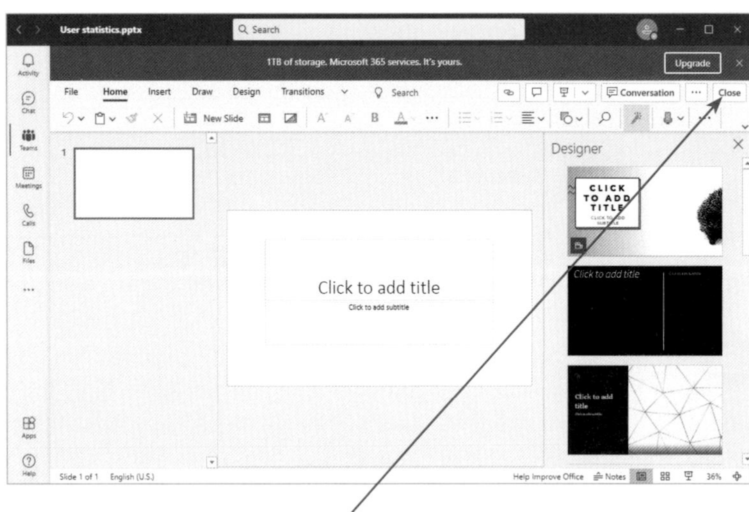

Files in the Microsoft 365 suite, such as Word, PowerPoint and Excel, will be autosaved when you are working on them within Teams.

6. Click on the **Close** button once the required content has been added

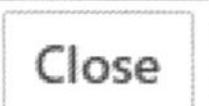

7. The new file is added within the **Files** section of the team, with the name added in Step 4 on page 159

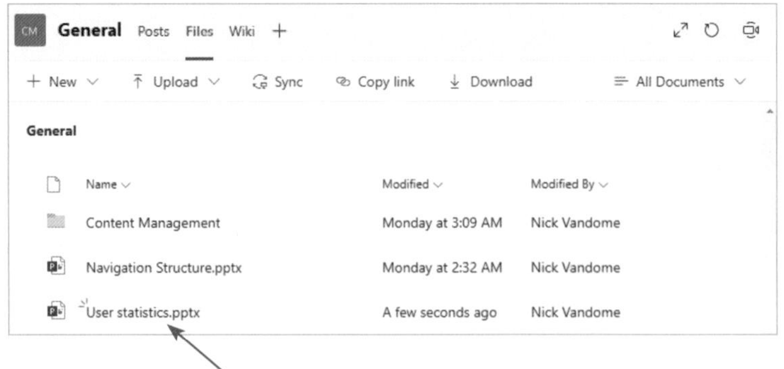

8. Click on the filename to open the file within the team

9. Click next to the filename to select the file

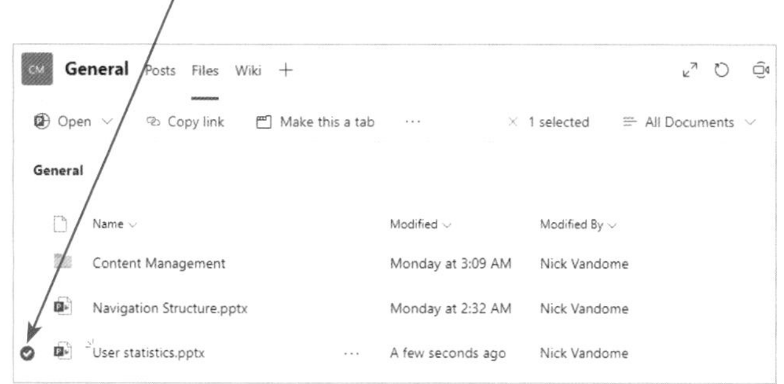

10. Click on the **Open** button on the top toolbar and select how to open the file

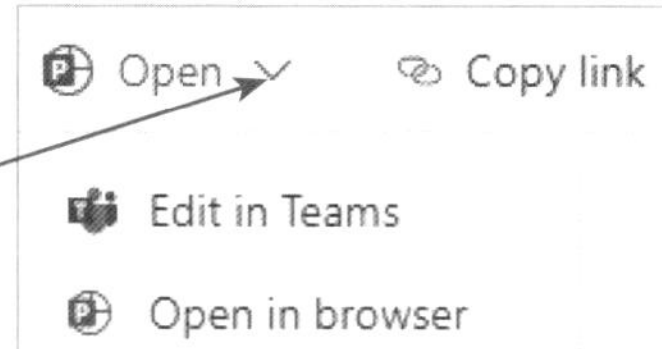

11. With a file selected, click on the **Make this a tab** option on the top toolbar

12. The filename is added as a tab on the channel's top toolbar. Click on the tab to view the contents of the file

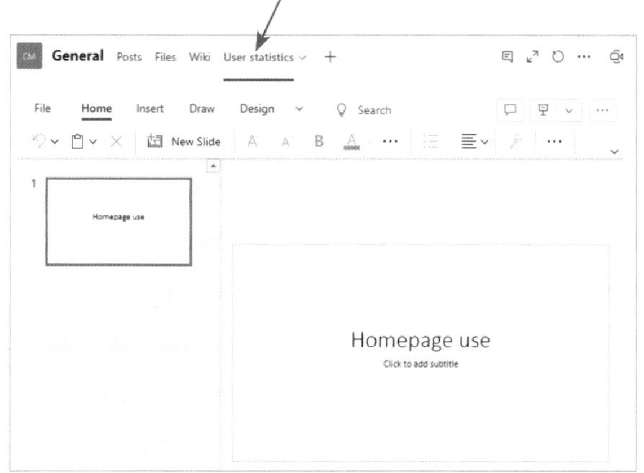

Click on the menu button to the right of the **Make this a tab** option, to access a menu of options for working with the file, such as deleting it, renaming it or copying it.

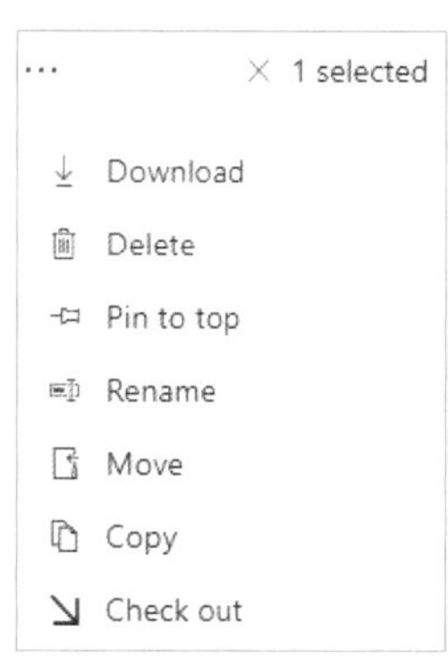

Editing Files

Once files have been added to a team, they can be edited by all of the team members. To do this:

1. Click on the **Files** tab of a team channel, as shown on page 156

2. Click on one of the files in the main window. The filename will be underlined, indicating that it is the active file and can be opened

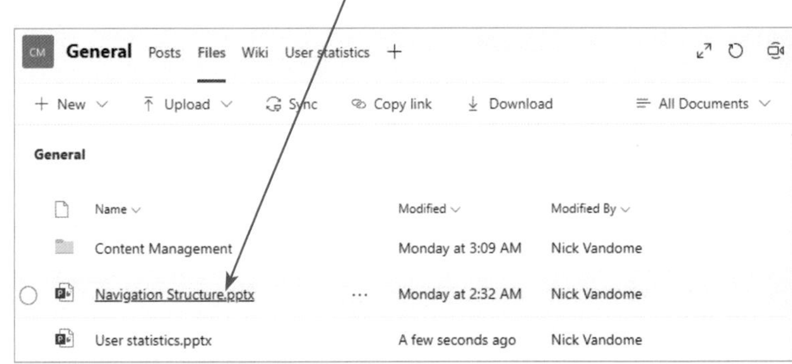

Files can also be checked out so that only one person can edit them at a time. For details about this, see page 164.

3. The file opens in its default app within the Teams interface, ready for editing

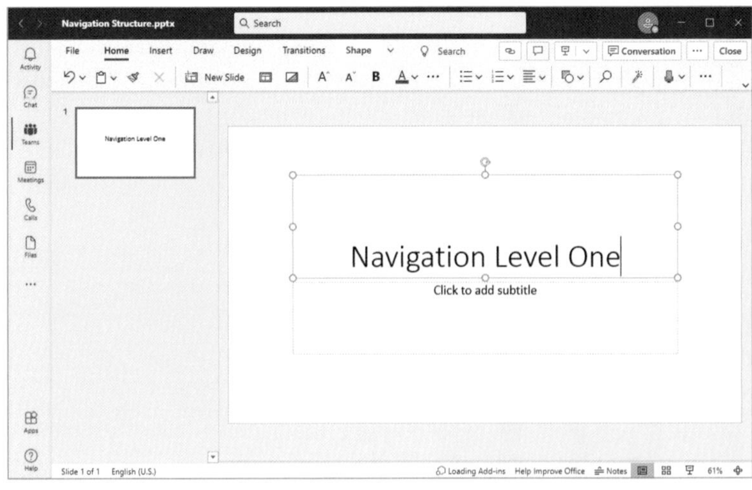

4. Make the editing changes to the file, as required

Drop-down menus

Click to add subtitle

5. The editing changes are displayed within the app. Click on the **Close** button to save the editing changes

Close

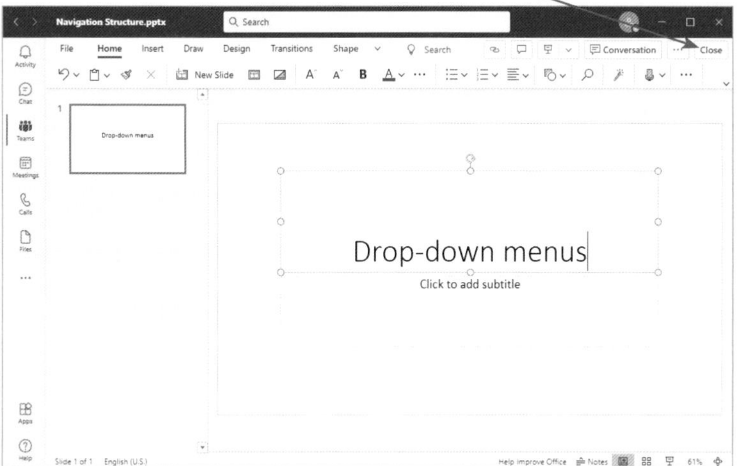

6. Details about the edited file are displayed in the main Files window, including time **Modified** and **Modified By**

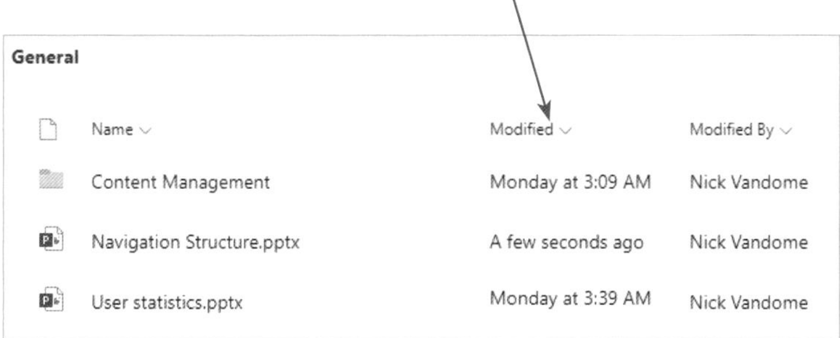

Name	Modified	Modified By
Content Management	Monday at 3:09 AM	Nick Vandome
Navigation Structure.pptx	A few seconds ago	Nick Vandome
User statistics.pptx	Monday at 3:39 AM	Nick Vandome

Click on the down-pointing arrow next to the **Modified** and **Modified By** headings to select different options for how files are sorted in the Files window. This includes **Older to newer** or **Newer to older** for **Modified**; and **A to Z** or **Z to A** for **Modified By**.

Checking Out Files

One of the issues with editing files within a team is if two people open it at the same time, and both make editing changes that could be contradictory to each other. This is overcome with the Check out feature, which enables one user to edit a file, while it is unavailable for anyone else to do the same. To do this:

1. In the main File window within a channel, select a file, as shown on page 161, and click on the toolbar menu button

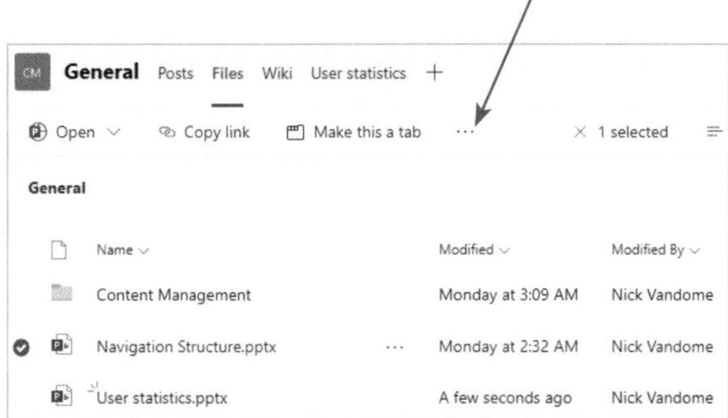

If you want to edit a file, it is best to check it out first to ensure that your changes are not overwritten by someone else editing it at the same time.

2. Click on the **Check out** option

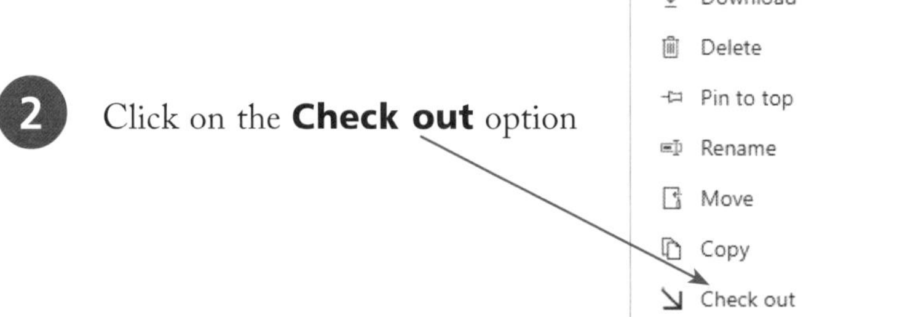

3. The checkout operation is confirmed. The file can then be opened and edited without anyone else being able to edit it

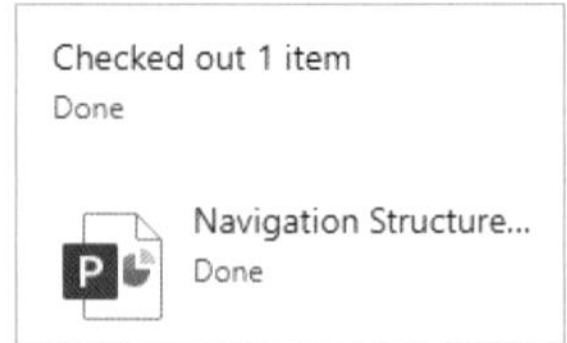

4. The checked-out file is indicated by this icon next to the filename in the main File window

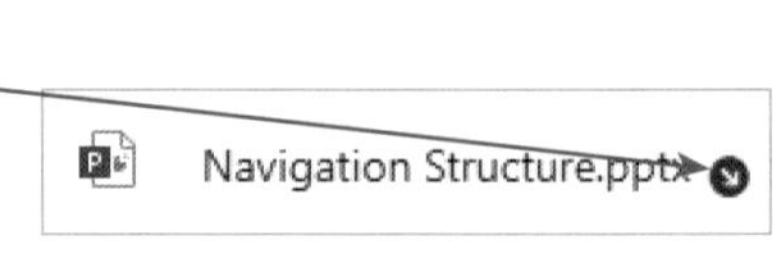

Managing Files

From within the Files section of a team it is possible to apply a range of options to specific files. To do this:

1. Move the cursor over a file in the Files section, and click on the menu button. A range of options can be applied to the file, including opening it, copying it, making it into a tab and deleting it

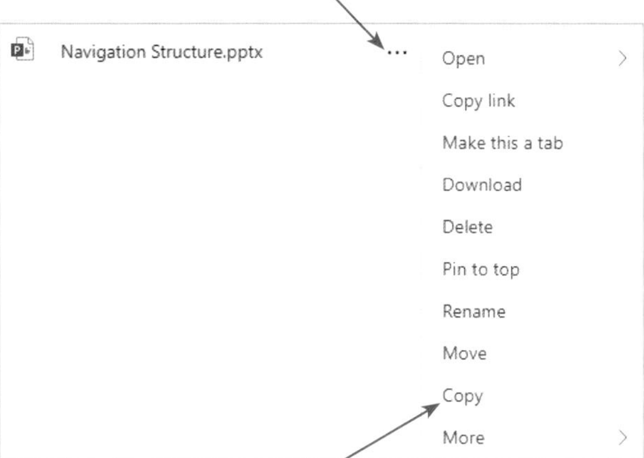

2. Click on the **Copy** option and click on the **Copy** button to copy a link to the file, which can then be sent to someone else

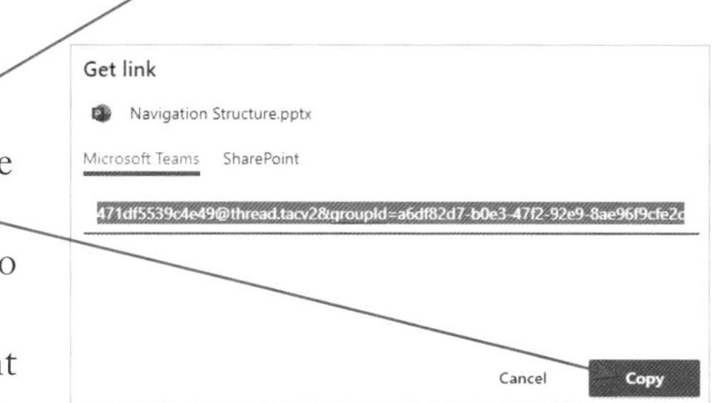

3. Click on the **Pin to top** option in Step 1 to pin the selected file to the top of the Files window

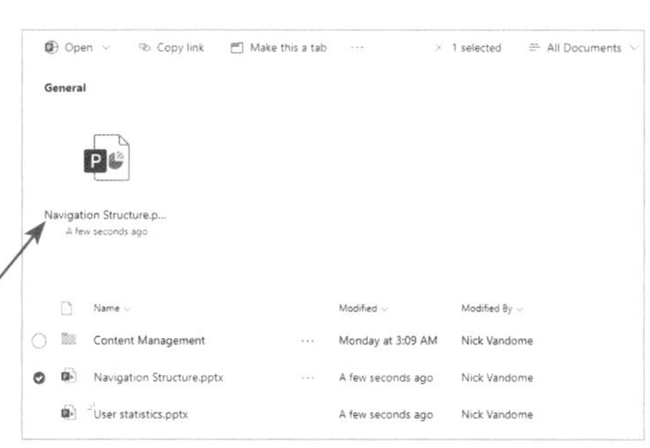

Links to files can be sent to people even if they are not in one of your teams, or part of your organization.

Using the Files Section

Files can be created by and uploaded to all of the teams in your network. However, there is also a location where you can view and manage all of the files to which you have access. To do this:

1. Click on the **Files** button in the left-hand sidebar

2. Click on the **Microsoft Teams** button in the left-hand panel to view all of the files within your Teams environment

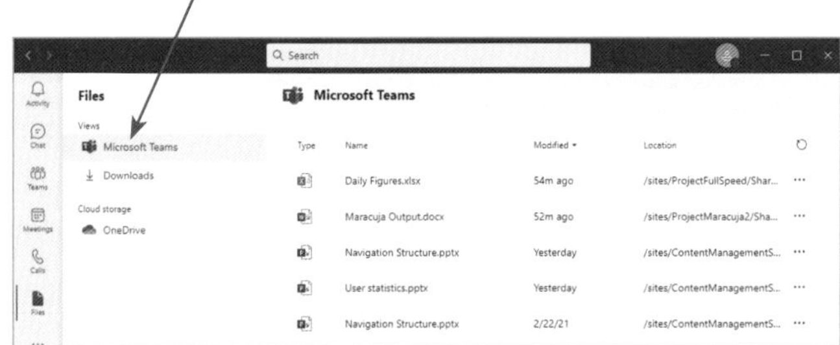

3. The location for each file is listed here; i.e. the teams in which the files are located

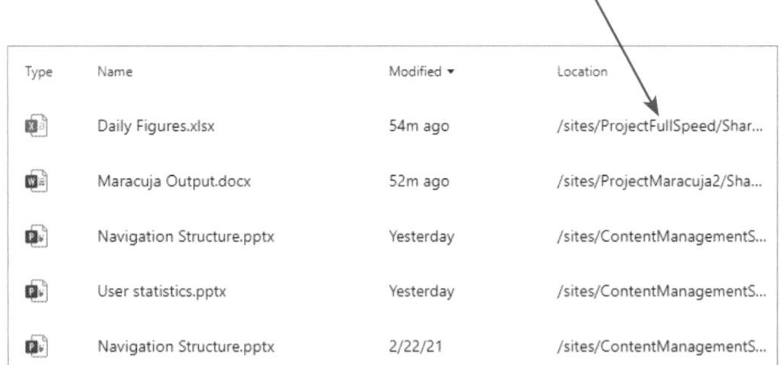

Type	Name	Modified	Location
	Daily Figures.xlsx	54m ago	/sites/ProjectFullSpeed/Shar...
	Maracuja Output.docx	52m ago	/sites/ProjectMaracuja2/Sha...
	Navigation Structure.pptx	Yesterday	/sites/ContentManagementS...
	User statistics.pptx	Yesterday	/sites/ContentManagementS...
	Navigation Structure.pptx	2/22/21	/sites/ContentManagementS...

4. Move the cursor over a file and click on the menu button to access options for editing or opening the file

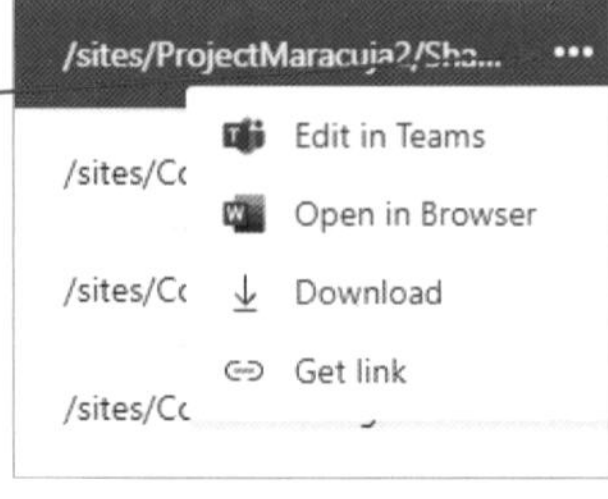

Click on this button on the top toolbar in the **Microsoft Teams** section to update the files list and view the latest ones that have been created across all of your teams:

5. Click on the **Downloads** button in the left-hand panel to view and manage the files that have been downloaded within your Teams environment

6. Click on the **OneDrive** button in the left-hand panel to view files that are available in your OneDrive online storage

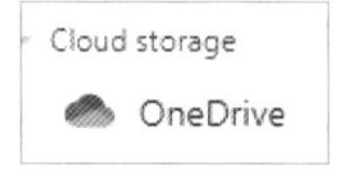

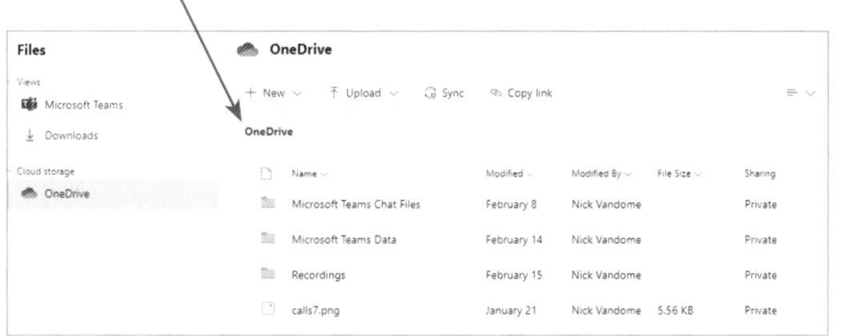

Files that are stored in OneDrive can be accessed from any of your devices that have Teams installed.

7. Click on the **New** button in the OneDrive section to access options for creating new files that will be stored within OneDrive

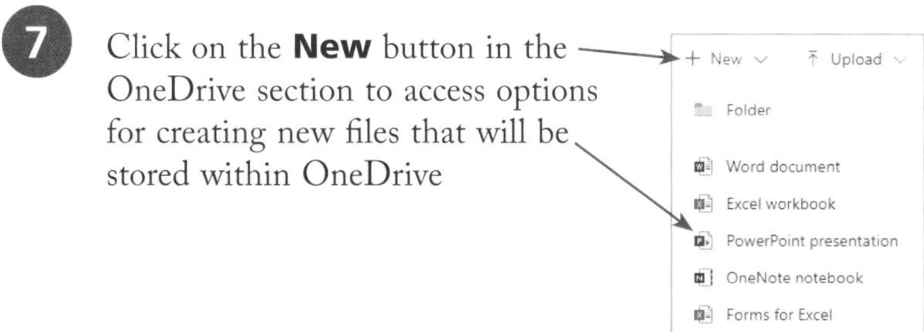

8. Click on the **Upload** button in the OneDrive section to upload **Files** or a **Folder** into OneDrive

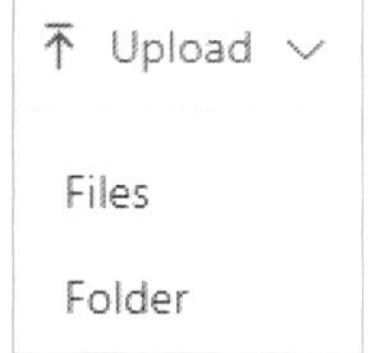

Sharing Files Externally

In a business or educational environment there may be occasions when you want to share files with people who are not part of your organization or your Teams environment. To do this:

Don't forget

Files can also be selected and shared externally from within the **Files** tab of a team in the **Teams** section.

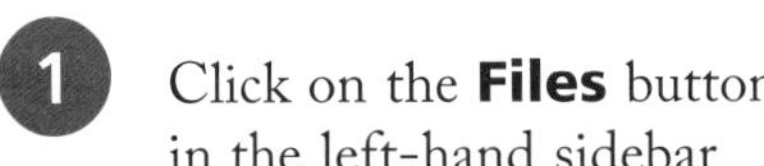

1. Click on the **Files** button in the left-hand sidebar

2. Move the cursor over a filename, click on the menu button and click on the **Get link** option

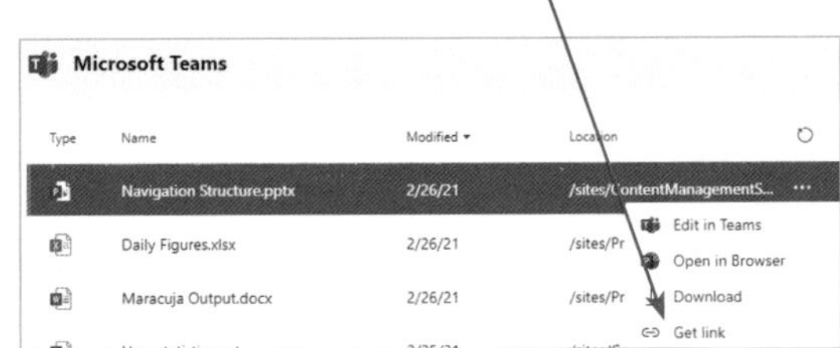

3. Click on the **Copy** button to copy the link

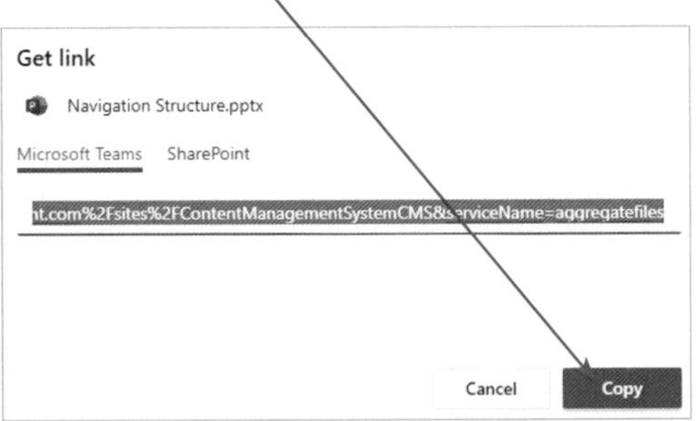

Hot tip

The recipient of a file that has been shared externally requires the Teams app to open the file, but they do not need to be part of your Teams environment. If they do not have the Teams app they will be prompted to download it to the device on which they are viewing the link.

4. Create an email and paste the link into it

5. The recipient will receive the email and will be able to access the file from the link

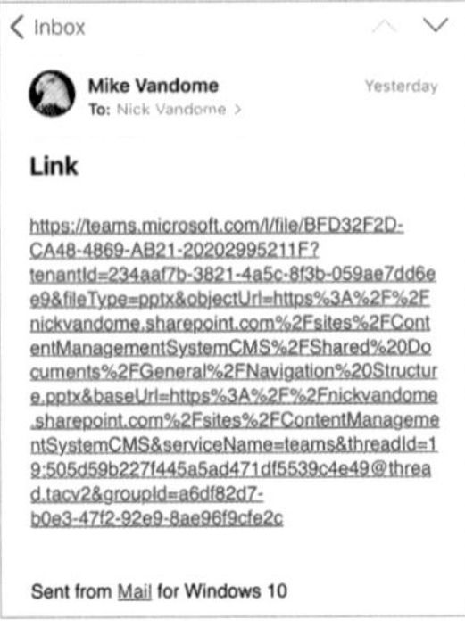

10 Adding Apps

This chapter shows how to expand the functionality of Teams, by using more apps.

Using Microsoft 365 Apps

Teams is a very effective collaboration tool in its own right, but it can be made even more powerful through the addition of other apps that can expand its functionality.

Using Microsoft 365 apps

The most obvious example of using other apps with Teams is the Microsoft 365 suite of apps, including Word, PowerPoint and Excel, which will be familiar to most people who have used Windows computers in the workplace.

In some organizations, the Microsoft 365 suite will already be available, both individually and within Teams. If it is being used within Teams, the apps can be added to individual teams, in which case they open within the Teams interface.

Adding Microsoft 365 apps within a team

If you want to use one of the Microsoft 365 apps within a team, the best way to do this is to add the app as a tab within a team (this has to be done in relation to an existing file that has been created with the relevant app). To do this:

1. Click on the **Teams** button in the left-hand sidebar

2. Select a team and a channel within it

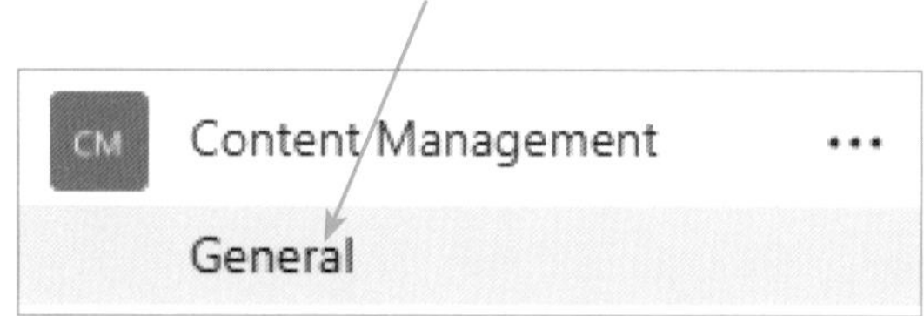

3. Click on the **+** button on the top toolbar

For more details about adding files to the Teams environment or creating them from scratch, see pages 156-161.

4 The available apps are listed in the **Add a tab** window. The Microsoft 365 suite of apps is usually toward the top of the window. Click on the required app

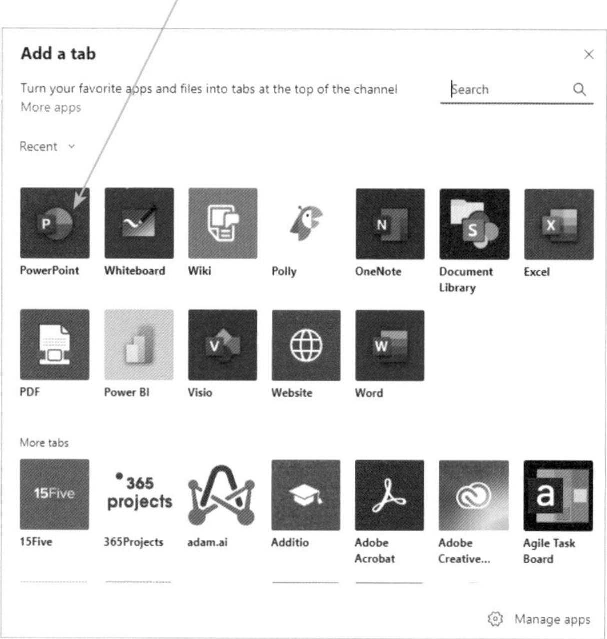

5 Enter a name for the app that will be displayed on the tab, select a file within Teams created in the app, and click on the **Save** button

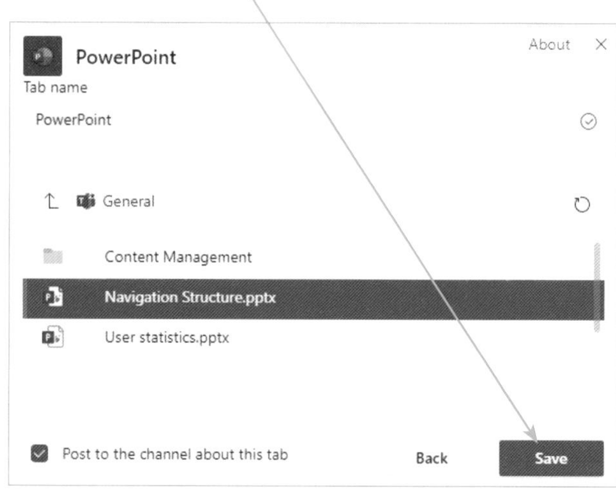

The name for the tab in Step 5 should either be the app name or the name of the file that it will display.

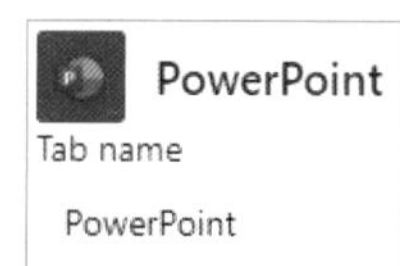

...cont'd

6. The name given in Step 5 on page 171 is added as a tab on the channel's top toolbar

7. Click on the app's name (or filename, if used) on the toolbar to open the related file

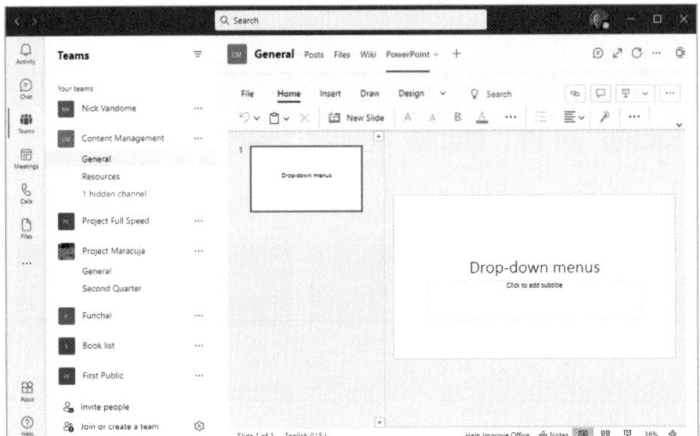

8. Click on the down-pointing arrow next to the app name on the toolbar and click on the **Rename** button to rename the tab name

Wiki PowerPoint

Settings

Rename

Remove

9. Rename the tab name and click on the **Save** button

Since the name on the channel's top toolbar in Step 6 is linked to one file, it is a good idea to make the tab name relevant to the file rather than the app.

The filename is not displayed by the app when a file is opened in Teams.

10 Click on the **Settings** option in Step 8 on the previous page to access options for changing the file that is related to the app

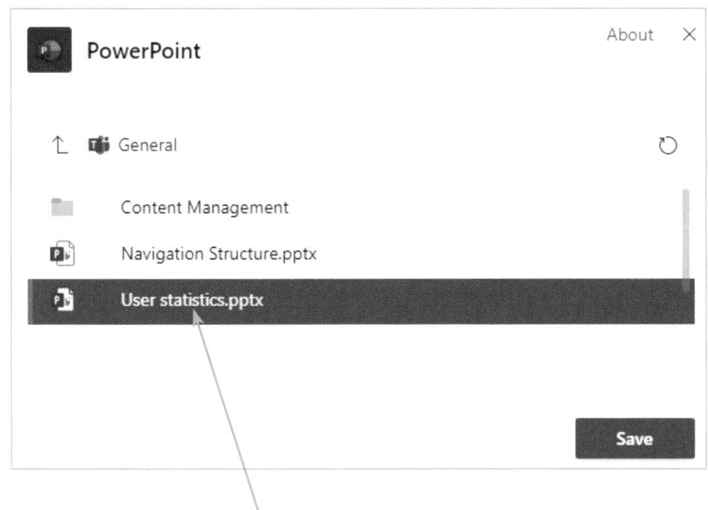

11 Select a new file and click on the **Save** button

12 The tab name on the toolbar remains the same, but if the name is clicked on, the newly selected file in Step 10 will be displayed

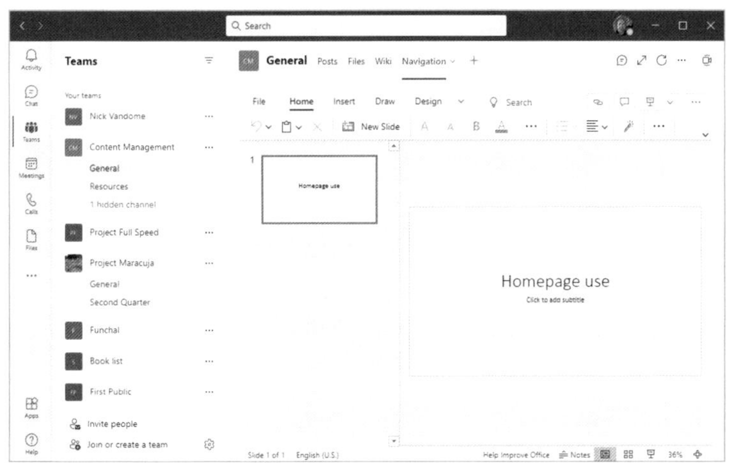

If a new file is selected, the tab name should be changed afterward, using the **Rename** option in Step 8 on the previous page, so that it matches the file that is displayed.

Using Non-365 Apps

Outside of the Microsoft 365 apps there is a wide range of apps that can be used within Teams. These offer different options for a working environment, and so all operate in their own specific way. However, accessing and using non-Microsoft 365 apps is similar for all of these apps. To access the apps within Teams:

1. Click on this button on the left-hand sidebar 

2. The **Apps** window displays the most recent app. Click on one to view its details

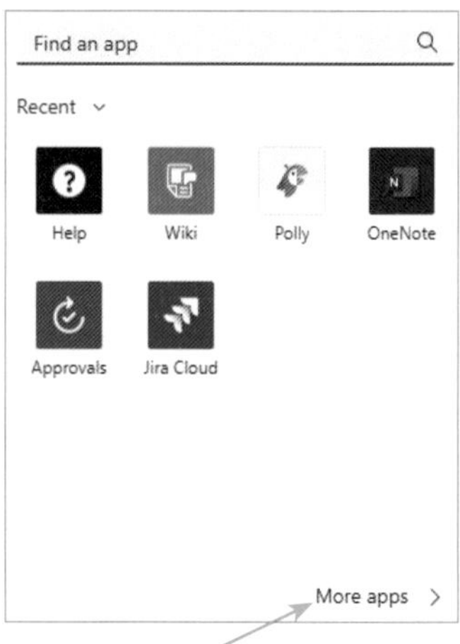

Use the **Find an app** Search box at the top of the Apps window in Step 2 to search for specific apps.

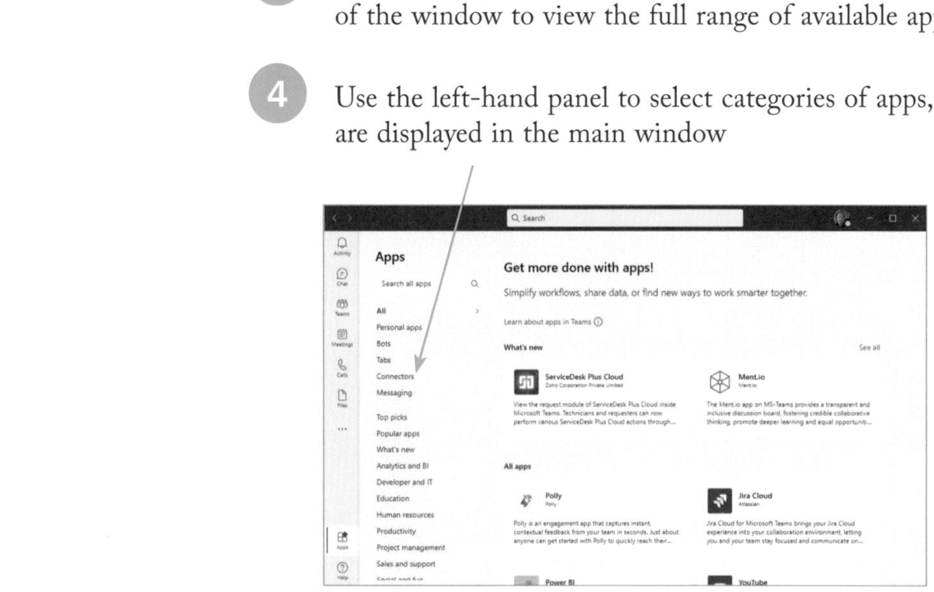

3. Alternatively, click on the **More apps** button at the bottom of the window to view the full range of available apps

4. Use the left-hand panel to select categories of apps, which are displayed in the main window

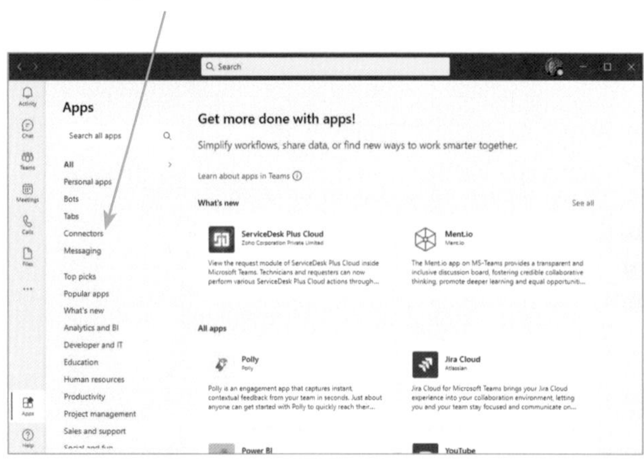

5 Click on an app to view its details. Click on the **Add** button to add the app to the Apps window

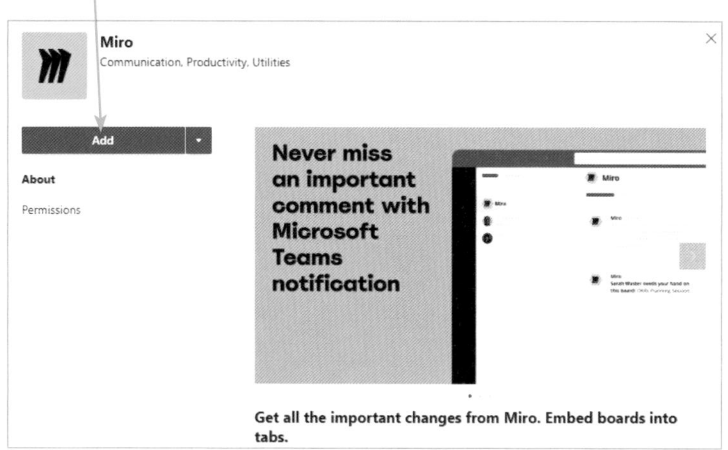

Once an app has been added, it can be accessed from the **Apps** button in Step 1 on the previous page.

6 Click on the down-pointing arrow next to the **Add** button to access options for adding the app to a specific team or an existing chat

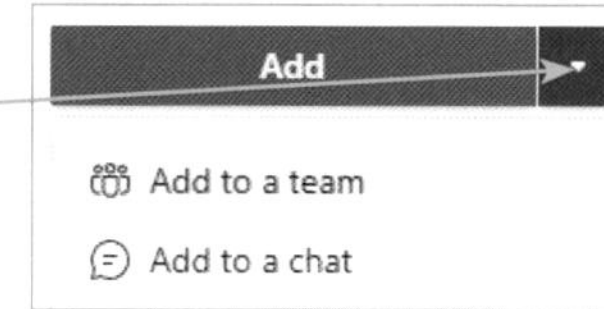

7 Click on the app in the Apps window to open it. It is visible on the left-hand sidebar, above the **Apps** button. Details about the app and how to use it are displayed in the main window

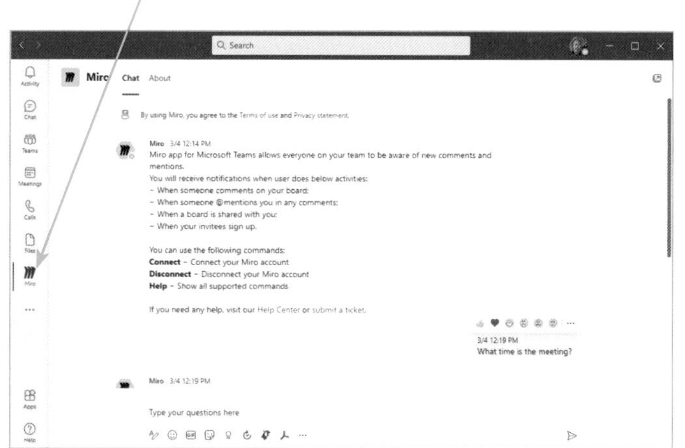

An app's icon only remains on the left-hand sidebar when details about the app are being viewed. Once another button is clicked on the sidebar, the app's icon disappears.

Setting Up Apps

Some non-Microsoft 365 apps require certain steps in order to set them up, ready for use. To do this:

1. Click on the **Apps** button on the left-hand sidebar and click on an app to set it up for the selected team channel

Details will differ for setting up different apps, but the relevant information for each one should be displayed in the window in Step 2, which will be specific to each app.

2. Details about setting up the app are displayed

3. Enter the required command(s) for setting up the app

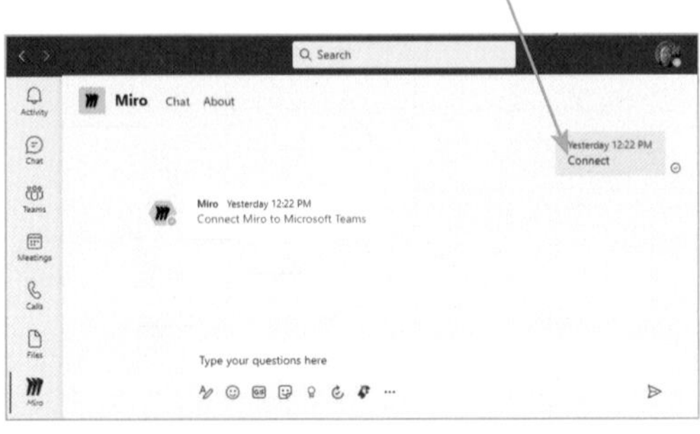

4. Once an app has been set up, select a channel and click on the **+** button on the top toolbar to add it as a tab

5. Click on the required app

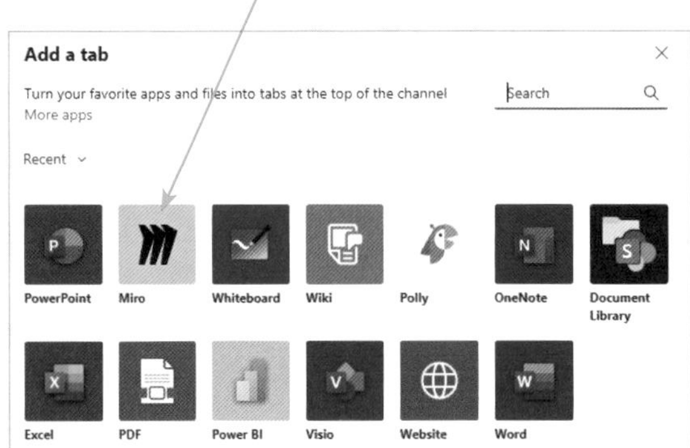

6. Click on the **Add** button

7. Each app will have its own process for being added to a team. Some require an account to be set up for the app. Follow the required steps to add the app to the selected channel

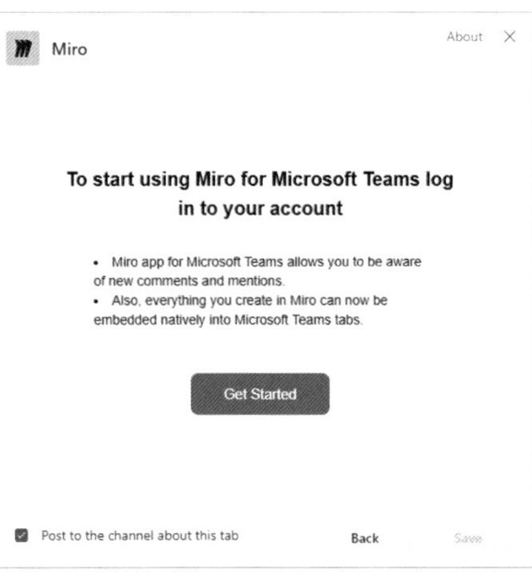

Each app that is added as a new tab has to be linked to some content or a process that is relevant to the app.

Authorizing Apps

Some apps require authorization before they can be used within Teams. This can be done if you are an administrator of a team:

1. Access an app to add it as a tab, as shown on page 177. If authorization is required, the app will ask for permissions to be accepted. Click on the **Accept** button

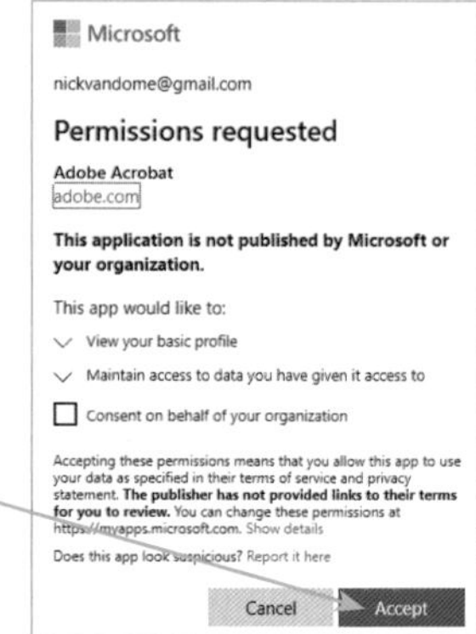

2. Click on the **Authorize** button

3. Authorization is done via your Microsoft Account. Enter your account details and click on the **Sign in** button

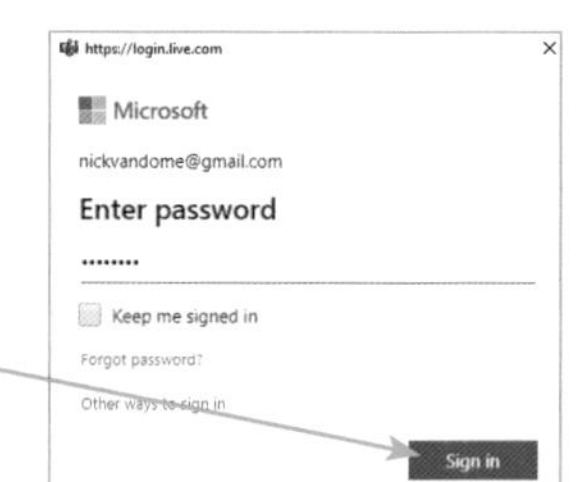

4. Click on the **Accept** button to accept the permissions required by Microsoft to add the selected app to Teams

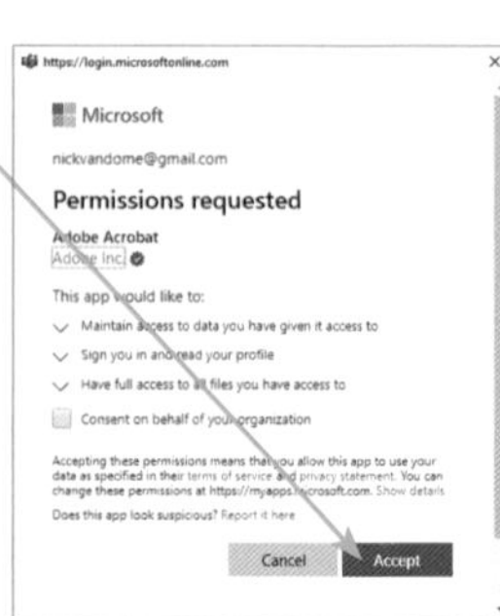

Authorization is usually required by apps that are not published by Microsoft or your own organization.

11 Creating Wikis

This chapter shows how to share information in Teams by creating Wikis.

Starting a Wiki

As shown on pages 56-57 in Chapter 3, knowledge Wikis can be created within a team channel. These can be used to share information and knowledge within the team, and team members can add to the Wiki once it has been created. The Wiki first has to be started and have content added to it:

1. Select a team channel, and click on the **Wiki** button

2. Content is added in the **Page name**, **Untitled section** and **Your content goes here** (body text) text boxes

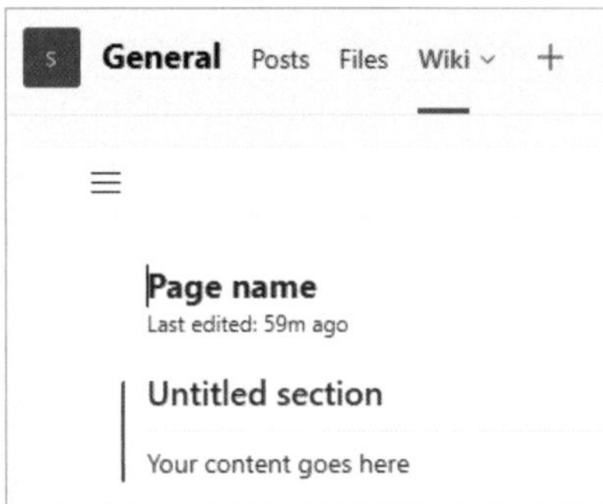

3. Enter content for the different sections of the Wiki

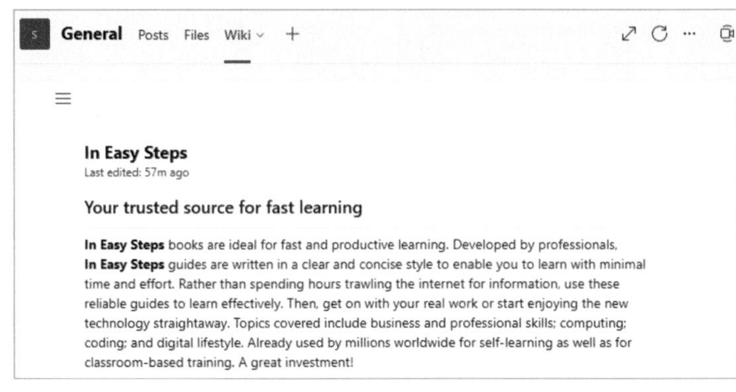

For each text body, the placeholder text in Step 2 (e.g. **Page name**, **Untitled section** and **Your content goes here**) disappears and is replaced when you start typing your own text.

4. Click in a body text paragraph to access the top formatting toolbar

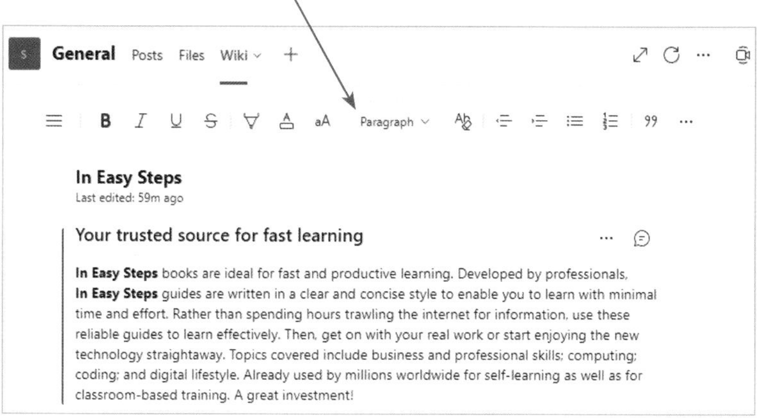

5. The formatting toolbar has a range of options for formatting the body text (see pages 182-184)

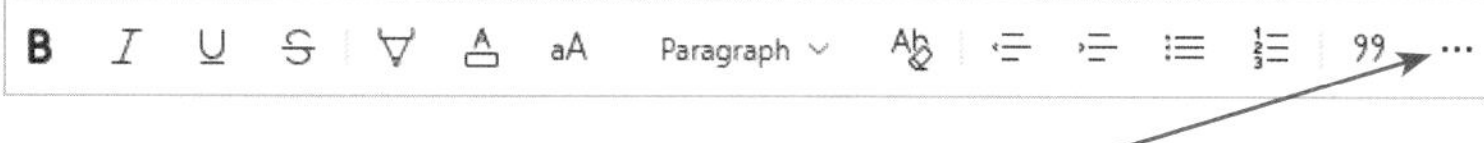

6. Click on this menu button to access more options for adding content to the Wiki

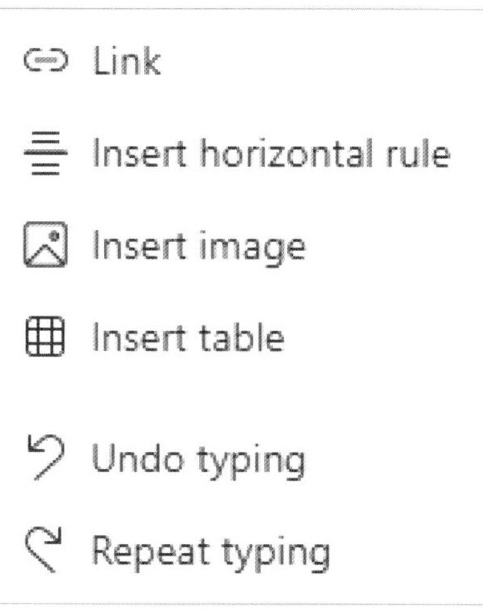

The page name and section title text boxes cannot have additional formatting applied to them; only the body text section can.

Depending on the size of the window in which Teams is being viewed, some of the additional formatting options in Step 6 may appear as icons on the toolbar.

Formatting a Wiki

Once content has been added to a Wiki, it can be formatted in a number of ways to give it its own distinctive style. To do this:

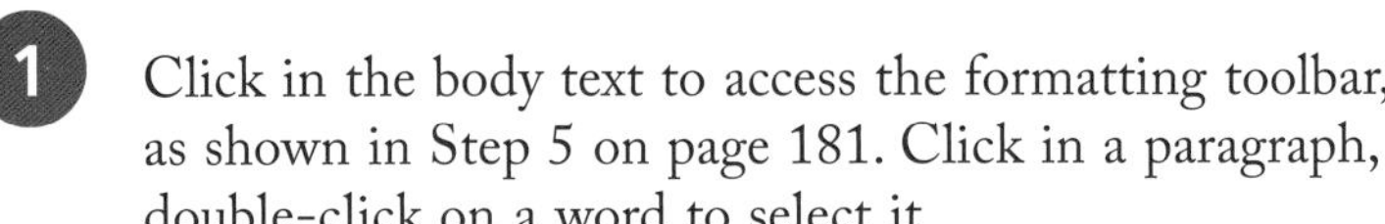

1. Click in the body text to access the formatting toolbar, as shown in Step 5 on page 181. Click in a paragraph, or double-click on a word to select it

Your trusted source for fast learning

In Easy Steps books are ideal for fast and productive learning. Developed by professionals, **In Easy Steps** guides are written in a clear and concise style to enable you to learn with minimal time and effort. Rather than spending hours trawling the internet for information, use these reliable guides to learn effectively. Then, get on with your real work or start enjoying the new technology straightaway. Topics covered include business and professional skills; computing; coding; and digital lifestyle. Already used by millions worldwide for self-learning as well as for classroom-based training. A great investment!

Clicking in a paragraph has the same effect as selecting a word (or words) in the paragraph, in terms of applying paragraph styles.

2. Click on the **Paragraph** button on the formatting toolbar and click on one of the preset styles

Paragraph
Heading 1
Heading 2
Heading 3
Paragraph
Monospaced

3. The style is applied to all of the text until the next paragraph break

Your trusted source for fast learning

In Easy Steps books are ideal for fast and productive learning. Developed by professionals,

In Easy Steps guides are written in a clear and concise style to enable you to learn with minimal time and effort. Rather than spending hours trawling the internet for information, use these reliable guides to learn effectively. Then, get on with your real work or start enjoying the new technology straightaway. Topics covered include business and professional skills; computing; coding; and digital lifestyle. Already used by millions worldwide for self-learning as well as for classroom-based training. A great investment!

4. Double-click on a single word to select it, or drag the cursor over several words to select them all

Your trusted source for fast learning

In Easy Steps books are ideal for fast and productive learning. Developed by professionals, **In Easy Steps** guides are written in a clear and concise style to enable you to learn with minimal time and effort. Rather than spending hours trawling the internet for information, use these reliable guides to learn effectively. Then, get on with your real work or start enjoying the new technology straightaway. Topics covered include business and professional skills; computing; coding; and digital lifestyle. Already used by millions worldwide for self-learning as well as for classroom-based training. A great investment!

5. Click on these buttons on the formatting toolbar to, from left to right: apply bold; apply italics; or apply underlining, or all three

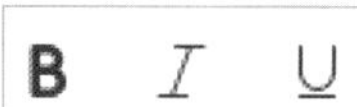

Your trusted source for fast learning

In Easy Steps books are ideal for ***<u>fast and productive learning</u>***.

6. Click on this button and click on a color for the background of the text

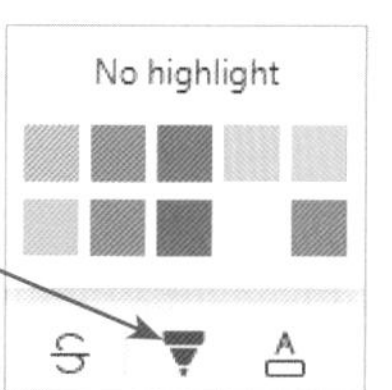

Your trusted source for fast learning

In Easy Steps books are ideal for **fast and productive learning**.

7. Click on this button and click on a color for the font of the text

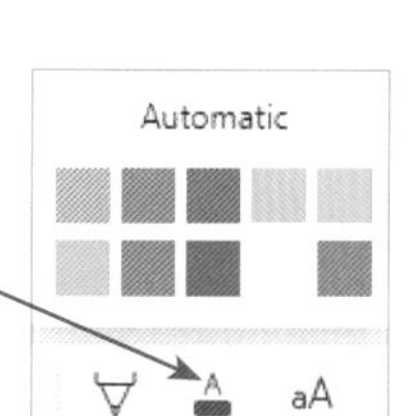

Your trusted source for fast learning

In Easy Steps books are ideal for **fast and productive learning**.

When selecting background text color and font color, ensure that there is a strong contrast between the color and the text/text background so that the text is as easy to read as possible.

...cont'd

If selected text is all within one paragraph, the indenting and list formatting will only be applied to that paragraph. Press the **Return** key at the end of a line of text to create a new paragraph.

Don't forget

Make a selection of text within the body text and click on this button on the formatting toolbar to remove all formatting that has been applied to the selection:

8. Select a word (or words) and click on this button to increase, or decrease, the font size

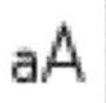

9. Select two or more lines of text (in different paragraphs)

Microsoft Teams In Easy Steps
Windows 10 In Easy Steps
Smart Homes In Easy Steps

10. Click on these buttons to decrease the indent of the text or increase the indent of the text

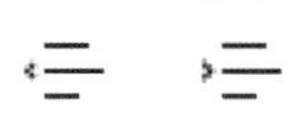

coding; and digital lifestyle. Already used by millions
classroom-based training. A great investment!

Microsoft Teams In Easy Steps
Windows 10 In Easy Steps
Smart Homes In Easy Steps

coding; and digital lifestyle. Already used by millions
classroom-based training. A great investment!

Microsoft Teams In Easy Steps
Windows 10 In Easy Steps
Smart Homes In Easy Steps

11. Click on these buttons to create a bulleted list or create a numbered list

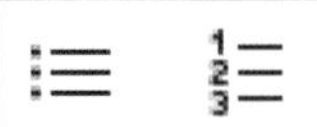

1. Microsoft Teams In Easy Steps
2. Windows 10 In Easy Steps
3. Smart Homes In Easy Steps

- Microsoft Teams In Easy Steps
- Windows 10 In Easy Steps
- Smart Homes In Easy Steps

Adding Images to a Wiki

Once content has been added to a Wiki, images and tables can be added to enhance its appearance. To add an image:

1. Click in a paragraph in the body text section, at the point where you want to insert an image. Click on the menu button on the top toolbar

2. 
Click on the **Insert image** option

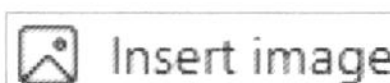

3. Click on a location for selecting the image

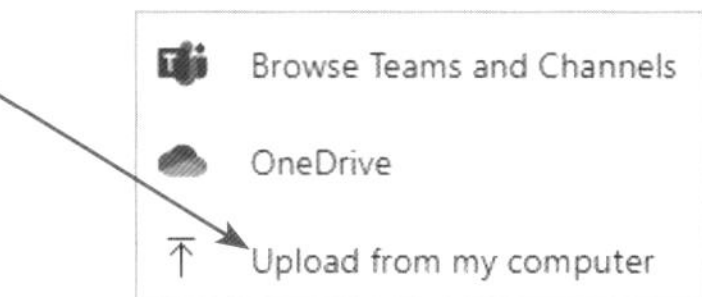

4. For the **Upload from my computer** option, navigate to the required image, click on it to select it and click on the **Open** button

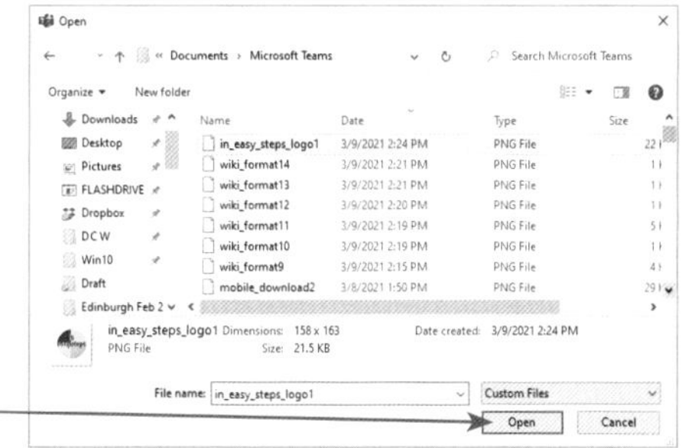

5. The image is inserted into the Wiki at the point at which the cursor was inserted in Step 1

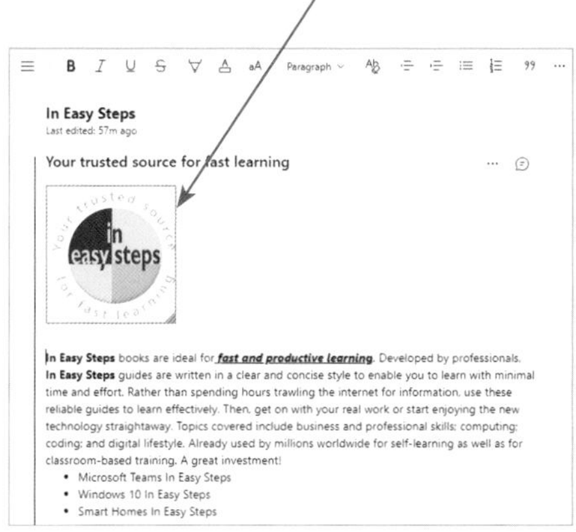

If an image is inserted into the middle of a paragraph, the text will be split above and below the text; the text will not wrap around the image.

Images can be resized within a Wiki by clicking on them, moving the cursor over the bottom right-hand corner and dragging the corner-resizing handle.

Adding Tables to a Wiki

To add a table to a Wiki:

1. Click in a paragraph in the body text section, at the point where you want to insert the table. Click on the menu button in Step 1 on page 185 and click on the **Insert table** option

Insert table

2. Drag on the grid to select the number of rows and columns in the table. The blue squares indicate the size of the table

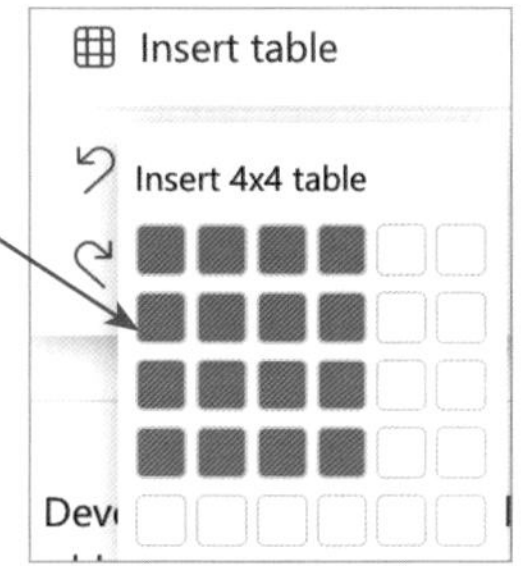

As with images, tables are inserted at the point where the cursor is located and the text will be split above and below this point, which could split sentences.

3. The table is inserted at the point at which the cursor was inserted in Step 1, with the number of rows and columns selected in Step 2

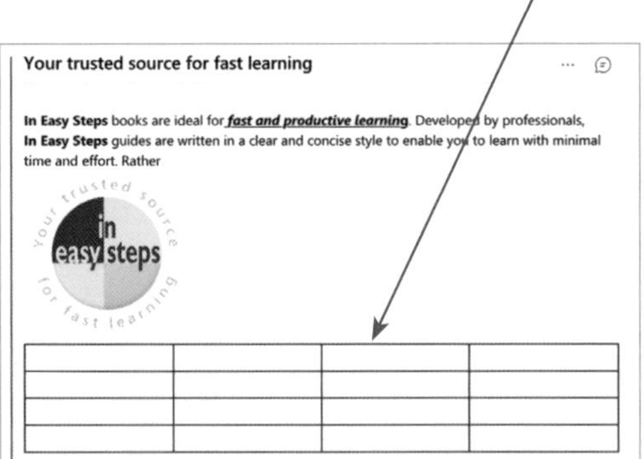

4. Enter text into the table, as required

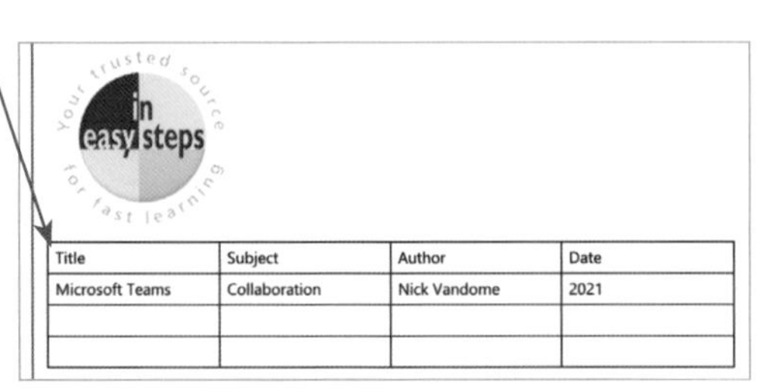

Title	Subject	Author	Date
Microsoft Teams	Collaboration	Nick Vandome	2021

Use the **Tab** key on the keyboard to move to the next column cell in the table. Use **Shift + Tab** to move back to the previous column cell.

Index

A

B

C

D

E

F

G

H

I

J

K

P

R

S

T

U

V

W

Z